An Army of Lovers

Women's Music of the '70s and '80s

Praise for *An Army of Lovers*

The women's music networks were for many of us where we gathered to sing and stomp and share the pulsing rhythms of our lives. This book captures that sense of exhilaration, enthusiasm and possibility so many of us celebrated. What it also does is detail the history of how women rewrote the rules of production and distribution, putting together all kind of women who could rent a theater or church or basement hall so that we could come together and sing the lyrics that detailed what we hoped to accomplish—a revolutionary poetry, an alternative network of women making their own way in the world. When there were no spaces where we could hear our musicians, we made those spaces and along the way remade the rules for what women could accomplish on the neighborhood level. I stood in those crowds, sang along with Meg Christian and Casse Culver and women who played rock & roll and bluegrass and all the music that echoed in my bloodstream. Jamie Anderson has caught the lightning and put it on the page.

- Dorothy Allison

An Army of Lovers is an epic undertaking to summarize a vast movement that changed the course of women's roles in the music industry. Jamie Anderson covers the breadth of the women's music historical narrative beautifully. But it is through her personal interviews with workers, producers and performers that make this book a wild romp through those crazy magical times and a must read.

- Sue Fink

Traveling troubadour and feminist historian Jamie Anderson has accomplished a feat befitting an Amazon Hercules. She has wrestled the wide-ranging story of the 20th-century musical explosion known as Women's Music into a compelling time line from bold heroines of the Harlem Renaissance to the mainstream acceptance of women-worshiping hits like Katy Perry's "I Kissed A Girl" (long after feminist Jill Sobule's groundbreaking song of the same title) and Ariana Grande's love songs to ladies. *An Army Of Lovers* is the riveting exploration of a cultural Wild Wild West for women, packed with daring adventures, narrow escapes, defied expectations and the intoxicating power of truth found in music music music.

- Alyson Palmer (BETTY)

It is daring to write about a social change movement, controversial to write about music and essential to leave a trail. Thank you Jamie for climbing the hurdles to write a book about feminist expression and lesbian identification through song. For chronicling "women's music" from personal transformation to songs to concerts to community building. Many have tried, few have made it to the finish line.

- Holly Near

Sappho's Reply

Rita Mae Brown

My voice rings down through thousands of years
To coil around your body and give you strength,
You who have wept in direct sunlight,
Who have hungered in invisible chains,
Tremble to the cadence of my legacy:
An army of lovers shall not fail.

An Army of Lovers

Women's Music of the '70s and '80s

Jamie Anderson

BELLA
BOOKS
2019

Bella Books, Inc.
P.O. Box 10543
Tallahassee, FL 32302

Printed in the United States of America on acid-free paper.

First Bella Books Edition 2019

Editor: Katherine V. Forrest
Cover Designer: LJ Hill

ISBN: 978-1-64247-045-1

Table of Contents

Table of Contents

For Therese Edell.
You were a bright light for so many of us.

INTRODUCTION

•◦✄◦•

Songs About Our Lives

In 1977, my friend Lois asked if I was going to a Therese Edell concert at a community college in Phoenix, Arizona. I'm not sure why I said yes, except Lois was an ex who'd remained a good friend and there probably wasn't anything happening at the lesbian bar that night. As we filed into the concert hall, I wondered why a couple hundred women would go to hear someone who wasn't Joni Mitchell or Carole King. As soon as I heard that rich alto voice caress "A Woman's Love" (an Alix Dobkin song), I was smitten. Leaving the venue, Lois turned to me and exclaimed, "What's great about her music is that she's singing about *our* lives."

Not long after that I found an album in a women's bookstore. I'd always ignored the little display of LPs in the corner, but one that sported a picture of an orange juice can caught my eye. *Lesbian Concentrate*, an Olivia Records compilation, featured Meg Christian, Cris Williamson, and a host of other names soon to have their own altar in the church of my lesbian-feminist life.

Women have always made music. However, there were few who spoke to lesbians and feminists, and they weren't well-known except in certain circles. At the time I didn't know about Gladys Bentley, an outspoken blues singer popular in the forties, who wore men's attire and had a wife, or cabaret singer Frances Faye, who recorded in 1953 the standard, "The Man I Love," and quipped, "...the man, the man, *the man?* What am I saying *that* for?" Later on, in the sixties, lesbian folksinger Maxine Feldman was kicked off the Boston coffeehouse circuit for "bringing around the wrong crowd." Their music was the seed for our burgeoning music movement. If only we'd known what to call it.

"Meg Christian invented the term 'women's music,'" says one of our most notable performers, Cris Williamson. When I asked what it meant then, she replied, "I had no idea. No one did."[1] In my interviews with women involved in this great phenomenon, I heard over and over again that no one knew what they were doing in the beginning so it's not surprising that defining it was hard. Olivia Records president Judy Dlugacz did a pretty good job, though. Sometime in the eighties she told *Bitch*, "(Women's music) simply reflects the consciousness of the audience. It doesn't have anything to do with a musical style." Lesbian cultural worker Sue Goldwomon defined women's music this way:

"To a certain extent the women's music movement was a lesbian music movement. There were a few straight women who were involved with it. Kristin Lems, who was the founder of the National Women's Music Festival, is a straight woman. But for the most part they were lesbian women and they were writing music about lesbians, about each other, about their relationships and singing it for other women who were, mostly but not exclusively, lesbians. And that was something that had never been reflected anywhere, as far as I know. Anywhere in the world, at any other time."[2]

Women's music impacted the lives of lesbians and feminists in a profound way not found anywhere else, touching on issues important to us. It could be a love song from a woman to a woman, a song about women's rights, or an instrumental piece composed and played by women.

"Women's music" became an accepted term and a huge force in women's lives. Toni Armstrong Jr., musician and publisher of *HOT WIRE*, recalls, "… we've all been touched *permanently*. These experiences have, over the years, changed the views and expectations of hundreds of thousands of women."[3] It was a way for us to feel good about ourselves, in a time when it was hard to be a lesbian and a feminist. Musician-activist Nancy Vogl says, "Music was the vehicle for us to experience a generation of women coming of age and creating a new vision of what it meant to be a woman…we were defining ourselves, as opposed to being defined by a dominant culture, i.e. patriarchy."[4] "It wasn't the same to be gay then," remembers choral director/songwriter Sue Fink. "There were so many people who thought we were awful. So many women were depressed or alcoholics or unhappy…I really wanted to be a force to make people feel better about themselves."[5] Fan Judy Jennings found women's music in the seventies, when she was fleeing an evangelical upbringing. "The effect on me was profound. I found hope and the belief that there was/is a better world to be found, inhabited by sane and loving people."[6] Another fan, M. J. Stephenson, remembers that "It felt so good to finally hear music that had messages and stories about me and my friends."[7] We found a community of women who supported us and understood what it meant to be a lesbian and a feminist. For Anne Haine that was found through Margie Adam's "Best Friend–The Unicorn Song." Haine says, "I ventured into a women's bookstore to buy myself a copy and discovered a whole new world and a whole new community."[8]

And what a community we became. Soon, I was traveling hundreds of miles to attend women's music festivals, clutching my well-worn LPs and waiting in line for a chance to talk with my favorite musicians. From 1979 to the present I attended at least one women's music festival a year, despite living in Arizona much of that time where it took many hours of travel to attend some of the events. One year I went to nine women's festivals. Thousands more discovered the same joy. We ran out to buy each new recording, we attended and some of us even produced concerts, radio shows, and so much more. We were Amazons! It was with this bravada that I started my own music and writing career.

It was a great pleasure to interview so many women active in this vital culture. A few preferred not to be interviewed, and if I had difficulty finding other resources about them then sadly, there is not as much in this book about them as I would like. Also, it was a challenge to decide who should be included and how they would be presented. I joked that I could write a set of encyclopedias. (Do they make those anymore?) I hold the faith that the women involved in this movement will look beyond word count and know that their contributions were important. If I missed details, I hope they write their own books. None of us should be forgotten. I will never forget that Therese Edell concert or that album with the orange juice can on the cover and what they started for me and millions of others. Women's music changed our lives forever.

CHAPTER ONE

••✐✐••

WHY DON'T YOU START A RECORD COMPANY?
Women's Music Begins in the Seventies

It's not your wife I want
It's not your children I'm after
It's not even my choice I want to flaunt
Just wanna hear my lover's laughter

- *Maxine Feldman*, "Angry Atthis,"
© 1969/1976 *Atthis Music BMI*, used with permission.

Maxine Feldman

On May 13, 1969, the night after she moved to Los Angeles, folksinger Maxine Feldman wrote "Angry Atthis." It was a play on the words "angry at this" and also the name of one of the poet Sappho's lovers. Most homosexuals of the day were deep in the closet. Popular on the Boston area folk coffeehouse circuit, Maxine never made a secret of her sexuality. A local folk DJ cautioned venues not to book her or they'd draw the "wrong" crowd. Only one coffeehouse continued to hire her, so she worked a variety of jobs—in a bookstore, as a bartender and in a department store.

No stranger to the stage, Maxine had worked briefly as a child actor. One of her earliest appearances included a part as a Girl Scout on the 1956 television show *The Goldbergs*. She took singing, dancing, and acting lessons as a young child and then, in her teens, attended the Performing Arts High School in New York City. She also performed professionally in children's theater. After high school, she enrolled in Emerson College in Boston, majoring in theater arts until school officials found out she was a lesbian and she was expelled. In New York, her parents sent her to an aversion therapist, Dr. Bieber, who claimed he could change her sexual orientation. Maxine didn't believe it. "We know that doesn't work. To me, being queer is like breathing."[9] Maxine refused to continue the sessions. Her parents turned their backs on her. By this time, she'd learned a few chords on a Martin guitar and worked in folk venues from 1963 until 1966, including a regular gig as an emcee at the Orleans's hootenanny.

Acknowledged as the beginning of the LGBTQ (lesbian, gay, bisexual, transgender and queer) rights movement in America, the Stonewall Riots exploded in New York City on June 28, 1969. Stonewall didn't immediately affect Maxine and others like her, but it was one of the catalysts that fueled women's music. It empowered women to be out and proud of being lesbian, and to seek out music by lesbians. The second wave of feminism also contributed, with feminist authors Betty Friedan (*The Feminine Mystique*), Germaine Greer (*The Female Eunuch*), Kate Millett (*Sexual Politics*) and the Boston Women's Health Collective (*Our Bodies, Ourselves*) publishing groundbreaking books. The feminist magazine *Ms.* started up in 1971. *Roe v Wade* was decided in 1973, confirming women's right to abortion. Feminist consciousness-raising groups began in many cities and served to empower women. Activist Angela Davis became a powerful feminist presence in the sixties and later. The National Organization of Women (NOW) formed in 1966 and gained prominence. In 1971 they passed a resolution proclaiming lesbian rights as "...a legitimate concern of feminism."[10]

Maxine Feldman, Michigan Festival, seventies.
Photo by Toni Armstrong Jr.

In 1971 Maxine may not have been aware of NOW and feminist groups. She was attending El Camino College in Torrance where she saw the feminist comedy team Harrison and Tyler (Patty Harrison and Robin Tyler) perform. For several years prior the duo had merrily made their way across nightclub and campus stages worldwide, appeared on national TV, and released two albums. In 1971 they started doing pro-gay/lesbian material. At a party after the El Camino show, Maxine sang "Angry Atthis." A year later Harrison and Tyler decided that she should open their shows in California.

At Ventura College for an audience of three hundred during Human Dignity Week, Maxine did her usual opening set, making it clear that she was a lesbian. The college's public relations person was horrified, telling Robin that this was not in the contract. Tyler strutted on stage and informed the audience, "...the college did not tell us to bring a lesbian here. But we are part of a revolutionary movement and this means freedom of expression for all people." Most of the audience leapt to their feet in a standing ovation.[11] Ventura College President Dr. Ray E. Loehr responded, "This does not represent the kind of freedom women's lib is all about."[12] He went on to say that lesbianism was a psychological issue and if it was discussed at all, it should be in a classroom.

Harrison and Tyler were threatened with non-payment at that gig and others because Maxine was opening for them. If the comedy duo wasn't paid, they still paid Maxine even if it had to come out of their own pockets.

The comedy duo had a lesbian following, but Maxine was different. "Maxine was doing songs that were far more aggressive than our humor," Robin remembers, adding, "We didn't use terms like 'big dyke' etc. Also, she looked far more radical than we did. We were still very commercial (sort of like Ellen DeGeneres) and not as threatening... There was no women's music at that time. There was this song 'Angry Atthis' and this huge dyke...and she was this big—and I use it in the kindest terms—big, because she was proud of it...dykey-looking dyke, singing 'I am proud to be a lesbian.' It was very, very difficult. People started going after her, and started going after us, and canceling our performances. When that happened, I knew we had come upon something very, very important, and at the time I didn't know we were making history."[13]

In spite of the controversies, Maxine enjoyed the shows because the students were always supportive, even if the administration didn't follow suit. After the concerts she loved meeting gay men and lesbians who led isolated lives and were thrilled to find that they weren't the only ones. She saw herself as a bridge for them, always ready with kind words and resources.

Maxine, Robin, and Patty decided that Maxine should record. Robin and Patty raised the money for a forty-five rpm and took Maxine into the studio where she recorded "Angry Atthis" and "Bar 1." Robin Flower and Naomi Littlebear Morena accompanied her. In 1972 they pressed one thousand forty-fives and sold half in the first month at $1.25 each.[14] The record received airplay on Los Angeles stations and one station in New York. Copies were sold at performances and via mail order but the disc didn't sell as well as it might have because there wasn't yet a network of distributors and stores where they could place it. However, it was an effective calling card to get Maxine more gigs. Proceeds from the forty-five were earmarked for a full-length album and then to finance albums by other feminist artists.[15] In 1979, as it turned out, Maxine finally did release *Closet Sale*, but with other financing and on another label.

Maxine claimed that the forty-five was recorded with tape left over from Harrison and Tyler's *Wonder Women* album and that 20th Century Fox had produced the first lesbian record even though they didn't know it. Perhaps that was meant as a joke; Robin says that she and Patty financed the disc and 20th Century Fox had nothing to do with it.

At a gig in Pasadena Maxine's cheap guitar broke, so she started telling
funny stories and jokes. The comedy was so well-received that she added it to
subsequent shows. After a 1974 concert in New York City, the *National Review*
called her "Jonathan Winters in drag," one of Maxine's favorite accolades.[16] In
a 2002 interview with *Queer Music Heritage* she stated, "I've always been butch,
I've always been loud, I've always been proud, and I've always been very Jewish,
and that hasn't always set too well with people, but with humor I was always able
to get in the door."

Maxine felt that adding comedy changed her role as the serious folksinger
opening for the comedy duo so she went back to solo shows. "Maxine felt she
could do better by not fronting us so she went off on her own without telling us,
which hurt us for years as we had risked so much in both bookings and money,"
Robin contended. "Had Maxine stayed fronting us, she would have reached a far
wider audience than she did when she left."[17]

The performances of Maxine, and Harrison and Tyler in the early seventies
coincided with the second wave of feminism. Women were forming groups
to advocate for women's health, support women's art, and much more; and
they needed funding. Maxine's concerts were sometimes fundraisers for these
feminist groups; however, some of them weren't comfortable with her out
lesbian presentation, believing it detracted from their message and discouraged
supporters. It was a problem that many lesbians in feminist groups after her
also encountered. Maxine blamed it on our conditioning as women. We are
not supposed to like each other, much less be supportive. She declared this
throughout her career, expressing dismay when concert crowds were small or
when record sales weren't as large as expected.

She continued to perform through the seventies at all kinds of venues, from
tiny coffeehouses to bigger clubs like the Ash Grove in Los Angeles. In 1974,
she played at the prestigious Town Hall in New York City. Also on the bill was
Yoko Ono and the all-female rock/jazz band Isis. At a 1977 NOW conference
in Houston, she received protection from the Secret Service, partly because they
were already there to guard speakers Rosalyn Carter and Betty Ford and partly
because protesters outside had signs such as, "Kill all dykes, kikes, commies and
abortionists." Maxine joked with her concert audience, "Well three out of four
ain't bad."[18] There were dry spells, though, and when music didn't pay the bills,
she worked other jobs, including one at Alice's Restaurant in Massachusetts, the
one made famous in Arlo Guthrie's song.[19]

Maxine wrote "Amazon" in 1976, a lesbian anthem that many know as the
one that always opened the Michigan Womyn's Music Festival.[20] It's on her
one album, *Closet Sale*. She once said that she was most proud of "Amazon" and
"Angry Atthis." Of "Amazon" she said, "I was living in the Berkshires and 'round
four in the morning something just woke me out of bed. I got up, went to my
guitar...my hands went into place as they had never done before...the words
just poured out of me so fast that I couldn't write and play at the same time.
The next day I went into a recording studio and put it down 'cause I was afraid I
was going to lose it. I'm not sure if it was the goddess or indigestion that got me

up but either way it was all right because out of it came a very fine song called 'Amazon.'"[21]

Maxine often appeared at the Michigan festival as an emcee where her booming "Welcome Women!" and funny stories were well-loved. Attendee Martha Meeks saw her at an early festival. "One of my friends thought she was a dude. All indignant she said, 'I thought there weren't any men here.'" Martha countered with, "Not a dude! A strong funny womyn! There are untold ways a womyn can be."[22]

Meg Christian and Olivia Records

At the same time, in the late sixties and early seventies, singer-guitarist Meg Christian was honing her skills in Washington, DC-area venues. She grew up in a musical family in Tennessee and Virginia. Taking up the ukulele at a young age, she was later encouraged to play the guitar by a babysitter and purchased her first guitar at sixteen. Influenced by artists popular in the folk music boom of the sixties, she devoured music by the Kingston Trio and Joan Baez.

At the University of North Carolina in Chapel Hill and two classes away from graduating with a degree in English, she switched to classical guitar even though she could barely read music. A couple of years later she was the first person to graduate from UNC with a degree in guitar.

In 1969 she moved to DC where she joined a consciousness-raising group. She also performed in area clubs, covering work by popular singer-songwriters Judy Collins, Carole King, Joni Mitchell, and James Taylor. She also gave guitar lessons. Meg told *Guitar Player* in 1978, "As time went on, I found myself more involved in the Women's Movement, and I began to examine the lyrical content of the songs I was singing, finding most of what they said about women's lives just disgusting. I started to look more and more for songs I felt were saying something that was good, that was positive, that was real."

Nightclub owners asked her to wear makeup and dresses. "It was one of my first revelations that I was not being treated as a musician but as someone who was supposed to be there as a woman."[23] They also didn't like her choice of material or how her audience looked and acted. She had to "...tell friends to please dress nicely and act nicely so I wouldn't get fired once again for singing the wrong kind of material."[24]

By 1973, Meg had reached her limit and made a commitment to perform exclusively for women. She wasn't yet writing songs but she was relentless in finding music by others that empowered women. She included "Did Jesus Have a Baby Sister?" by Dory Previn and "Joanna," a song by Cris Williamson, from an album she found in a discount bin in 1972. "Cris was the first woman that I ever heard perform music that I just knew was coming from the same place my music was," Meg told KPFT's *Breakthrough* in 1983. "In her deepest heart, I knew it was woman-identified music and I knew it was coming from a very deep common place." Meg was so taken with Cris's music that she started performing her songs. When she found out that Cris was to perform in DC at Georgetown University, she encouraged women at all of her concerts to attend the show. Cris was surprised to find the room packed. Not only that, they seemed to know the words to every song she sang. When she stumbled on the words to "Joanna," Meg's voice called out the missing lyrics. After the show, Meg introduced herself and asked Cris if she'd like to be interviewed on a local women's radio show, *Sophie's Parlor.* During the interview with Meg Christian and Ginny Berson they talked about the difficulties facing women musicians. Cris recalled, "We sat around a table and they were asking me questions about sexism in the music industry. I was pretty lucky, I certainly witnessed it, but hadn't had any really bad experiences...but I certainly understand it."[25] Then she casually asked them why they didn't start a women's record company.

Meg and Ginny were part of a group of women who wanted to change the world with their ideology while also financially supporting themselves. Included were women from the Furies, a radical lesbian collective that published a feminist newspaper, the *Furies.* Members also included women who'd recently relocated from Ann Arbor, Michigan and were part of another group, Radical Lesbians. Prior to Meg's involvement in 1972, Ginny remembers:

"We decided we'd try to get more of the DC lesbian community on our side. We didn't even know what 'on our side' meant, but there was a certain amount of hostility to anyone who was doing *anything*, pretty much. We chose some people who we thought would be good to be friends of the Furies. My assignment was to 'organize' Meg...we went to the bar...I asked her to dance. That was the end of my organizing Meg (laughs)...I started to fall in love with her."[26]

As they got to know each other, Ginny encouraged her to record a tape to send to colleges and women's centers to help her get gigs. They were already discussing this when the radio interview with Cris occurred.

In 1973, at a meeting of these radical feminists, Ginny excitedly presented the idea of forming a women's record company. At first, the other women were apprehensive, but it didn't take long for them to decide that yes, this could work. That Meg and Ginny were the only ones who had experience in music was no deterrent—Meg a performer and Ginny her manager/booker. Meg had been performing in the DC area and had done at least one tour elsewhere in the country with Ginny in their Toyota station wagon. Those shows had exposed them to the excitement building over women's music so they knew a women's record company would work. "We would go into little cities, big cities...(and) the middle of no place for a show of Meg's," Ginny remembered. "The women's community would be together and they would see each other in their largeness for the first time. It was thrilling to be there...to feel the potential."[27]

The Olivia name came from the title of a forties-era lesbian pulp novel by Dorothy Strachey. Judy Dlugacz, another member of the group, recounted that, "One day Meg came running down the stairs saying 'Gee I have this novelette *Olivia*, this would be a good name...'" It was much better than Siren Records, one of the other names considered, so Olivia they became. "...(It had) a nice round sound, very melodic," Judy remembered. "...we also liked the idea of taking from difficult roots and creating something beautiful…sort of owning the history of the way in which our culture has survived…"[28]

They had no money and knew little about business. They wrote letters to record companies and, in the guise of students doing research, asked for information about running a record company. They met with Yoko Ono and asked her to help with funding. She said she couldn't do that; however, she offered to record for them. The Olivia collective thought her music was too odd and turned her down.

Meg Christian, Michigan Festival, seventies.
Photo by Toni Armstrong Jr.

They started to let people know about their plans. An ad in the radical feminist paper *off our backs* drew a response from Joan Lowe, an experienced sound engineer from Oregon who had a degree from MIT. Her small record label had already produced several artists, including folksinger Malvina Reynolds. Meg and Ginny had heard about Joan earlier while they were on tour in the summer of 1973. They decided to go to Oregon to meet with her. Ginny recalls, "(It was) a fabulous encounter, she was a godsend to us."[29] Thrilled about their new endeavor, Joan promised to help them and suggested that a forty-five rpm record might be the right first step. The Olivia collective agreed.

Meg announced to her audiences that a new women's recording company had emerged. Excitement was high. Joan came to DC and recorded Meg Christian singing the Gerry Goffin/Carole King song "Lady" and Cris Williamson singing her own "If It Weren't for the Music." Ginny doesn't recall where they got the money to do the forty-five, but she does remember a $10,000 gift.[30] They sent the forty-five to anyone they thought could help them fund their fledgling company and then waited for the money to roll in. Beyond a fifty-dollar check from Meg's uncle they didn't receive much. Ginny doesn't blame the high-profile musicians they attempted to contact. "Part of the problem was that we didn't have anyone's address. We sent things to their record labels and agents and God only knows if they ever saw them."[31] In a time when making just one LP cost thousands of dollars, their meager fundraising efforts were barely a start.

The forty-five was meant only as a fundraising device, not as something for sale at concerts or in stores; however, word got out. Ginny laughed as she remembered,

"Women said, 'No, we're going to kill you if you don't sell it.'"[32] Armed with mailing lists garnered from *off our backs* and *The Furies*, they wrote to potential fans. They sold the recording via mail order and at Meg's shows for $1.50. There was a fifteen-cent postage fee for mail orders; the sales form also had space for an additional donation. Some fans included enough to make it an even $2 while others contributed much more. Checks of $50 or $100 were not uncommon. Five thousand forty-fives flew out the door. The income from that plus what was left of the earlier gift gave them enough to produce their first full-length album, Meg Christian's *I Know You Know*.

Ginny recalls that it was very exciting to record it. Before it was officially released, they played it for women at a New Year's party. Women would "...listen to it and just cry—there wasn't anything like this before."[33] Containing the iconic "Ode to a Gym Teacher," it also included "Valentine Song" and Cris Williamson's "Joanna." Cris performed on the album, as did many other women.

It had become clear that DC was not a good place for a feminist recording company because most of the services they needed were in entertainment capitals like New York City, Nashville, or Los Angeles. Nashville was thought to be too conservative. A couple of

Olivia Collective, seventies—bottom row: Meg Christian, Ginny Berson, Judy Dlugacz, top row: Jennifer Woodul, Kate Winter. *Photo by Joan E Biren (JEB) © 2018*

collective members were from the East Coast and didn't think New York was right. Meg and Ginny had been touring for a while and were most impressed with the West Coast where they had met musicians Margie Adam, Vicki Randle, and others. There was interest from the Los Angeles lesbian-feminist community in having them come out.

In March of 1975, five members of the Olivia collective quit their jobs and moved to Los Angeles—Meg Christian, Ginny Berson, Kate Winter, Jennifer

Woodul, and Judy Dlugacz. There were five more who didn't make the move and didn't continue with Olivia. A week or two after they arrived in California, so also did *I Know You Know*. Olivia thought they'd sell 5,000 over the life of the LP. They sold that many in two or three months. Between 10,000 and 12,000 records were sold the first year. By 1983, they'd sold 70,000.[34]

Meg Christian's music resonated with so many. Fan Julie Peddicord was just out of high school when she heard Meg's "Ode to a Gym Teacher." "I realized I was not alone. The song described completely the crush I had on my middle school gym teacher/coach."[35] Another fan, Julie Sherwood, heard Meg at a fundraiser for the publication *Lesbian Connection*. "She picked out each note with perfect precision and of course sang like an angel...I don't think my feet hit the ground for weeks!"[36]

The Olivia collective lived together in a house that also contained the Olivia office. Only Kate Winter had a job outside the record label. They pooled their resources, allowed each member a small amount for personal spending money, and put as much as they could back into the company. Meg Christian brought in most of their income from money earned at concerts. Judy recalled this about Meg, "...she was really the person we depended on to bring home the money for the first three or four years."[37] Their 1974 financial statement, published in the women's music journal *Paid My Dues* in 1975, listed expenses of $12,208, an income of $24,442, and stated that collective members were not yet paying themselves. The statement does not say how much Meg earned from concerts.[38] They published the information because they believed that feminist organizations should be held accountable to the women who supported them. Their financial picture improved in two years. In 1976 the *Advocate* reported that they expected gross sales of $300,000.

Cris Williamson

Born in Deadwood, South Dakota in 1947, this daughter of a park ranger and a nurse also lived in Wyoming and Colorado, in a family that enjoyed singalongs and music from an old Victrola. She listened to a variety of music, from jazz singer Nina Simone to folk performer Judy Collins. Schooled in piano and voice, she took up the guitar as a teen and started singing professionally at age sixteen. She released her first album, *The Artistry of Cris Williamson*, when she was seventeen and still in high school. Only five hundred were pressed on Avanti, a label created just for her. She released two more albums with them. Recorded at radio station KWYO in Sheridan, Wyoming, most of the cuts were covers of popular folk songs including Bob Dylan's "It Ain't Me Babe" and "Mr. Tambourine Man," as well as Tom Paxton's "You Were Always on My Mind" and the folk classic "House of the Rising Sun."

In 1965 she vied for the title of Miss Wyoming. For the talent portion, she sang and played one of her own songs. She didn't advance further to represent her state in the Miss America contest; however, she did walk away with Miss Congeniality.

While in college in Denver, she performed as a folk artist and as the female lead in a rock band, the Crystal Palace Guard. After graduating with a degree in English, she briefly taught high school English. Years later, she would perform in a concert at the same school where she taught. In 1969 she moved to California. Eventually settling in Los Angeles, she recorded an album for Ampex Records. Unfortunately, the label folded six months later. Fortunately, this was the album that Meg discovered when she was searching for woman-identified music early in her career.

Meeting the Olivia collective was groundbreaking for Cris Williamson. They loved that she was a strong musician, but Cris mused, "They were puzzled by me. They loved my music, but I had no politics." At the time, "I was being a hippie in northern California, living with a whole bunch of people in one house, boys and girls. It was free love."[39]

When the collective had amassed $18,000, they recorded Cris Williamson's *The Changer and the Changed* with Joan Lowe as their engineer. It was released on November 15, 1975. The iconic album contained original songs, one co-written with Jennifer Wysong ("Sweet Woman"), and one by Margie Adam ("Having Been Touched [Tender Lady])." Cris accompanied herself on piano and acoustic guitar. It also included Meg on classical guitar and vocals, as well as side players soon to become well-known to women's music fans including rocker June Millington (from the mainstream band Fanny), banjo player Woody Simmons, singer Holly Near, and, according to the liner notes, Margie Adam on "tacky piano." The joyous chorus on "Song of the Soul" consisted of Cris's sister Becky, members of the Olivia collective, and Vicki Randle. Songs included "One of the Light," about her spiritual quest; "Sister," originally written for a musical about Sister Aimee McPherson; and "Hurts Like the Devil," a breakup song with a cheerful feel, recorded with a lively banjo accompaniment.

Probably her most popular song, still requested by many audiences, was "Sweet Woman." One of the first love songs ever recorded about one woman to another woman, she wrote the beautiful melody to a poem sent to her by her girlfriend Jennifer Wysong. In the album liner notes, Cris wrote, "I returned from the first National Women's Music Festival filled with such warmth in my soul, and I ran to my piano to capture the beautiful strength of women and its impact on me."

"With 'Sweet Woman,' all of the sudden there were women who would get it. And they'd about drive off the road. They'd write me. 'Oh My God!...It's a woman singing about another woman. How powerful!'...Power can come from the simplest place, which for me is about the truth. There is nothing quite so fine as telling the truth straight like that and not being afraid. I didn't know to be afraid."[40]

This album was important to many women. Fan Michelle Marquand heard it in the seventies, during her first year of college. She'd left home at eighteen, driven out by anti-gay bullying that included someone spray-painting their driveway with "Michelle the queer lives here." Her lover played *Changer and the Changed* for her. "I was blown away—women singing about loving women.

It was an epiphany to me because growing up in Indiana I was sure there were four lesbians in the whole world besides me. I held that music in my heart, like a talisman against all the harassment and prejudice I experienced in my youth… That album was a lifeline to me."[41] Barbara Goldman, another fan, also found strength in the album. Faced with living alone for the first time in her life, she recalls, "I played it all day. Nearly wore it out."[42] Ginger Starling was a seminary student when she first heard Cris Williamson. "I had no idea my life was about to careen in a whole new direction."[43] Karen Escovitz discovered *Changer and the Changed* when she was a teenager. Her parents brought it home after hearing one of the songs at a self-help seminar. "I remember listening to 'Tender Lady' and crying and not knowing why."[44] It led to her discovering more women's music and to her identity as a lesbian.

Julie Nicolay was a college student when she first heard this album, not long after it came out. She was in her dorm when "…from down the hall I heard someone singing 'Sweet Woman.' I immediately froze, my heart beating…I got up and walked down the hall to the room and sat against the wall, listening with big tears. I had yet to meet another lesbian. When the album side was over, I screwed up my courage and with a bit of a shaky hand, knocked on her door. As the door opened and this woman smiled at me, my life went exactly where it was meant to…I bought *Changer* and of course, everything else Olivia sold."[45]

As they had been with Meg's album, the Olivia collective was modest in their expectations and thought they'd sell 10,000 of *Changer and the Changed*. Instead, in just a couple of years, they sold between 75,000 and 80,000 and the album charted on *Billboard*. Cris Williamson went on to sell thousands of recordings, and *The Changer and the Changed* is the bestselling women's music album of all time.[46]

Women's music journal *HOT WIRE* described her music well: "Her images are stark and wild: fire, shooting stars, flowing water, light, angels, and the endless, sweeping wind. Her historical themes stir our collective unconscious: Peter Pan, Dorothy of Oz, the renegade Crazy Horse." Friend and fellow performer Teresa Trull describes her this way, "…Cris is a real poet. She writes in a lot of images, beautiful images…"[47] Cris says about her own work: "I've never really defined my music. I like to stress the interconnectedness between ourselves and the environment and all creatures."[48]

Holly Near and Redwood Records

Like Cris Williamson, Holly Near loved singing from an early age. Growing up in a music-filled household in the country near Ukiah, a small farm town in northern California, she found few opportunities to perform unless you count standing out in a field and crooning to the cows. Later she named her music publishing company Hereford Music.

Growing up, she honed her skills at talent shows, hospitals, and afternoon teas. In high school she sang with the Freedom Singers, a quartet that fashioned themselves after the Kingston Trio and the Weavers. She was also enamoured of musical theater and played Eliza in the school's presentation of *My Fair Lady*. In the late sixties, after high school, she studied theater arts at UCLA. Horrified by the Vietnam War, she joined the activist group Another Mother for Peace. She stuffed envelopes for them while continuing to perform in school musicals. In 1969 she got her first film role, in *Angel, Angel, Down We Go*, starring Jennifer Jones. The next year she landed a part in the Broadway production of *Hair*. "I made a perfect candidate for *Hair*. First of all, I had the *hair*, lots of it. Second, I had a big voice, strong enough to survive the chorus numbers. Third, I was willing to do the nude scene..."[49]

One night she showed up for work to find cast members gathered in the green room intently discussing the recent killings of students by the National Guard at a Kent State anti-war rally. She admitted that she hadn't heard about the event and even though she came from a political family, wasn't sure she wanted to do anything to protest the killings. The cast decided to eliminate their big finale, "Let the Sunshine In," and instead, offer a silent vigil. Holly abstained from the voting, afraid that it would make the audience mad and also violate her contract. She changed her mind when she saw how stunned the audience was, deciding that it was an effective tool. About a year later in 1971, Kent State students would ask her to write a song for their memorial. On the plane traveling there, she wrote "It Could Have Been Me."

Around this time, she joined another anti-war group, Entertainment Industry for Peace and Justice. It was at one of their meetings that she first heard Jane Fonda speak about an anti-war show called FTA (Free the Army and also known as Fuck the Army). Produced by Jane Fonda, Donald Sutherland, and Francine Parke, the variety show toured the country entertaining soldiers, featuring Dick Gregory, Country Joe McDonald and others. When a cast member dropped out, Holly auditioned at Fonda's house and got the part.

Holly admitted that she wasn't politically sophisticated at first. She figured that if Jane was thrilled to have someone with stage presence and talent, she could teach her. Shortly afterward, they left for Hawaii, Japan, and the Philippines. On the tour she received a sobering education in racism, colonialism, and cultural disruption. The tour ended late in 1971. She toured again with Jane Fonda and Tom Hayden in 1972 and 1973. They were received with great enthusiasm in many places but there were times when the show was disrupted with a bomb threat.

She continued work in film and TV, including a guest spot on *The Partridge Family*. Her character, Gloria Goldstein, ran against Keith Partridge in a school election. Her character cried after losing but confided that they were tears of joy because the resulting publicity encouraged the school's newspaper editor to ask her out. Holly pleaded with the director to change that demeaning line. She was given a firm no. She also appeared on *All in the Family* and *Mod Squad*. But her heart by now was in peace activism and folk music. Even though she didn't perform with a guitar and her influences were more Broadway than folk, she found a ready audience at places such as the Ash Grove, a well-known folk venue that also hosted the Byrds, Janis Ian, and Tret Fure.

Holly started cutting demos for record companies. Executives loved that she was drawing big crowds at LA-area clubs. They didn't like that her music was so political. A producer at one label said her voice lacked "an element of submission." In those days, there weren't many role models for women in music. You had to be Dusty Springfield or Janis Joplin and she didn't fit into either mold.

People who'd heard her in Free The Army and elsewhere started asking about a record. It seemed logical to make one on her own even though she'd never been in a real recording studio. She didn't think about the enormity of starting a record label—only that she wanted to get the music out there. Redwood Records, named for the beautiful trees near her Ukiah home, began in 1972. Her long-time friend Jeff Langley had been playing piano for her at her shows, and so he joined her for the album. At first the arrangements were simply voice and piano but as they saw and explored the possibilities, other instruments were added. Holly and Jeff learned as they went. Her parents organized the business. "As far as I know there'd never been an artist who had an independent label like I did. We were making this up as we went along."[50] *Hang in There* was released in 1973. Even after this release and several more albums, she didn't give up her dream of working in the mainstream. "I would just go ahead and make this record and still thought that I would make my way back to the music business and figure out how to live in both worlds—do anti-war material in the mainstream."[51]

Her music grew in popularity. She sold *Hang in There* at shows and gathered names for a mailing list. In each city where she played she'd find the record stores, sometimes ripping that page out of the phone book, and sending them to her mother who was handling her shipping. She performed all over the US and in Vietnam. Her next release, *A Live Album*, contained "It Could've Been Me" plus others that she'd been performing at shows.

In 1975, the LA Women's Building was planning a fundraiser. Some of the organizers were uncertain about this heterosexual anti-war singer but in the end, she was invited, as were Margie Adam, Meg Christian, Lily Tomlin, Cris Williamson, and The Alice Stone Ladies Society Orchestra (a six-piece old-time jazz ensemble). Holly was thrilled to be a part of this huge production, the first time she'd participated in an all-woman event. She invited Meg, Margie, and Cris to her house for rehearsals. In spite of being told that she wouldn't get along with lesbian separatist Meg, they all immediately formed a rapport, enjoying the beautiful harmonies and a lot of laughs.

The show was a great success, incorporating Cris's "Waterfall," Holly's "It Could Have Been Me," Margie's "Would You Like to Tapdance," and Meg's "Ode to a Gym Teacher." Margie thought she heard a buzz in the speakers but quickly realized it was something much nicer—the audience singing along. They all performed in a skit, "Goodbye, Miss Sweeny," Cris playing a precocious seven-year-old who had a crush on her teacher. Holly played the object of her crush, the formidable Miss Sweeny. Not long afterward, the four musicians did a TV show, *Come Out Singing*, that won a local Emmy.

That summer Holly performed at her first women's music festival, the San Diego Women's Music Festival. Nervous because most of the women were lesbians, Holly kept to herself. When it came time for her to perform, she was relieved to fall into familiar harmonies with friend Meg.

As she was invited to perform for different groups, she expanded her activism, adding feminist elements. "My voice has always been my passport and then I ran like hell to catch up."[52] While many women fans loved this direction toward feminism, she also got angry letters from others who thought she should be singing about "more important" issues.

As Holly was finishing her third release, *You Can Know All I Am*, she was asked to join the landmark Women on Wheels tour, with Cris Williamson, Margie Adam, and Meg Christian. They wowed audiences in eight concerts all over California. On the way home

Holly Near and band performance at Artemis Café in mid-seventies: JT Thomas, Carolyn Brandy, Holly Near, Suzanne Vincenza, Barbara Cobb, Meg Christian. *Private collection, Holly Near.*

from their last show, Holly gave Meg a ride to a party. Meg was in a committed relationship and Holly was a straight girl thinking about marriage, but that didn't stop them from sitting in the car for four hours, Holly's hand on Meg's knee. They never went inside to the party. Holly soon broke up with her boyfriend. Meg and her lover Ginny split also. Holly and Meg were together for three and a half years. Ginny continued as Meg's manager.

Margie Adam and Boo (Barbara) Price

Like Holly, Margie Adam was from California. She was born in 1947 in Lompoc to a newspaper publisher and a piano instructor. In a household bursting with politics and culture, her piano instruction began as soon as she could get up on the bench. Songwriting started early. Her first song was penned at the tender age of fifteen, a love song to her sweetheart Kathy. She had a brief career as a junior high teacher but her real passion was music. She loved Dusty Springfield, Carole King, and Laura Nyro. When she discovered Cris Williamson's Ampex album, she was thrilled.

In April 1973, she was in Los Angeles, making the rounds of record labels with a demo tape of her original songs. All of them turned her down, and in the process she learned that her songs didn't fit in with mainstream music. She was staying with her girlfriend who told Margie she'd be attending the National Lesbian Conference. This groundbreaking event was held at Moore Hall on the UCLA campus and produced by Lesbian Activist Women, a group that included *Lesbian Tide* newspaper publisher Jeanne Cordova. Margie decided to attend, even though she knew little about it. There were 1,500 women there, double the capacity of the hall, and energy was high. Performers included pianist/singer

Margie Adam, 1981.
Photo by Pat Gargaetas (PGar).

Linda Shear and folksinger M'Lou Brubaker.[53] Their songs were different from Margie's music. She remembers, "Linda would say all this incendiary stuff then sing a beautiful song. They called it lesbian music."[54] Even though she admits that Linda scared her she went to a workshop she offered, signed her mailing list and even offered her and her friends a place to stay for the night. Margie played them a few songs, so shy that she performed with her back to them.

Author Kate Millett gave a speech at the conference and invited everyone to come to a music festival at Sacramento State where she was teaching. A month later, Margie nervously gave her first public performance at the small event's open mic, confessing to the crowd that she wasn't a performer and didn't actually know what she was doing.

On Sunday morning of the festival Kate Millett opened up a building so they'd have access to a piano and asked Margie to sing the songs she'd sung at the open mic. Woody Simmons was also there, playing the piano and banjo. Margie comments, "We were lovers immediately. It didn't matter that I had a lover already. I look back now and think everything was sexualized...the passion we felt was 360 degrees—the music we wrote in bed was the music we wrote—there was no seam." Later, she sang with Cris Williamson and remembers, "...not being able to hear where her voice ended and mine started... *that* was women's music."[55]

Jeanne Cordova was also at that festival and invited Margie to do a fundraiser for the *Lesbian Tide*. On the way home from Sacramento Margie offered her a place to stay. Sitting in her living room, Margie played songs for her. "Jeanne said, 'You know, there's more going on in women's lives...than just love.'" Margie recalls, "I had no idea what she was talking about. 'What about writing music about the world, about feelings besides love?' *Bingo*."[56]

A similar energy was happening all over the country. Margie recalls, "Lesbian feminists in small circles all over the country were simply on fire! The word-of-mouth promotion of events was extremely effective during this time. Part of it was that a critical mass of us knew each other—or knew of each other. And we were gripped by the unfolding possibility that we could build a community with our bare hands, with our bursting woman-loving hearts."[57]

In 1974 she was asked to perform at the first National Women's Music Festival in Champaign-Urbana, Illinois where she heard Cris Williamson and others. Energized by each other's music, Cris invited Margie to share her shows at the Full Moon Coffeehouse and the Wild Wild West in San Francisco. Margie invited Cris to her concert for the Los Angeles Women's Building. Cris played in Denver and invited Margie there. Margie also did gigs with Vicki Randle and Meg Christian. In the fall of that same year, 1974, Margie, Cris, and Vicki did a show at the Shrine Auditorium in Los Angeles. Margie recounted that so much happened in the months between the first and second National Women's Music Festival that it was hard to keep the timing of all these events straight.

Boo Price, then a politically active young student who'd just started studying law at UC Davis, happened to be in Los Angeles the same weekend as the show at the Shrine. Ginny Berson, a friend who'd been at the National festival, urged Boo to attend.

Margie remembers, "What she witnessed was each of us taking hold of the audience with equal intention and artistry and then stepping out of the spotlight to accompany and sing backup for each other. She immediately grasped that what we were doing was a practical model for feminism that was easily transferable from town to town, from community to community...she saw the concert as a tool to raise consciousness and attention regarding the issues within the community and beyond through over-ground media."[58]

Boo asked Margie if a comparable concert could be done in Davis, California. She had recently started a lesbian caucus at the law school there. The students were looking for a fundraiser to support affirmative action because of the groundbreaking Bakke case in which a white student argued before the Supreme Court that his exclusion from the UC Davis medical school was based on a racial quota and therefore unconstitutional. Boo had produced shows before and thought a concert was a great idea. The students suggested including Tower of Power, a popular mainstream R&B band. "I said, well, that's a good idea but I have a better idea. Let's do a women's music concert," Boo recalled. "The term was so brand new. No one knew what I was talking about."[59] They all agreed to do the event.

She rented the largest space on campus, Freeborn Auditorium, hoping to fill all of its one thousand seats. She went to every campus women's organization, from the garden club to the sororities, to tell them about the show. She played a tape of Vicki Randle in the hallways of the law school every day at lunch. Three hundred and fifty people showed up to hear Meg Christian, Margie Adam, and Vicki Randle. "The next morning, I said to myself that was fun and I'm glad I did it and I *never* want to do it again. Within a couple of weeks, I was planning another concert in the spring in a hall that held five hundred people which we totally crammed."[60] From that first show in the fall to the second one, the lesbian community exploded with new possibilities. Women came from all over California and from other states for that next concert featuring Margie Adam, Cris Williamson, and Meg Christian.

Boo and Margie discovered a similar passion for feminist principles and a strong belief that women's music could play an important part in relaying that ideology. Margie said, "She also was crazy about my music which was no small thing."[61] They became lovers a few months later and not long after that, Boo became her manager.

Margie's touring life developed organically. Margie remembers, "I was propositioned by complete strangers who said variations of the following: 'I saw you perform at National and I'm a student at the University of Connecticut in Storrs. The Women's Center has some money and we want to bring you!'"[62] It was an ironic development for a musician who didn't really consider herself a performer, only a songwriter. She was completely amazed that these venues kept calling her. She'd tell them, by way of "full disclosure," "Now…you know I'm not a performer, right?" The response was always the same: "That's okay. Just come sing your music."

Linda Shear and Family of Woman

Women's music was happening in the heart of the country too. In May 1972, when Holly Near was touring with Jane Fonda, and Meg Christian was playing in DC-area bars, Linda Shear was part of a duo in an out-lesbian performance at the University of Illinois, Chicago, at an event organized by a group called Lesbian Liberation. Family of Woman formed shortly after that. They expanded from a duo into varied performers and started playing concerts, a radical effort at a time when most lesbian music could only be heard in bars. In a 1973 edition of *Sisters: By and for Lesbians*, a publication of the Daughters of Bilitis in San Francisco, members of the band asserted, "We refuse to play bars or clubs because most of the club owners are men. We play only women's concerts because we are not background music for other activities."

Linda was writing a little but most of the songs were popular covers, some with changed lyrics. Their goal was to include songs written only by lesbians. Performances included poetry and stories. "The energy in the concert rooms was palpable," Linda remembers.[63] They started to tour and appeared at the Los Angeles Lesbian Conference where they met young Margie Adam.

There was no lesbian movement then, just individual musicians and bands performing. At one point, Linda got a letter from Meg Christian saying that she'd been playing in bars and maybe she'd try doing concerts too.

The band lasted a difficult two-and-a-half years. There was love among them but as Linda said, they "… didn't handle conflict well."[64] Linda continued to perform solo, and after moving to Massachusetts released *A Lesbian Portrait* in 1974 on cassette and reel-to-reel. In 1977 it was issued on LP. It contained woman-affirming songs written from 1972 to 1975 including "Family of Womyn," and "Lesbian Wombmoon." Ads for the release proudly said "… I am not a Woman Musician, I am a LESBIAN MUSICIAN." The liner notes emphatically stated that the music was for lesbians only. She'd started doing lesbian-only concerts in 1976. In 1978 she stopped performing to go to graduate school, then became a CPA.

The Chicago and New Haven Women's Liberation Rock Bands

Not all of early women's music artists were pop/folk-oriented singer-songwriters. The Chicago Women's Liberation Rock Band was formed in 1970 by keyboard player Naomi Weisstein because she was tired of the woman-hating lyrics often found in rock. She was a part of the Chicago Women's Liberation Union, founded in 1969, that also included a graphics collective, a legal clinic, a speaker's bureau, and the groundbreaking abortion counseling service Jane—very radical in an era when women's studies college curriculums were just gearing up.

In true feminist form, all women were welcome into the new band, regardless of skill. Six women played instruments ranging from drums to banjo and there were eleven vocalists. Founder Weisstein surmised, "This many vocalists was no surprise because the boy bands tolerated 'chick singers' fronting for them, so singing is what females gravitated towards."[65]

Their first performance at Chicago's Grant Park for International Women's Day was a musical disaster. It was

Chicago Women's Liberation Rock Band.
Used with permission, Virginia Blaisdell and Naomi Weisstein.

clear their idealistic vision needed modification. Eventually, the lineup was pared down to Susan Abod (bass, vocals), Sherry Jenkins (guitar, vocals), Patricia Miller (guitar, vocals), Linda Mitchell (manager), Fania Mantalvo (drums), Suzanne Prescott (drums), and Naomi Weisstein (keyboards). Some of the vocalists were asked to leave or get voice lessons (Weisstein called them "tuneless hippy singers") and it made them angry. Weisstein recalls, "The protest revealed a deep division in the goals of different players, which persisted for the life of the band and ultimately was a factor in destroying it, despite the addition of new and more skillful musicians from time to time. The division was between those who wanted to play liberatory feminist rock to the widest possible audience, which meant getting good enough to record and broadcast; and those who just wanted to play with their sisters no matter how they sounded..."[66]

There had been other all-women rock bands but they were the first feminist rock band. By today's standards they might be considered folk-rock; however, back then, it was highly unusual to see a woman with an electric guitar or behind a set of drums.

They replaced the sexist lyrics of popular rock songs with feminist ones. "Papa Don't Lay That Shit on Me" used a traditional blues tune with new lyrics by two band members. Audiences screamed, danced, and sang along. At some shows women ripped off their shirts. Crowds mobbed the stage at the end. Women musicians were encouraged to perform their own music. After one gig, one of the band's guitarists found a note in her guitar case from a fan who was so thrilled about the group, she'd decided to start guitar lessons. The band toured mostly in the Midwest and Northeast.

The New Haven Women's Liberation Rock Band included Jennifer Abod, sister of the Chicago band's bassist. Like their sister band, their hard-hitting feminist lyrics shone in songs like "The Abortion Song" and "Sister Witch." In a 1974 article in the *Lesbian Tide* members outlined some important points. "We must make our own standards so that we don't judge ourselves in terms of pig values...We must preserve the consciousness of our oppression and our need of collective action and our response to it. We can't let promoters, rip-off artists and bandwagon writers con us into writing and singing 'sad songs by the river' and songs about being a liberated chic (sic) while the conditions that cause us suffering go unchanged." They go on to say that they chose to perform for mixed audiences (men and women) but their performances were for women because "men are superfluous."

In 1972 the New Haven and Chicago bands recorded *Mountain Moving Day* for Rounder Records, the bands' only recording. The Chicago band disbanded in 1973 when Naomi Weisstein moved from the Midwest. The New Haven band also broke up.

Alix Dobkin

On the East Coast another feminist musician was making her mark. Alix Dobkin's early years were mostly spent in New York City. There was always music in her home, from baroque to folk. She was a tomboy who was usually chosen first for sports teams and loved hanging out with friends, all of them boys. The daughter of progressive Jewish parents who were also Communists, there was constant worry about the FBI. Her mother instructed her not to open the door if they came around.

At a camp run by the Jewish People's Fraternal Order, she enjoyed singing folk songs such as "Follow the Drinking Gourd" and "Joe Hill." She formed a tight bond with other campers. They loved attending folk concerts where they heard the Weavers, Earl Robinson, and Sonny Terry and Brownie McGhee. In eighth grade, Alix found herself drawn to a female cheerleader. She knew to keep her feelings hidden. In her teens, she joined the Communist Party. In 1956, the FBI opened a file about her.

She was inspired to learn the guitar after her friend Eliot led the way. The old acoustic had strings so high off the neck it was nearly impossible to play. That didn't stop a determined Alix who practiced daily, using techniques learned from her friend and those she found on her own. After buying a new guitar with money saved from a summer job, she and Eliot started to attend frequent jams where musicians would take turns playing union songs, Scottish and Irish tunes, and old folk songs. As the folk boom gathered steam, the rooms became more and more crowded.

In 1960, while attending college in Philadelphia, she once again fell in love with a woman. She and Nancy broke up when Nancy met "the man of her dreams."

In Philadelphia Alix got her first singing job. It led to other gigs, sometimes opening for Bill Cosby. In the early sixties, after college, she headed to Greenwich Village in New York City. Basket houses—venues where musicians could perform and pass a basket for pay—were very popular. She played at many, including the Gaslight, where this kid in her twenties could hone her repertoire of international folk songs. Even the FBI noted that she was becoming well known in Greenwich Village clubs. When the gigs didn't support her, she found work as a secretary. Around this time, she started dating Sam, a guy she met at the Gaslight.

While playing at Gerde's Folk City, she met Suze Rotolo whose boyfriend was a young skinny folksinger named Bob Dylan. He was soon added to their group of friends that included comic Flip Wilson, folksinger Tom Paxton and protest singer Phil Ochs. After the Gaslight closed for the business day, the group had raucous late-night poker sessions. Alix was never invited to play—"chicks" were not allowed—instead, she refilled their drinks and emptied ashtrays.

For a time, she and Dylan took turns taking each other out for late-night breakfasts. He called her his favorite female singer and that may have been true although Alix realized later that he used that line on other women folkies. One night at a gig in Philly Dylan told her he'd just written a song that he wanted her to sing, "Don't Think Twice It's All Right." She presented it at a few gigs but ultimately decided it wasn't for her. He was decidedly unhappy about her response. In later years her daughter urged her to put it back into her concerts so she did.

At the time, two women singers on the same bill were frowned upon. They were expected to sing certain songs and wear dresses and makeup. Former tomboy Alix didn't fit in that way so she made a special effort to offer a unique presentation of songs written by others. It wasn't until Tim Hardin ("If I Were a Carpenter") made a sexist comment while in her living room that she started to write her own songs. More songs followed, although at the time, most of her repertoire was still written by others. Traveling by bus and drive-away cars, she toured the East Coast and Midwest. The FBI continued to monitor her activities even though she had drifted away from the Party.

Back in New York City in 1965, she married Sam. In her autobiography, *My Red Blood*, Alix wrote, "I would join the ranks of Dick and Jane's all-American mom, smile by the back door, wipe my hands on my apron, and 'live happily ever after.' With Sam I could be a wife and also retain my career…" Just six days before, gay protesters, the men in suits and the women in dresses, had carried signs and marched in front of the White House. Even though nothing like that had ever happened before it went unnoticed by the new bride.

They soon moved to Coconut Grove, Florida, to open a folk club. When she was left out of business decisions, she said nothing but felt conflicted. The club featured popular acts like Joni Mitchell, Simon and Garfunkel, Gordon Lightfoot, Ronnie Gilbert from the Weavers and Alix's old friend Bob Dylan, but attendance fluctuated wildly with overdue bills being a constant headache. They closed after a short run, returned to New York, and eventually settled in Woodstock, N.Y.

She had an opportunity to record for two different mainstream recording labels, Columbia and Elektra. Negotiations stalled for the former when she told them she wasn't sure about singing for men. When she asked Elektra for a woman engineer and musicians, they agreed. When she added that she also wanted final say over publicity, they said no and she walked away.

Her life changed in 1970 when she joined a feminist consciousness-raising group. "It felt comfortable and exciting, sort of like Party meetings combined with the easy intimacy of a girls' team venturing inward together, making our way into risky unfamiliar personal terrain with no map."[67] Her feminist journey continued with the discovery of Germaine Greer's *The Female Eunuch*. Soon after, her daughter Adrian was born.

Her new feminist consciousness helped her to realize that her marriage wasn't working. She left Sam and took her infant daughter to New York City. One night in her dark living room, she stood with her guitar and had a vision of rows of women attentively listening to her.

Public radio was a frequent companion, especially WBAI in New York City. One night Alix heard DJ Liza Cowan complain about the lack of women singer-songwriters. Alix called and introduced herself. A few months later, she played live on her show. Liza loved her songs, saying that it was the first time she'd heard music that was specifically by and about women. It also didn't hurt that they "grinned stupidly at each other" the whole time. Alix was soon making frequent appearances on the show.

One night Alix came to WBAI with a tape of a new song, "The Woman in Your Life is You." Liza started using it as the sign-off for her late night show. In the liner notes of her first album Alix remembered, "...Tuesday after Tuesday...I fell asleep contentedly listening to her broadcast of the tune I'd written for her." Soon, Liza was the woman in her life.

At performances in New York City, women asked Alix about recording. She recalls, "Women kept saying, 'You've *got* to record these songs!' and '*When* will you put out a record?' Women really wanted it."[68] She raised $3,300 for her first album—all the money she needed—on a private lesbian cruise around New York City in 1973 and then went into the studio. With new friend and flute player Kay Gardner and bassist Patches Attom (the pseudonym of a lesbian afraid to come out) they recorded *Lavender Jane Loves Women*, the first album financed, engineered, and performed by women that received national distribution. Arranged by Kay Gardner, it featured original songs by Alix including "View from a Gay Head," a song that used "lesbian" more times than any previously recorded song, "A Woman's Love," written for Liza's birthday, and "The Woman in Your Life is You." Also included were songs written by others like "Eppie Morrie," a traditional folk tune previously performed by Ewan MacColl but with a different ending, and "I Only Want to be With You," a song made famous by Dusty Springfield.

Alix originally pressed one thousand albums because that's all she could afford. Covers were printed free at a community press. Groups of supporters pasted covers on the records and put in the inserts. She sold them at shows and through an ad in *Ms.*, at the time, a new publication. With the proceeds from that pressing, she was able to produce more copies. This time, it came with printed jackets.

Fan Mary Forst recalls, "I will never forget getting the record *Lavender Jane Loves Women*...marveling at the feeling of validation and legitimacy of having our values and experiences mirrored back to us in a media form!"[69] Another fan, Pat Gargaetas, met a woman at a women's bookstore right after the release of the album. She insisted that Pat listen to it. "She was right. I HAD to hear it. That album changed everything about listening to music. At that point I essentially checked out of 'popular' music."[70] Writer and activist Elana Dykewomon was profoundly moved after hearing *Lavender Jane Loves Women* in the early seventies. "I remember putting it on the record player, listening, staring out the second-story window. Oh damn, I thought, if they get ahold of this they'll kill us. They: whatever ancient patriarchal army had destroyed the Amazons of North Africa and Southern Europe. I was transported to that archetypal struggle—and then moved beyond it, back into the women's realm, where every creativity was again possible..."[71]

While Alix's earlier career in folk music helped with stage presence, it didn't help her book her first tour. She needed audiences with a feminist consciousness, so she got the names of venues and other resources from the feminist newspaper *off our backs*. Word of mouth contributed as did the burgeoning feminist scene sprouting up at colleges. "I learned as I went along...everybody was making it up then. It was the right place at the right time with the right people. Women who had experience in the civil rights movement and oh, just so many things that were interacting and exploding when feminism met lesbianism."[72] Alix toured with Kay Gardner, drawing crowds of sixty or seventy.

Kay Gardner

When Kay Gardner met Alix Dobkin, she had recently completed a master of music degree in flute performance and was fresh from the dissolution of an eleven-year marriage. She'd played the piano since the age of four and since the age of eight, the flute. Even though she'd never seen an orchestra conductor who was a woman, she longed to do just that. Composing was also a big part of her musical life.

She first found feminism in 1963 through Betty Friedan's *The Feminine Mystique*. In the women's chamber music ensemble where she played, the book and its ideas were intensely discussed but there was no women's movement at the time to back them up. Kay's husband so discouraged her that she returned to her life of homemaker and mother to two daughters. It would be several years before their divorce.

In the late sixties her feminism was further sparked by other writers including Sylvia Plath, Kate Millett, and Germaine Greer. It wasn't long before she was reading every piece of feminist writing within her reach. She was a very busy woman, playing in two orchestras as well as her own chamber group, teaching flute at two different colleges and raising two children. Somehow, she found time to fall in love with a woman. It changed her life.

In the early seventies, while earning another degree, she discovered Sophie Drinker's *Music and Women: The Story of Women in Their Relation to Music*. This important work helped spark Kay's interest in music and spirituality and how it all related to women. In November 1974 she told the *Lesbian Tide*, "I've spent my entire life immersed in music…I am also a lesbian…My training (I have a Master of Music degree) has been in re-creating men's classical music. No more, folks! Women's music, and the creation of it is where I'm at and where I'll stay."

In the summer of 1974, she toured New England with her woman lover. Their improvisational music touched the crowds. She boasted to the *Lesbian Tide* that, "Our music healed and lifted spirits in ways that no male music can." The women in their audiences were so moved that they spontaneously whooped and hollered, sang, and danced with the music.

In addition to touring and gigs with Alix Dobkin, she did her own performances on flute, guitar, and piano. Her instrumentals reflected her classical background. She also incorporated original folk tunes, accompanying herself on the guitar. Some of her fondest memories were of performing at early women's music festivals including The Boston Women's Music Festival in October 1975. She did her own set, offering some of the songs she would later include on her first release, *Mooncircles*. She also loved playing with others at the festival.

After forming Urana Records with engineer Marilyn Ries, she set about finding financing. It took a tremendous effort to raise money for her music as well as the others on their label (which included folksinger Casse Culver). She made up brochures and handed them out at the Boston event and other performances. A letter was sent to family and friends, even those she rarely saw. She also organized fundraising parties where she'd talk about her music and hand out letters. In addition, there were women who loaned or gave her large amounts of money including a health food store owner who contributed $7,000 toward one of her label's recordings and E. Shirley Watt, also known as Squirrel, who gave almost $72,000 for the production of two recordings. Squirrel financed other early women's music recordings including those from Maxine Feldman, Robin Flower, and Willie Tyson.

Kay Gardner's first album was released in late 1975. In subsequent years it might have been labeled New Age but that genre had not yet been established. Also, this was far from the tepid arrangements that some associate with New Age. In the liner notes Kay commented, "My music is naturally suited for subtle activities…I think it's perfectly alright for music to be in the background. It can often have a very healing effect." Her vibrant folk/classical compositions featured Kay on flutes, vocals, finger cymbals, autoharp, and guitar. Meg Christian played guitar on three cuts while pianist Althea Waites and a host of string and percussion players rounded out the band. "Prayer to Aphrodite" is based on a poem by Sappho. It's played in the mixolydian mode, a scale based on the fifth note of the western scale. Some believe this mode arouses passion so it's perfect for a song honoring a lesbian poet who wrote about love. "Lunamuse" has a circular structure, with the climax in the middle. In the liner notes Kay remarked that the form "…symbolizes the wholeness of women, our connectedness to the rest of the biosphere. It also parallels the rhythms of women's lovemaking, meditation, and circle dancing." It's in the key of E minor, thought to aid digestion and help with meditation because its vibration has a calming effect on our bodies.

Unlike some of the other women's music made at the time, her work did not focus on a political message but rather on healing and spirituality. She maintained that both were important feminist principles.

Sweet Honey in the Rock

Offering something very different was this group started by Dr. Bernice Johnson Reagon. A member of the Freedom Singers, a group founded in 1961 that sang at civil rights demonstrations throughout the South, in the early seventies, she was the vocal director of the DC Black Repertory Company. Urged to start a singing group, she took ten members from the vocal workshops she was leading and taught them the traditional song "Sweet Honey in the Rock." This group didn't jell but a later one did. Their first performance as the a cappella ensemble Sweet Honey in the Rock occurred at Howard University in 1973. They continued to perform traditional songs such as "No More Auction Block for Me" and the blues tune "See See Rider." They added original compositions. "Joan Little" was written by Bernice about a woman accused of killing her jailer rapist. Songs composed by her and other members covered important topics like racism, sexism, and unfair hous-

ing. They sang about mothers, daughters, and community at universities, concert halls and music festivals all over the world, including the 1979 Michigan Womyn's Music Festival.

Engineer Boden Sandstrom often ran their sound when they were in DC and in

Sweet Honey in the Rock, 1982.
Photo by Irene Young © 1982.

other locales. She never tired of it, calling their music uplifting, appreciative of the wide variety of sounds they offered, a pleasing challenge to an engineer. They also proved to concertgoers that unaccompanied singing with occasional percussion is not limited in what it can do. For many women's music audiences, it was the first time they'd heard something outside of a standard guitar/bass/drum band, or a solo singer-songwriter with piano or guitar.

Their first recording, *Sweet Honey in the Rock*, was released in 1976 on folk label Flying Fish Records. The lineup changing over the years, they went on to release more than twenty albums on various labels.

Casse Culver

Casse Culver was another East Coast-based performer. Growing up, she was influenced by many genres of music, from show tunes to country. She learned to play her own music and in the late sixties and early seventies worked as a street singer. Like many young people, she headed to the Woodstock festival in 1969. She met Albert Grossman there, manager for many musicians including Bob Dylan and Janis Joplin. Based on his recommendation, she auditioned for a music publishing company and signed a contract with them. In 1972 this newly out lesbian also recorded an album but Grossman wasn't happy with it. Casse recalls that he called her into his office and said, "I don't care what you do in your bedroom, just don't go screaming it down the streets."[73] Not only was the album never released, but until she spent a lot of money to get out of the contract, she couldn't record anything else. When she found women's music, it was an epiphany.

"It was the first time that people really listened to what I had to say. They were quiet. They paid attention. Not only did they do that, then they acknowledged me after what I said. They applauded or they cheered. Or they cried. Or they came up to me afterwards and said, thank you so much for singing some particular song, that makes something for me so much easier to get through. For me it was an opportunity to be totally authentic. Totally honest. No fear of censorship."[74]

Her album *3 Gypsies* was released in 1978 and included Margie Adam (keyboards), Kay Gardner (flute), and Susan Abod (bass). Casse offered mostly original songs on guitar, autoharp and harmonica. One song held special meaning for her. "'Good Old Dora', which spelled GOD ... was my vision of what God is really like. God

Recording of Casse Culver's *3 Gypsies* — bottom row: Joan E. Biren (JEB), Joan Gibson, second row: Betty MacDonald, Roz Richter, Susan Abod, Mary Wings, Maxine Feldman, third row: Marilyn Ries, Paula Spiro, Margie Adam, Willie Tyson, Casse Culver, top row: Boden Sandstrom, Barbara Edwards, Robin Flower, Kay Gardner. Many of these women were musicians on the project. Marilyn was the engineer and Joan, a financial supporter. *Photo by Joan E Biren (JEB) ©2018.*

is there as a supportive mother-like figure helping us do what we need to do to have a decent life."[75]

She toured. Boo Price said she was, "...one of the very strongest songwriters of the first group (of women's music performers) ... (a) really natural performer. Lots of joy in her performances."[76]

Willie Tyson

Also known for the joy in her work as well as a charming stage presence and funny songs, Willie recorded and released her first women's music album *Full Count*, on her label Lima Bean Records, in 1974. An earlier album, *Sweet William of the West*, was released in 1972. Two more albums followed, *Debutante* and in 1979, *Willie Tyson*. A folkie who dabbled in other styles, she wrote sharp-witted songs like "Mommy Will There Be Muzak in Heaven?" and performed the occasional cover such as Peggy Seeger's "Gonna Be an Engineer."[77] She toured extensively, sometimes with bassist Susan Abod (Chicago Women's Liberation Rock Band). After her third album, Willie stopped performing. She worked for years afterward as a civil engineer.

The Berkeley Women's Music Collective

The early seventies were a rich time for women musicians. Nancy Vogl attended the landmark 1973 lesbian conference at UCLA and later that year, the Sacramento women's festival. "After I had those two experiences," she remarked to *HOT WIRE* in 1988, "I knew that there was something I wanted to be a part of. I moved into a collective household of women on a Saturday, and by the following Wednesday we said, 'Let's be a band.'"

Nancy had long been a music fan. When she was twelve, she found an old guitar in someone's garbage and her dad fixed it up. She listened carefully to her brother playing the guitar—she could hear him through the heating vent—and worked to copy what he played. A few years later, after hearing the Chicago Liberation Women's Rock Band and mainstream band Fanny, she had an epiphany—she could be in a band.

Other members of the BWMC included Suzanne Shanbaum, Debbie Lempke (who she had met at that UCLA conference), and Nancy Henderson. Drummer Jake Lampert was an original member of the collective but didn't stay because she had a commitment to BeBe K'Roche, another San Francisco Bay area band. Henderson left around the time of their first album—liner notes say she attended school to become a gym teacher. Bonnie Lockhart replaced her. In a folk/rock/jazz style, they explored a variety of issues including class, sexuality, and women's rights with songs like "The Bloods," "Gay and Proud," and "Class Mobility."

Everything was performed after a great deal of thought and discussion and it wasn't always easy. Nancy Vogl remembers, "…(we) had huge blowouts with each other because we were taking on the contradictions of capitalist society at every single level—racism, ethnic bias, class ignorance…based with the inequalities of what it meant to be in patriarchy, but also it was way more than patriarchy, it was colonialism, imperialism and the band gravitated (because of our personalities)… toward more of a political overview that was world view—looking at socialism as the ideal at the time rather than commercial feminism which was just analyzing women being the same as men or adding the same privileges as men."[78]

It was exciting to be a member of a movement without clearly defined leaders and one that was guided by the simple principle that women were a priority. "You don't have to be constrained…everyone gets to do and try everything and we didn't know what the hell we were doing. We were five women and said let's do an album. We didn't know how to do that—we just figured out how…that's how women approached everything."[79]

They released *Berkeley Women's Music Collective* in 1976 and *Trying to Survive* in 1978. The liner notes for the second album included thanks to the people who loaned them $13,000 to make the album. Both albums were distributed by Olivia.[80]

Their several national tours began in 1975, the first one in a van that musician and novelist Mary Wings loaned to them. Mary and Robin Flower had just returned from the National Women's Music Festival and told them they *had* to go. Tours were interesting and sometimes a challenge. Nancy Vogl comments, "We were all pretty butch...(we) had an absolutely dedicated intense following, but we didn't appeal to the more refined young woman who was not as radical politically, socially, or visually...we turned off some people, especially older women...(and) more established feminists. We did a conference in Denver with Robin Morgan and I think we creeped them out a little (because) we were young punks; we had tattoos, for chrissake (laughs)."[81]

They played a variety of venues. One college gig stands out for Nancy: "A woman professor hired us for a college in Vermont...there we were—four twenty-five-year-old dykes... at this catholic men's college. All these football players in letter jackets stood in back with their arms crossed and all the feminists in town sat in front on the floor. It was the funniest gig we've ever done. Thank God she brought us to Vermont—kind of like a lifeline to the local dykes who were starving."[82]

Their last performance together was in 1979 at the Michigan Womyn's Music Festival. They went on to work in different bands. Nancy Vogl later recorded solo.

Linda Tillery

Linda Tillery took a different route. From 1968 to 1970, she made her name as the singer for a Berkeley rock band, the Loading Zone. They toured while under contract with RCA. She recorded a solo album, *Sweet Linda Devine*, with CBS in 1970 and sold about 20,000 copies. In the seventies she made her living as a musician, singing rock and soul standards at parties and weddings. She loved performing. "I go onstage to perform because I really love the interaction with people. My purpose is to bring as much joy, through music, to as many people as I can."[83] Also, in the seventies, she worked at a women's bookstore in Oakland. When flyers for the area Women on Wheels concert with Cris Williamson, Meg Christian, Holly Near, and Margie Adam came to the store, she didn't get it. "It's not Aretha, so why are these women all excited?"[84]

Gradually, she became aware of the absence of women in certain areas of music. In 1976, she met women from Olivia. "I didn't know Olivia Records from Minerva Records...but I did know some members of a band called BeBe K'Roche. The BeBes had signed a contract with Olivia and needed a producer for their album. They asked me to do it and I said yes."[85] After that, she was approached by Teresa Trull to produce her first release. "Teresa's music was a lot closer in nature to that which I was accustomed, so I agreed to do that project."[86]

Women's music provided her opportunities she might not have had in mainstream music. "I was allowed to produce albums because I was a woman as opposed to not being allowed to produce records because I was a woman."[87]

In 1977, her self-titled Olivia album was released. She was the first Black woman to record on a feminist label. It wasn't always a comfortable place to be. "...I never felt like I fit in, which didn't necessarily have to do with the environment or the movement itself, but how I perceived myself...for those of us who are not white women, not folksingers...That's why I introduced the song 'Steamroller' as a folk song. That is my folk music—it's the music my folks raised me on."[88] At the start, she was very involved with

Vicki Randle, Rhiannon, Linda Tillery, 1990 Michigan Festival
Photo by Toni Armstrong Jr.

Olivia. "Now I was in an environment where every job was being filled by a woman, and it was a very empowering experience."[89] She worked with Olivia until 1979 and continued to perform in women's music, including Olivia's 1983 Carnegie Hall concert, an event she really enjoyed because it "...commemorated ten years of survival for a real maverick movement."[90] In addition to women's music, she did studio work for Santana, Boz Scaggs, and others, appearing on over thirty albums.

Jade and Sarsaparilla (Janet Hood and Linda Langford)

On the other coast, from 1973 until 1978, this duo was known for their work at colleges and resorts all over New England, including popular watering holes in Provincetown like Piggy's and the Post Office. They also played at the 1975 Boston Women's Music Festival. Janet Hood played piano, sang, and co-wrote some of their songs with manager Bill Russell. Her lover, Linda Langford, contributed vocals. Their only album, *Jade and Sarsaparilla*, was released on Submaureen Records in 1976 and included the upbeat "She's That Kind of Woman," the ballad "I'd Like to Be" and the funny "I Need a Drink of Water in My Mind." After their breakup, Linda continued on to a solo career.

New Harmony Sisterhood Band

In 1973 Marcia Deihl, inspired by the Chicago and New Haven Women's Liberation Rock Bands, started jamming with a group of women friends in the Boston area. The five-member band that evolved featured fiddle, acoustic guitar, bass, and more. They played at protests, benefits, and union drives. In a style best described as folk/bluegrass, their primary purpose was to support feminist and leftist issues. They made an album and toured through the seventies, mostly on the East Coast. They broke up in 1980.

Malvina Reynolds

Malvina Reynolds also performed folk music. Born in 1900, she grew up as the daughter of socialists, surrounded by family political discussions, and didn't become an active songwriter until she was forty-five. Malvina sang her original children's music as well as material for adults in a variety of venues. Humor, politics, and poetic lyrics were a major part of her songs. She became well-known when Harry Belafonte recorded her "Turn Around." "Little Boxes," written in the sixties as a comment on the conformity of suburban life, was a hit when Pete Seeger recorded it. Later, it was used as the opening song in the popular TV show *Weeds*, sung by a variety of musicians. She wasn't a lesbian but she was a feminist. Her list of original songs included the feminist anthem "We Don't Need the Men." She wrote hundreds of songs and performed all over the country including at an early National Women's Music Festival. Known mostly on the folk circuit, she was well-loved by those in women's music. Concert/festival producer Lin Daniels loved her. "I was just blown away at Malvina's courage. She had the courage to go against the boys, and start her own publishing house, started her own label, (and) she had the courage to do that in the fifties."[91] When Malvina passed away in 1978 at the age of seventy-seven, she still had gigs on her calendar.

Elizabeth Cotten

Another performer better known on the folk circuit, Elizabeth Cotten also played at women's music festivals. Feminist/lesbian multi-instrumentalist Robin Flower performed with her for a short while.

Born in 1895, Elizabeth Cotten grew up in a musical family. While just a child, she saved the seventy-five cents a month that she made as a domestic and bought her first guitar for $3.75. A self-taught musician, she learned to play it and a banjo upside down, perhaps because she was left-handed. While in her teens, she wrote many songs including the folk classic "Freight Train." After getting married and having a daughter she set her instruments aside until her fifties, when she worked for the Seegers, including Ruth Crawford Seeger, Pete

Seeger, and Peggy Seeger. They were surprised to find that she wrote the well-loved "Freight Train" and helped her secure the rights to it. Her fingerpicking guitar style is so unique it's emulated by many musicians and is known as "Cotten style." Cotten performed at an early National Women's Music Festival and in 1983 at Sisterfire. The sixth National Women's Music Festival was dedicated to her. She loved to perform. Robin Flower remembered, "If there was one person left in the audience, she'd still play."[92] Elizabeth performed until her nineties and passed away in 1987.

Madeline Davis

Also a folksinger known in the seventies, this out lesbian performer attended her first gay pride march in 1971 and afterward wrote "Stonewall Nation." The New York-based folksinger performed the song at the next march and many marches after that. The song was released on a forty-five rpm record that served as a fundraiser to establish a gay community center in Buffalo, N.Y. She sold five hundred of the first pressing and then made more. A member of the Mattachine Society, an early gay organization, she was active from the early seventies until the late eighties. In 1972 she was elected as the first out lesbian delegate to a major political convention, the one that nominated George McGovern. Music took a backseat to her political activities. Her only full-length recording, a cassette called *Daughter of All Women*, was released in 1983.

Kristin Lems

This young National Women's Music Festival organizer was also a folk performer. She played twice at the first festival, including a rousing performance of the Carole King/Gerry Goffin classic "Natural Woman" with Cris Williamson, Margie Adam, Meg Christian, and Kay Gardner. She was also featured at the second and third festivals. Margie Adam remembers Kristin singing her original "Mammary Glands" at one of the festivals. A piano and guitar player, Kristin polished her performance skills at local watering holes in Champaign-Urbana, IL, including long-term gigs at two restaurants. By 1976, she was playing around Illinois in support of the ERA. In 1977 "Mammary Glands" with "Women Walk More Determined" were released on a forty-five disc. She recorded two others after that and in 1979, she released a full-length album, *Oh Mama!* Fan Sherry Cmiel remembers hearing Kristin in the seventies at a campus venue, Treno's. "Many, many women would show up, some dancing on tables (yes, alcohol was served). When Kristin would play 'Women Walk More Determined,' women would form a circle around the room and dance. It was like an anthem."[93]

Vicki Randle

This singer and multi-instrumentalist appeared at the first National Women's Music Festival in Champaign-Urbana, IL in 1974 as well as many other women's music events. As the daughter of a jazz pianist and a singer there was often music in her home. When her mother was pregnant with her, the baby shower was held in the club where her father was accompanying Billie Holiday. At the age of nine she found a Silvertone guitar that someone had thrown out and taught herself to play it, learning every Beatles song she could find. As a teen, she started playing in rock and pop bands and also tried her hand at traditional Irish and English music. At eighteen she sang at LA jazz clubs and cabarets while maintaining a schedule at singer-songwriter oriented venues. For several years she had a regular night at the Bla-Bla Café, a well-known showcase in the seventies and early eighties for a variety of entertainers from Rosanne Cash to Robin Williams. When she turned twenty-three she moved to the San Francisco area and continued to make a living with music, alternating between singer-songwriter gigs and working with others as a backing musician. Starting in 1978, she secured spots with a variety of touring bands. While she continued to write songs, she was known mostly as a supporting musician, adding her rich voice and percussion to the music of others including Cris Williamson, Meg Christian, Holly Near, and Linda Tillery. She also worked with a variety of mainstream musicians including Aretha Franklin and Laura Nyro.

Early Compilation Albums

In addition to albums released by individual artists, the early seventies also featured two notable compilation recordings. *Virgo Rising*, released in 1972 or 1973, was a collection of songs by various feminist musicians engineered by Joan Lowe, who also worked on Olivia's early recordings. Released on Thunderbird Records in Reno, Nevada, it featured folk songs, some that were originals and some traditional tunes with altered feminist lyrics. Profits went to a women's organization. Liner notes proudly state, "The album is sort of a private consciousness-raising session: songs to diaper babies by, songs to rivet or sculpt by, to drink or type or draw up the terms of your divorce by, to shelve books by, to make laws or run for office by, mow the lawn or fix the door by, songs to raise the heart when low, songs of sisterhood." The best-known artist was Malvina Reynolds, who included three of her own compositions including "We Don't Need the Men" where she sang about how we didn't need them except when it was time to "move the piano." While *Virgo Rising* was feminist in content, it wasn't specifically lesbian although in the liner notes Joan Lowe is described as someone who "…always preferred toy dump trucks to dolls."

A Few Loving Women was definitely made by lesbians. It was recorded at the Firehouse, an early LGBTQ center known for cultural events in New York City. Released in 1973 by the Lesbian Liberation Organization, an offshoot of The

Firehouse, it featured several performers including the band Women Like Me (Roberta Kosse, Bici Forbes and Arleen Mindis) with their song "Big Orgasm." On the LP cover, producer Claire (no last name listed) commented, "I was standing in the middle of the Firehouse surrounded by women making posters proclaiming their pride and their beauty. The television in the background played tapes made on the preceding *Performer's Sunday*. I thought, 'Gee, I'd love to have a copy of that music to play at home anytime I wanted but it's impossible, they'll never make a record' ...I suddenly got a hot flash, broke into a sweat and headed for the nearest telephone. We recorded five days later."

Also on that album was "I'd Like to Make Love with You," by Margaret Sloan-Hunter. "I chose to sing on this record, not because I am a singer, but because I wrote a poem once and happened to set it to music," Margaret said in the liner notes. "I had become aware that there were hardly any direct—not subtle—love songs to women by women. Women must learn to write about, speak about, shout and sing about their feelings for one another. If the words of my poem ride on winds that blow closet doors open, then all women will have to sing it at least once." A few years later Teresa Trull recorded it for her first album on Olivia. Margaret went on to become one of the early editors of *Ms.*

Mainstream Artists

Mainstream record executives were taking note of the burgeoning women's movement and started to sign women's bands and artists with a strong message. Some later became involved in women's music and some simply served as inspiration for those who followed.

Helen Reddy

Her 1971 hit "I Am Woman" sold over a million copies and was heralded as an anthem for women's liberation. When she won a Grammy for Best Female Performance she thanked "God because *she* makes everything possible."

Birtha

All-female rock band Birtha began in 1968. They toured up and down the West Coast with their hard-rocking sound and then signed with Dunhill Records in 1972. Later, their touring schedule included more of the USA plus Europe and Canada. *Can't Stop the Madness*, their second album, came out in 1973. They continued to tour, sharing stages with Fleetwood Mac, Alice Cooper, The Kinks, B. B. King, and Three Dog Night. They disbanded in 1975.

Isis

Named for a goddess, this all-women band was started by Carol MacDonald and Ginger Bianco after being in all-women ensembles, Goldie and the Gingerbreads, and Blithe Spirit. Isis incorporated jazz, funk, and rock in its repertoire and served as a training ground for the seventy-three female musicians who rotated in and out of the band during its seven years of existence. Songs included "She Loves Me" and "Bobbie and Maria," both written by out-lesbian MacDonald. They auditioned for record labels including A&M. In the book *She's A Rebel*, Carol said at that audition Herb Alpert (the "A" in the label's name) commented, "They're great but I think women look stupid playing horns." Undaunted, they continued to other labels and eventually recorded two albums for Buddah and one for United Artists.

Saxophone/flute player Jean Fineberg joined the band in the early seventies after seeing an ad in the *Village Voice*. She'd been a flute player most of her life but had only played the sax for a year and half. She made it through the audition and played with them for about six years. She remembers, "It was completely radical, both socially and musically. We were a bunch of young, crazy women playing this insane original rock and roll, dressing up with body paint and living the life of rock musicians to the hilt. We stayed up all night, did alcohol, drugs, and everything else that goes along with that. We toured cross-country playing huge arenas with the likes of Three Dog Night, Leon Russell, and playing TV rock shows like Merv Griffin, Mike Douglas and *Don Kirschner's Rock Concert*."[94]

Also a part of that band was horn player Ellen Seeling. The two of them later played with Laura Nyro, then formed DEUCE, a popular jazz band that played at the Michigan Womyn's Music Festival and other venues.

Unfortunately, Isis never achieved wide acceptance. Carol didn't think they got support from the women's community because they were viewed as an "establishment group" who played on TV.

Fanny

Fanny, with June and Jean Millington, was the best known all-women rock band in this time period. In the early seventies they released six albums, toured almost nonstop, recorded at the Beatles' Apple Studios and shared stages with Tina Turner, Chicago, and others. Sisters June and Jean Millington started out on ukuleles while growing up in the Philippines then switched to guitars after they moved to the US in 1961. They figured out things on their own. "There were no models for young girls to learn how to play," Jean recalled.[95] In 1968 they formed an all-women's band called the Svelts that played Motown and other covers at venues on the West Coast. It wasn't easy. June remembered men looking up their skirts. They continued to hone their skills, changed personnel, and renamed themselves Wild Honey. A secretary from Warner Brothers heard them at an open mic and told her boss, Richard Perry. He heard them, was impressed and signed them. In the beginning, the label thought they'd be a novelty act like Tiny

Tim, until the women proved themselves. The band changed its name again to Fanny. Warner Brothers cranked out the corny slogan "Get behind Fanny." Did the band care? "Most people couldn't even accept an all-girl band," said June. "That was a much bigger issue for us."[96]

It was assumed that male musicians handled the instruments, the women were just singers or even worse, performed topless. "The first time we played anywhere, people expected us to prove ourselves," Jean remembered.[97] June added, "We got used to that and just played our asses off and people loved it."[98]

Fanny was considered a feminist band by some although they didn't claim that label. Jean explained, "We didn't want the emphasis to be that we were girls, lesbians, or politically active—we wanted it to be just about the music... Unfortunately, the label wanted us to wear skimpy outfits...It did bother me that there was so much emphasis on beauty. You don't want your reputation built on that."[99]

Even though they rocked as hard as male bands, they didn't sleep with groupies or destroy hotel rooms. Drummer Alice de Buhr remembered, "We never did a whole lot of partying because no one knew how to approach us. It wasn't 'Hey baby!' Men politely asked what kind of drums I played and other questions like that. Women didn't know how to respond to us. Maybe lesbians would've gone back to the hotel with us, but there was no protocol for that."[100]

The band continued through different lineups, with June and Alice leaving after the release of their fourth album. The band broke up in 1975. June went on to work with Cris Williamson and others, as well as releasing solo efforts.

The Deadly Nightshade

The members of the Deadly Nightshade had an ominous beginning in 1968 as part of the five women "symphonic" rock band Ariel. Helen Hooke (guitar, fiddle), Anne Bowen (guitar), and Pamela Robin Brandt (bass) were students at Smith and Mt. Holyoke colleges. Their music drew attention from recording labels. Helen recalled, "We were sitting in one record executive's office, and another executive popped his head in the door and said, 'Don't sign an all-girl band. We'll just have to pay for their abortions.'"[101] They didn't get signed and disbanded. They reunited not long after that for a benefit for the Northampton Women's Center. Calling themselves the Deadly Nightshade, the successful concert resulted in more gigs. They played a variety of venues, from rock clubs to country bars, singing covers as well as original songs on a range of topics, from food to plastic surgery. No one could accuse them of being quiet wallflowers. "The Deadly Nightshade was high energy. We'd always hit the stage at 110%, and escalate from there," Pam remembers.[102] After three years of touring they signed with RCA Records, putting out two albums, *The Deadly Nightshade* and *F & W (Funky and Western)*. Album side players included sax player Jean Fineberg and other members of Isis. They received a Grammy nomination for Best New Artist and appeared on several TV shows including *Sesame Street*.

Gigs included large events like the Philadelphia Folk Festival as well as three appearances at the National Women's Music Festival. At the New England Women's Music Retreat, they blew out the power. They were also popular at gay pride rallies and NOW events. During a NOW convention in Atlantic City they locked the janitor in the closet because he was ready to go home and they definitely weren't.

Their performances were fun. Pam recalled, "What I liked best about how the Deadly Nightshade affected audiences is that people always had a fabulous time together, even in the weirdest places. I looked out on the dance floor one night, in this tough hole-in-the-wall C&W (country and western) bar, and there were straight-as-boards couples in square dance outfits dancing next to these lesbian couples who'd told me they usually only felt comfortable at all-women's venues. And doing a circle dance around the room was a bunch of gay guys wearing long dresses…and beards. It was like a microcosm of the world as it ought to be."[103]

They broke up in 1977. Helen Hooke also played with Casse Culver and put out a solo album in the eighties.

Singer-Songwriters, Rock, and Country

In the sixties and early seventies, charts were dominated by men but a few solo female performers such as Carole King, Joni Mitchell, Carly Simon, Bonnie Raitt, and Laura Nyro stood out. Janis Ian released "Society's Child" on Atlantic in 1966 when she was a teen, after she'd been turned down by twenty-two companies.

Girl groups and pop singers also made an impression. Lesley Gore's "You Don't Own Me," released in 1964, was an anthem for women who wanted to change the status quo and not be defined by their relationships. She realized she was a lesbian while in college but didn't come out publicly until 2005.

Also, in the sixties Aretha Franklin was burning up the charts with hits like "Respect." The Staples Singers, led by Mavis Staples, was singing "Respect Yourself." The outrageous singer from Jefferson Airplane, Grace Slick, released her first solo album in the early seventies. Joy of Cooking was a Bay Area rock band fronted by two women, Terry Garthwaite and Toni Brown. They recorded three albums for Capitol Records. Both Terry and Toni continued to solo careers. Terry performed at early women's music festivals including National and Michigan.

Good things for women were happening in country music too. Loretta Lynn sold millions of records, many featuring her original songs. In her memoir *Coal Miner's Daughter*, she wrote, "Most of my songs were from the women's point of view…I'm not a big fan of Women's Liberation, but maybe it will help women stand up for the respect they're due…most of my fan club is women, which is how I want it." She released her controversial song "The Pill" in 1975. "…I'm thinking of all the poor girls who get pregnant when they don't want to be, and how they should have a choice instead of leaving it up to some politician or doctor who don't have to raise the baby."[104]

Continued Growth for Women's Music

Inspired by these mainstream artists and also by women's music, women excitedly started concert production companies, radio programs and more, even if they'd never done anything like it. Musician Sue Fink wasn't surprised by this. "Anytime you see something growing it's because people feel ownership and investment…when we were community building we were at our biggest and best. We did some incredible things."[105] Even more incredible things were ahead.

CHAPTER TWO

··•✄•··

IT'S TOO LATE TO STOP US!

Festivals, Venues, and Multi-Performer Tours of the Seventies

In the early seventies feminist and lesbian performers recorded and started to tour nationally. Women started coffeehouses, festivals, and more to celebrate this new culture.

Sacramento Festival

What is generally regarded as the first women's festival happened in Sacramento in 1973. In a speech given earlier in the year at the National Lesbian Conference in Los Angeles, author Kate Millett invited the audience to attend her festival at Sacramento State. Margie Adam did her first performance at the event. She remembers, "I don't think she (Kate) used the phrase 'women's music festival.' I think that belongs to Kristen Lems and the National Women's Music Festival. Kate may have called what she wanted to create a cultural festival or a lesbian festival. I know that she was determined to shift the focus away from political discourse and toward women's culture—poetry, music, film. She saw the conference model as essentially male-identified—a structure that invited speeches, argument, and in-fighting. If you were to deconstruct Rita Mae Brown's 'army of lovers' Kate would have been on the 'lover' end of the continuum."[106]

Festival attendee Karlene Faith recalled, "…women dancing on the riverbank in the sunshine, and at night we had a dance that was raucous and fun. The band was Eyes, a dynamic all-women R&B group…the room was jammed…it was very hot, and a lot of dancers took off their shirts, celebrating their first experience of an all-women space, sort of a freedom orgy. We were a tribe."[107]

At one point, a male motorcycle group showed up outside. The women surrounded them, chanting "Go away, you're not wanted." Kate Millett stepped forward to ask the men to leave. The guys stayed put and revved their bikes. The women formed a tighter circle and kept chanting until one of the guys told them they didn't want any trouble and rode away.

Amazon Music Party

In August 1974 in the redwoods near Felton, California, the Berkeley Women's Music Collective performed as did others, including several singer-songwriters.[108] It was musician Teresa Trull's first time at a women's music festival, and even though she was in a leg cast, she traveled with several friends across the country from North Carolina. Gwen Avery—later known for her song "Sugar Mama"—was also there and performed in the nude. She wasn't a scheduled musician but jumped on stage during a set change. Teresa laughs when she recalls Gwen's performance— "Security is like, okay ma'am you have to leave. She plays a scale on piano and they try to pull her off. They try again, and they're starting to freak out because they don't know how to contain her. She looks into the audience and slams into this blues thing (Teresa sings) 'I'm on my way back home.' It tore the place down…I thought that was amazing."[109] Teresa played at the open mic before she and her girlfriend hitchhiked home to North Carolina. Or at least, tried. They got waylaid in Nevada where it was illegal to hitchhike. She jumped off a bridge to avoid cops and broke her cast in two places. The two of them made it as far as Utah where they gave up and got on a bus. It was just a few years later that Teresa recorded with Olivia and went on to do much more in her music career.

Teresa Trull, 1974 Amazon Music Party.
Photo by Pat Gargaetas (PGar).

Midwest Wimmin's Festival

In the Ozarks of Missouri, this festival started in 1975 and continues today. While there's music, it's informal—jams, a talent show, campfires. Sharing skills and information is important, with how-to workshops ranging from tuning your car to quilt making. It's very laid-back. If you want to offer a workshop, you put yourself on the schedule. Want to sell crafts? Spread a blanket and set out your wares. Want to perform? Sign up for the talent show. Musicians who've played at the festival include Mosa (aka Mimi Baczewska) and Jori Costello (Big Bad Gina).

San Diego Women's Music Festival

In October of 1975, a collective of a "…very loosely knit core group of women with a smiling cast of tens…" (according to their program) presented this festival on rented land at the Sherilton Valley Ranch. The festival had barely begun when the owner of the land tried to cancel. Speculation was that she wasn't ready for all those lesbians, some of them not fully clothed. According to one of the organizers, Mary Forst, "There was a tense few hours while negotiations went on…many of us organizers had finished our work and were reveling in being able to sit around and anticipate the festival starting shortly and so we had indulged in some special brownies…I thought that was the end…But the central organizers stood up to her and told her it was too late—women were on their way from all over the country and would be arriving and couldn't be stopped! …To have it stated so strongly had a huge effect on me, it felt like a hologram of the whole women's movement. We are on the way and it's too late to stop us!"[110]

The program outlined the possible fire dangers of "Colewoman" stoves, told of a security committee wearing armbands, and stated that childcare was available for the whole weekend. Women were warned to move to a lower lake and pool for nude bathing since the upper lake was visible from the road and might "attract curious and/or gross onlookers." Workshops included instruction in improvisational theater, Bessie Smith piano, and feminist spirituality. Various camping areas were named Diana's Legs, Emma Goldman Tree, and Sappho's Arms.

Entertainment ran each day from midmorning to late night on Friday and Saturday and until early evening on Sunday. Most performers were solo, including many singer-songwriters, although bands were represented, including Moon, a Bay Area jazz trio, and Indavana Blues Band, a rock band from Phoenix, and the Berkeley Women's Music Collective. Rounding out the list were BeBe K'Roche, Meg Christian, Holly Near, Woody Simmons, and others. Holly and Meg were joined by friends Cris Williamson and Margie Adam. Margie remembers that the stage was in a precarious place next to a stream and that she slept in her car.

It was Boo Price's first women's festival. She was there as Margie's partner and manager. She remembers, "I looked around and thought, this is something that has to be done more and, in my mind, bigger."[111] She went on to produce concerts, co-produce the Michigan Womyn's Music Festival, and much more.

The festival ended early because of bad weather. "Imagine the parking lot, a sea of mud, women making a mad dash for their cars with all their wet camping gear and luggage…blinding rain…some of us valiantly trying to help direct traffic," remembers organizer Mary Forst, "…and there was Margie Adam, helping out! I was shocked and grateful—she pretty much stayed to the end." [112] Margie recalled that it "…was a blast because I got to say goodbye to all the girls. We were so excited."[113]

Boston Women's Music Festival

Organized by Artemis Productions, this event occurred on the Harvard University campus October 17-19, 1975. Boo Price helped to guide them through the organizing process since she had had experience producing concerts and working with artists like Margie Adam. At her suggestion that they hire a woman to run sound, Artemis found a company with a female staff member they could send. Myrna Johnston, who had never run sound alone before, went on to form her own sound company, working at countless events over the years including the Michigan Womyn's Music Festival.

Friday night opened with a polished performance by Jade and Sarsaparilla, an enthusiastic crowd of six hundred responding to them with cheers and whistles. The high energy continued through Ginni Clemmens's set. Performing on banjo and guitar, she had the audience singing along with her exuberant collection of traditional and original folk tunes. Rounding out the evening was Willie Tyson, who announced that she promised her friends she'd talk less and play more. It was not to be. Willie had them all in stitches with her funny stories—as much a part of her show as her songs.

Saturday night saw the local New Harmony Sisterhood Band play, plus solo performers Margie Adam, Holly Near, and Meg Christian. "Meg walked out on the stage," Ginny Berson remembers, and "she was literally knocked back by the energy that was pouring out of women."[114] Even though it wasn't planned, Cris Williamson showed up to play with her friends. There was a pronounced cooperative energy onstage. Margie played piano for Holly, Meg offered her guitar on several of Holly's songs, and Kay Gardner played her flute and sang with others. Another surprise guest was Holly's sister, Timothy, who interpreted some of the music in American Sign Language, one of the first times ASL was used at a women's event. Before Timothy left, she showed them all a sign for "sisterhood" and women copied her, their cheers raising the rafters.

A month later was the Boston Women's Music Weekend. Not to be confused with the earlier festival, this one had more of a local focus and included workshops, more of a participatory music weekend than a series of concerts although there was a show on Saturday night.

Artemis Productions continued to produce concerts for a few years in the Boston area, featuring many in women's music—Cris Williamson, Margie Adam, Holly Near, Kay Gardner, and others.

The National Women's Music Festival

In 1973, Kristin Lems and a group of Midwest college students produced Womenfolks, a small folk festival created in response to a local event that included only male performers. The overflow crowd inspired them to do it bigger in 1974. Lems told the university paper, the *Daily Illini* (March 26, 1974) that, "A women's festival is long overdue in this country. Its purpose is to both instruct and entertain, to examine the problems of women in music and to provide women musicians a chance to meet and play together…" Held at the University of Illinois during the break between quarters, the six-day event with six acts per night drew three hundred and fifty people.

The festival almost didn't happen. Ten days earlier, the university refused to let them use their facility because they weren't co-sponsored by any of the campus entertainment entities. Officials changed their minds when they learned the festival might garner national TV coverage. More trouble came with the performer lineup. It was supposed to feature Roberta Flack, Yoko Ono, Isis, Fanny, and Janis Ian but the woman hired to produce the event skipped town on the second day of the festival, taking her salary and contacts. In spite of that, Kristin remembers, "We realized we had something bigger and more historic than we had ever imagined."[115] They were left with open spots so organizers and festival participants sat on the floor of the auditorium stage and organized a new lineup for Friday and Saturday nights that included musicians who had performed earlier in the week—Margie Adam, Meg Christian, Vicki Randle, Cris Williamson, and the Clinch Mountain Back Steppers. Kristin remembers, "Those two concerts were the most euphoric and overwhelming events that any of us had gone through."[116] Margie Adam recalls, "I'd never heard Meg before…I remember putting my head in my hands and crying my eyes out."[117] Friday and Saturday night shows received standing ovations.

On Sunday, a group of musicians including Kay Gardner and Susan Abod (Chicago Women's Liberation Rock Band) stormed the stage to air their concerns about the lack of rock and classical music on the evening stages and perceived divisions between professional and community-oriented musicians. The audience and organizers listened and talked. Kay, Susan, and others performed.

Casse Culver performed at the festival and was bowled over by the energy, especially from the lesbians. She recalls, "At one point onstage I said, 'I want to welcome you all to the First National Lesbian Music Festival.' And of course, there was this enormous cheer—I mean, all these women stood up and practically took their shirts off to wave them as flags. I mean, it was awesome. After that died down there was one woman in the audience who was a straight woman who objected, very strenuously to this… I said, 'You know what? Ninety percent of the women up here onstage that you're looking at today are lesbians. And seventy-five percent of the people in the audience are lesbians. So, you call it what you want and I'm gonna call it what I want.'"[118]

Jam rooms were open during the festival and all attendees were encouraged to make their own music. They also swapped songs in the hallways and outside when intermittent rain didn't interfere. Workshops covered a variety of topics, from audio equipment instruction to women in radio. Energy through the festival was high. Margie Adam called the whole event life-changing. The festival was covered by mainstream press, including *Rolling Stone* and *Ms.*

As fulfilling as it was in many ways, they were still left with debt, including a $700 phone bill. Checks started to roll in from all over the country to assist, including one for $25 from Pete Seeger.

They raised money with events such as a crafts fair and spaghetti dinner. The second festival was held in June of 1975. Tickets were $15 and included admission to six full concerts and all workshops. The weeklong festival was dedicated to conductor Antonia Brico and was highlighted by a film about her. Also scheduled was an open mic, Ginni Clemmens's song swaps, over fifty workshops including one about songwriting by Melissa Manchester and several evening concerts featuring more than two dozen performers. Appearing were the DC area rock band Hysteria, singer-songwriter Deidre McCalla, blues/folk singer Barbara Dane, folk/rock trio Deadly Nightshade, singer/songwriter Vicki Randle, folksinger Rachel Faro, folk/rock performer Terry Garthwaite (Joy of Cooking), Judy Roberts with her jazz trio, and others. A reporter from the campus paper took special notice of one of the Saturday night acts: "The loud volume and aggressiveness of The Deadly Nightshade ...was a shocking, but as it turned out, pleasant change. Humorously reversing sex roles in 'Dance, Mr. Big, Dance' they could also rock with competence ('Truckin'). Lead guitarist-fiddler Helen Hooke took extended exploratory solos, showing her considerable talent."[119] Like the first year, organizers made another attempt to hire mainstream performers with a list that included Judy Collins and Loretta Lynn. Neither appeared.

Musician Lisa Rogers recalls the third festival, in 1976. She threw her guitar in the car and drove from New York to Illinois by herself. While at the festival, she slept on a gym floor. She discovered Malvina Reynolds, "...this riveting compelling twinkle-eyed grey-haired woman. I followed her around and sat at her feet...I could imagine myself doing it (music)."[120] Not long after that she joined the women's band Jubilee. In the eighties she co-founded the folk group the Therapy Sisters.

Malvina Reynolds passed away in 1978. The fourth festival was dedicated to her. At that festival, Maxine Feldman graciously gave up part of her set to Deidre McCalla and Therese Edell. Like other festivals, there was an atmosphere of sharing among the performers. It wasn't unusual to see them sitting in on each other's sets or introducing musicians new to women's music.

The Michigan Womyn's Music Festival

Lisa Vogel, her sister Kristie, and Mary Kindig (aka Digger) decided to journey from Michigan to the Boston Women's Music Festival in fall of 1975.[121] Digger remembers hearing Holly Near, Ginni Clemmens, Willie Tyson, Meg Christian, Maxine Feldman, and others for the first time. "...we were all smitten by the music, and I was particularly smitten with Margie Adam."[122] Digger and Kristie approached Boo Price, Margie's manager, and asked if Margie would perform at a concert they hoped to do next year. Boo told them to call her.

On the way home, they excitedly talked about the experience. Lisa remembers the conversation going something like, "Oh my God! Wouldn't it be great if there was a festival (where) we didn't have to travel all the way to Boston?"[123] A recent visit to the Midwest Wimmin's Festival in Missouri also fired them up.

A month later, Digger, Lisa, and a friend headed to Chicago, driving on snowy streets to hear Margie Adam and Ginni Clemmens at Second City. "After the women's weekend atmosphere (the Boston festival)," Digger recalls, "we were a little surprised that this venue looked a lot more like Saturday Night Date Night for straight people."[124] She situated herself near the stage so she could take photos. Sitting next to her was a familiar face from the Boston event, Boo Price. She encouraged Digger to produce a concert and gave her both her address and phone number. Digger remembers, "Then, in a moment I did not understand at the time, both Boo and Margie began actually jumping up and down, saying, 'It's happening!' Later I came to realize that women from Michigan traveling to other states to hear women's music meant the movement was both important to women and growing."[125]

Digger and Lisa dreamed about producing a concert at Central Michigan University in Mt. Pleasant, maybe with Margie. Then, they thought it could be a Meg Christian and Margie Adam show. It turned into a weekend, and finally, an outdoor festival. Lisa was determined to pull it off. Digger recalls this about Lisa, "I was the only person who was not calling her crazy. One

Lisa Vogel and Penny Rossenwasser, 1996 Michigan Festival.
Photo by Toni Armstrong Jr.

night during our frequent phone calls across town, Lisa was filling out her fantasy with more details, and I stopped and said, 'We're serious, aren't we?' At that moment, the dream got real and a little scarier. 'What will we call ourselves?' Lisa asked. I replied, 'We Want the Music,' to which Lisa replied, 'Collective.' Collectives were big in 1976. WWTMC was officially born."[126]

Digger's job was to phone Margie and Boo. They talked for hours about women's music and production issues. Margie opened her address book and gave Digger contact information for every woman musician she knew. Digger and Lisa contacted performers. Agreements were made on a handshake. If anything was signed, it was a simple paragraph. Ginny Berson, Meg Christian's manager, called Boo to ask what she thought of this new festival. Initially, they were skeptical but, in the end, decided to trust these young women from Michigan.

Others joined the festival collective, including people from the local food co-op and from Boogie Records, known for its support of independent music and various events. Originally envisioned as an event that welcomed men and women, it changed to women-only when it was decided that communal camping and showering would be easier. People from Boogie Records then dropped out.

They hired a sound company owned by a man who worked with his sister. He asked how many would be there and Lisa's reply was "maybe as many as a thousand women." "How many men?" he asked. "None," she replied. That was an utter surprise to him. He thought he was going to be on-site the whole time.

Funding was sparse. They held a yard sale to raise money for postage. They borrowed money from a friend—Digger remembers it as $1,000–then mimeographed hand-drawn flyers announcing the First Annual Michigan Womyn's Music Festival—"Pretty bold of us at the time to call it 'annual,'" comments Digger.[127] They headed to the National Women's Music Festival where they sat in the lobby with an ice chest and anyone agreeing to take a stack of flyers back to their hometown was rewarded with a cold beer. Deidre McCalla was at that festival, picked up a flyer and thought, "A festival without men? That'll never last."[128] Just a year or two after that, she was performing there. Other grassroots efforts were made, including networking with college students, friends, women's centers, and women's bookstores.

"By then, Lisa was on a roll," remembers Digger. "She found the land to rent, a generator, an electrician, a refrigerated truck, produce vendors...talked someone into renting us a baby grand piano—the list went on and on."[129] "We had absolutely no idea what we were doing when we produced the first festival. None," recalls Lisa Vogel. "I personally had produced nothing more than a few major keggers..."[130]

The land had no water. At first, they tried to dig their own well by pounding down a two-inch pipe. After many frustrating hours, they found a local woman whose father offered to help. A day before the gates opened, the well was successfully dug. Because it was rented land, the piping had to be removed after the event was over. Showers were installed on a hill because the drainage was good there. Organizers put up plywood walls when they realized that people on the road were getting a good view, which explained the long lines of cars driving slowly past. Someone was even selling views from a telescope nearby.

Tents were another issue. Lisa made calls to an army base and got the name of an officer, then contacted someone at a different base and said she was a reservist and that the officer at the other base had suggested they call and get tents and other items they needed. The only tent they actually rented for a fee was for the stage. They pulled this off for the first three festivals.

Tickets were $15 in advance and $20 at the gate. Their first mail order came from Chico, California. Lisa remembers being completely amazed that someone would come from that far away.

They didn't have money for lumber so they rented it. Lisa recalls, "They'd ask, you want to *rent* wood?…Our requests were so weird that people went along with it."[131] They were careful to only use one or two nails in the end of each piece so they could return it in good condition.

On August 20, 1976, a month after Lisa turned twenty, they opened the gates on land near Mt. Pleasant, Michigan. Organizers thought they were optimistic when they estimated that a thousand women would attend. Two thousand women showed up.

Digger took over as stage manager and emcee. "We had hired neither, and the performers kind of indicated that was a need. I think it fell to me because I was probably the only one not overly intimidated by the microphone or standing onstage."[132] They kept ticket money in Lisa's cowboy boots in the trunk of Digger's car. Performers were housed in collective members' homes. There was no official crafts area but after craftswomen showed up, they borrowed tables. Digger offers, "We were delightfully unprepared for what we were getting ourselves into. And nobody especially cared. Every moment was a new adventure."[133]

Initially there were no security workers. Lisa Vogel slept on the stage because she didn't have a tent and because she was afraid the grand piano that she'd rented for $150 would get damaged.[134] However, it wasn't the women attending the festival who were the problem—gawkers from the local community started to drive slowly by the festival. Tension grew as ogling turned to name calling. Vogel recalls a typical incident with a not-so-typical response from a festival attendee: "'Always wanted to give a dyke ten inches,' he said, safely behind his truck door. 'If you want to leave with those five inches you better get out of here now' she said, brandishing a machete like she knew how to use it."[135] After musing why a festie-goer would even bring a machete, Vogel admits, "We were in over our heads. We were in the crazy position of being between the local dudes who were trying to prove their manhood on the road and the dykes who were ready to send their manhood home with them in a bag. Let's be calm sisters…your inclination and anger are understandable, but this is really not a good idea."[136] Danger escalated when men were discovered sneaking into the festival through the woods. So, festival organizers quickly assembled crews, organized according to hometowns. If a warning horn went off, crew members from Michigan were to go to the "shower road." If you were from west of the Mississippi, your post was at the front gate. Festival attendee Tess Wiseheart recalls one night when men were reported on the land. "Two entrances…we were sent by state. All in the dark, a few flashlights and me, wuss of the world, scared silly. One of the organizers said, 'If you're from Michigan, you should be in the front.' I immediately joined the California delegation."[137]

Rock band BeBe K'Roche played Saturday night, then did a security shift at a place where men had been spotted coming onto the festival land. Lisa Vogel recalls, "I joined them, and we proceeded to party and get to know each other in the dark of the night. None of us were particularly nervous about the situation, so when we heard some noise in the woods, Peggy, the bass player, went off by herself to check it out. She came back with a drunk man hanging from his shirt collar at the end of her hand, barefoot, scared out of his mind."[138] They escorted him to the main road and laughingly told him to run.

Communal food was in the plans from the very beginning. Unlike most festivals, they didn't want food vendors or for attendees to cook their own food. The women from the local food co-op were supposed to help with meals but not long after the festival began, they went to a swimming hole and decided not to come back. Volunteers stepped in to do their work. Attendee Suji remembers eating boiled corn and potatoes out of fifty-five-gallon drums set in fire pits. Watermelon served as dessert. Martha Meeks attended an early festival and didn't know food was provided so she'd brought peanut butter, a loaf of bread, and a case of beer to share among her buddies. When she volunteered for a work shift, someone gave her food from the festival kitchen. She didn't have a plate so she used her Frisbee. "We made do with what we had back then," muses Martha.[139]

Teresa Trull, Holly Near, Meg Christian and Linda Tillery, 1976 Michigan Festival. *Private collection, Lisa Vogel.*

There was a first aid station at the first event but at subsequent festivals, the Womb, a more elaborate health care area, developed. Not only did it offer western medicine methods of care but also allopathic, with massage therapists, naturopaths and others on duty.

Attendees at first could drive right to their campsite in a big field and park wherever they wanted. The organizers realized that this created a negative impact on the land, so in following years a shuttle system evolved.

They hadn't thought much about trash. They decided to take the $400 left after the festival and hire a garbage company to haul the bagged garbage away. However, no company wanted their business. So, they borrowed a neighbor's truck and took bag after bag to the dump. On the surface, it didn't look like a pleasant task. The bags had sat in the hot sun for several days and were rife with maggots. Still, the small group of women remaining after the festival found a way to make it work, as they had for many tasks.

Much of what went on at the Michigan festival was true for other festivals. There was an atmosphere of sharing and support. Not enough women to cook dinner? Volunteers showed up to cook potatoes and stir soup. Need some help carrying equipment? More women stepped up to the plate to tote amps and mic stands. A musician needs a ride to the airport? A woman volunteered to drive her.

The energy at that first Michigan festival was celebratory, with stirring music from Meg Christian, Willie Tyson, Holly Near, BeBe K'Roche, Maxine Feldman, Margie Adam, Andrea Weltman, Sally Piano, Teresa Trull, and Linda Tillery. Festie-goer Suji recalled, "...on the last day climbing up the scaffolding of the stage, peering over the flooring of the high stage...and seeing all the wimmin standing up arm in arm singing 'Natural Woman' with all the performers. It was incredible."[140] Attendee Jane Kreinberg called the first festival "very primitive but very exciting."[141] Mary Byrne (who would later produce the National festival) was also at those beginning festivals and remembers, "I was hardly out at the time and here I was with all these naked women and listening to this incredible music. I was really blown away."[142] Martha Meeks also felt empowered at the early festivals. "The music was all brand new to me...and the crews, just women. This told me that I could do anything!"[143] Kristie Vogel was a part of the collective for that first festival "...there is something magical that happens when womyn gather together! ...After the first festival, because of all the hard work, we didn't think we would do another. But after some needed rest and continuous requests from womyn to produce another, we decided to do a second festival..."[144]

Sisterspace Weekend

Also beginning in 1976 and still in operation today is Sisterspace Pocono Weekend, later shortened to Sisterspace Weekend. Taking place at three different locations, it's now at Camp Ramblewood in Darlington, Maryland. Organized by a group of volunteers, it has featured many in women's music and culture including Toshi Reagon, Cris Williamson, Marga Gomez, Bitch, Edwina Lee Tyler, Ubaka Hill, SONiA, and many others. They average three hundred to five hundred in attendance and one year they drew one thousand.

The Pacific Northwest Women's Music Festival

This 1977 event in Portland, Oregon was produced by Women's Energy and featured Therese Edell as the headliner. It happened again at least one more year, in Olympia, Washington when Malvina Reynolds headlined. Other performers included Portland-based musicians Baba Yaga, Izquierda, and Mary Rose. It has no relation to a later festival with a similar name.

Long Island Women's Music Festival

This event occurred in 1979 in New York State and it appears to be be the only year. Featured performers included folk singer Ruth Pelham, rocker June Millington (with her band), and singer-songwriter Judy Castelli.

Early Concert Venues, Production Companies and Multi-Performer Tours

Women were excited about the musicians they heard at the festivals and on albums, so in addition to festivals, they started women's music venues in their hometowns. Tours that included more than one performer were also created.

Women in Production

In 1974 Boo Price started Women in Production, an all-women production company for shows in the San Francisco Bay area. As Margie Adam's manager, she worked with many new producers all over the country, walking them through the process of organizing their first shows. She created a production manual. If there wasn't a venue in an area where she wanted to book Margie, she'd call the women's bookstore—there was an extensive network of them then—and asked for contacts. Sometimes she talked the bookstore into producing the show.

Allegra Productions

Concert producer Polly Laurelchild went to her first women's music concert, Holly Near and Meg Christian, in 1976. "I'd never seen so many neat women in one place in my life…" she exclaimed to HOT WIRE (November 1985). In early 1977, she attended the National Women's Music Festival and by October 1977, she was part of Allegra Productions and producing the Berkeley Women's Music Collective in the Boston area. By 1985, Allegra had organized over one hundred music, theatre, and other events.

Las Hermanas Women's Cultural Center and Coffeehouse

One of the earliest venues opened in December 1974 in San Diego. It was a cozy space that offered home-cooked food and live entertainment. They featured performers known from the budding women's music network such as Meg Christian and Holly Near as well as other women musicians—Joan Armatrading, June Millington, and Malvina Reynolds. They also booked local performers, including pianist Sue Palmer. Like many entertainers, she found it an empowering place where she "was learning my craft and practicing in front of a very forgiving audience…It was just so cool because they were celebrating women and how wonderful we are…I hadn't been out very long, so it was a real thrill."[145]

It was primarily a women-only space, prohibiting women from bringing in male friends, relatives, and even their own children. Men were allowed on a very limited basis and only if no woman was available to run sound or lights. They were hired only if they trained women to do those jobs.

Disagreements between the original organizers, mostly Latina women, and later members, many of whom were white, created instability. Add to that a declining interest from the community and a rent increase, and the coffeehouse could no longer continue. It closed in early 1980.

Mountain Moving Coffeehouse

Across the country in Chicago, also beginning in 1974, was a crisis line run by WICCA (Women in Crisis Can Act) housed in a storefront. They found they had too much space and not enough money to pay for it. A few members thought they could present events there and Mountain Moving Coffeehouse was born. The name came from a poem by Yosano Akiko and included in a song recorded by the Chicago Women's Liberation Rock Band. Run by a collective that ranged at various times from four to eighteen women, it brought in local musicians and poets as well as touring acts almost every Saturday night for many years. Members learned everything about putting on a show, from booking performers to running sound.

Wild Sister Coffeehouse / Bloomers

Starting in 1975, this Pittsburgh gathering space offered women's art, entertainment, and a place for women to meet. Founders Dana Ventriglia, Ann Begler, and Felice Newman moved their coffeehouse around to various spaces in town until 1992 when they had raised $55,000, enough to purchase a building and a liquor license. The *Pittsburgh Post-Gazette* called it "…a South Side bistro with a sympathy for a liberated clientele."[146] They closed in 1985 and reopened as Bloomers, another women's space. It hosted a variety of art and performers including Jamie Anderson. It closed in the early nineties.

Women's Energy Productions and Mountain Moving Café

Both venues based in Portland, Oregon, they were active in the seventies. Women's Energy brought in many performers including Sweet Honey in the Rock, Cris Williamson, Meg Christian, Nancy Vogl, and Robin Flower. The café (not to be confused with the venue in Chicago) had more of a local focus, with art and music happening almost every night of the week. Kristan Aspen and Naomi Littlebear Morena played there as a duo before they started the band Izquierda. Mountain Moving became the hub for anti-war protests and other activism. Starting as a collective of men and women, it evolved into an all-women's group. They were open three years. Kristan recalls, "It had an impact on many, many lives."[147]

Other Venues

Full Moon Coffeehouse in San Francisco presented women's entertainment in the mid-seventies. Good Taste Productions produced shows in the Los Angeles area in the seventies, including a classical concert in October 1974 featuring women musicians and Cris Williamson in November 1974. Mother's Brew, a women's bar in Louisville, Kentucky, featured women's music—Maxine Feldman was their first, followed by many including Casse Culver, Holly Near, Mary Watkins, and Alix Dobkin. Also, in the South, Lucina's Music started in 1975 in Atlanta and featured local musicians as well as touring acts. Richmond, Virginia hosted several one-day women's festivals starting in 1974. Venues not started by women also featured women's music. Freight and Salvage, a live music venue in Berkeley, California, was one of the places to go. In Los Angeles, the Bla-Bla Café featured singer-songwriters and comics, some before they became known in women's music—John Bucchino, Tret Fure, Diane Lindsay, Vicki Randle, and Robin Tyler. Universities were also starting to present performers, usually sponsored by the women's center, feminist groups, or women's studies. So many venues and production companies were cropping up, it was hard to account for them all.

Multi-Artist Tours

Women on Wheels Tour

Marianne Schneller approached Holly Near, Cris Williamson, Margie Adam, and Meg Christian, and asked about putting together a tour for 1976 as a fundraiser for women in prison. Marianne's father had loaned her five thousand dollars so they had the money to start and she could produce the tour.[148] This new era of women's empowerment, in spite of cultural, racial, and class barriers, made for a lot of process, including whether or not to include Holly, who was straight.[149] "We were very into having a wonderful process but some of it was not so wonderful," remembers Olivia member Ginny Berson. "There was a lot of disagreements about politics. We were pretty fiercely lesbian—Holly was pretty fiercely not—she wasn't fiercely not for too much longer. (laughs)"[150] After it was decided that Holly would be included, they met for a year over planning. They labored over important questions like how could they call this women's music when they were all white? Should the concerts be women-only? What about ticket prices? Child care? Should the concerts be recorded and if so by whom? In the end, they decided not to record—a decision Holly Near regrets now—and made the shows open to everyone.

They played in seven cities, the final show at a state prison, the California Institution for Women. One of the reasons for the tour was to raise awareness around women in prison and included the collection of musical instruments, LPs, and sheet music to donate to these women.

Their Oakland concert was produced by Boo Price. She tried something new with tickets. Up to that point, women's events had one ticket price. "I decided (because we were raising money) that I wanted a higher-priced ticket and a general admission ticket. I didn't want the ones with more money to sit up front so I devised a plan so that the first row was general admission, the next two would be reserved seats or whatever, the next two general admission. I staggered it for the whole first third so that the people who paid more did get to sit in the first third."[151] She laughs because it was a complicated system that wasn't used for other shows. However, it did open eyes to the possibility of different price levels and not in a standard way where those paying more sat in the front. At women's music events for years after that, it was usual to have a sliding scale, where the admission wouldn't be set as one price, but as a range, say $5 to $10, or one price would be set but qualified as "more if you can, less if you can't." There was also childcare at the event—a new offering for women's events.

At the start of this Oakland concert, a group of twenty or thirty women started chanting "Free Inez!" Inez Garcia had been convicted of the second-degree murder of the man who raped her.

"My first thought was we should stop that then I thought no, we have to incorporate it…we got those women together and they chose a spokesperson," Boo remembers. "We put her onstage and she spoke about the Inez movement. They had collection baskets for her defense in the back of hall. These concerts weren't just 'pay your money, get your seat, listen to concert and leave'—they were all political community gatherings. Just being there was a political move."[152]

The performances of Women on Wheels were successful in several California cities in addition to Oakland—Los Angeles, San Diego, Santa Barbara, Santa Cruz, and Sebastopol. Some shows brought in one thousand or more audience members. In Los Angeles, 1,600 people attended. There was such a demand for tickets that second shows were added in Santa Cruz and Oakland. A total of 10,000 people attended the concerts. It was estimated that 80% of the crowds were young white women; 10% were older, younger, and Third World Women; and 10% were men.[153]

There was TV coverage and coverage in mainstream daily papers like the *San Francisco Chronicle*. For interviews, performers were careful to point out that they didn't represent the whole of women's music, it was a movement that encompassed a large part of history and many cultures.

Musicians presented songs that were well-known to audience members such as Cris Williamson's "Song of the Soul." Holly Near's "Sister-Woman-Sister" had a huge impact, partly because it was written after her visit to the California Institution for Women the year before and illustrated the stark reality of women in prison. All of the musicians performed solo as well as with each other.

Timothy, Holly's sister, interpreted a few of the songs in ASL (American Sign Language). It isn't known if any deaf people attended but for hearing audience members, it was a way for them to learn a bit of the language and to begin to gain awareness of deaf culture. The crew at all shows included sound engineer Margot McFedries and lighting coordinator Johanna Gullick. Local producers coordinated hall rental, graphic design, ticket sales, and more. The day following every show, a workshop was open to all. A film made by women in prison, *We're Alive*, was shown. There were discussions about culture and activism, sometimes heated.

The last show on the tour was scheduled for the prison but it almost didn't happen. The show had been approved by prison officials, then it wasn't. This cancellation was made public at shows earlier in the tour and through a tremendous publicity effort from many activists, including hundreds of signatures on a petition, the concert was reinstated with a few exceptions—some members of the tour were excluded from entering the prison. Officials didn't publicly state why but tour organizers were sure it was because of their earlier work with an activist organization that prison representatives did not see as supportive of them. The prison initially wanted Margie Adam excluded but then changed their minds. All of the performers were allowed in, as well as some of their touring staff.

During the performance the inmates were visibly moved, as were some of the guards. One guard, after hearing Meg's sound check, commented, "The girls here develop affection for one another, you know, and they're going to like that song."[154] Karlene Faith, the tour's workshop coordinator, was one of those denied entry. She remained outside the prison gates with others and held a vigil as the concert was going on inside.

At every show of the Women on Wheels Tour, audiences leapt to their feet. "Women were screaming like we were the Beatles," Holly recalls.[155] She told *HOT WIRE* in 1993 that Women on Wheels was one of the highlights of her career. Fan Pat Gargaetas attended the Oakland show where she loved every performer, including Holly and Cris. "Three thousand women singing 'Song of the Soul' (a Williamson song) was more than amazing."[156] Marcia Schwemer feels lucky that she was able to attend one of these concerts. After a particularly difficult time in her life, she listened to her women's music albums over and over again. She credits women's music with saving her life.

Varied Voices of Black Women

This important multi-artist East Coast tour featured poet Pat Parker, and musicians Linda Tillery, Mary Watkins, Vicki Randle, and Gwen Avery, supported by their band: bassist Barbara Cobb, keyboard player Colleen Stewart, and guitarist Jerene Jackson. The featured artists took their turns on instruments too, with Mary Watkins on piano, Linda Tillery on drums, and several women on vocals. It was a full show featuring their best work including Gwen Avery singing "Sugar Mama," Mary Watkins playing "Witches Revenge," and Pat Parker performing "Movement in Black." Watkins remembered that it "… was truly exhilarating and special. The energy was so high among us at times that it seemed you could almost hear crackle!"[157] Produced by Roadwork, a production company and booking agency, and Olivia Records, this celebration

Varied Voices of Black Women: Pat Parker, Mary Watkins, Vicki Randle, Gwen Avery, Linda Tillery. *Photo by Joan E. Biren (JEB) © 2018.*

of Black lesbian culture took place in October and November of 1978. They played in eight cities in a variety of venues including the University of Rhode Island, Vassar College, the University of Massachusetts, and Rutgers University. They sold out in several cities. Cobb recalls, "Wherever we went there was so much fun and community."[158] Writer Amy Hoffman, in her book *An Army of Ex-Lovers*, talks about the excitement of a standing-room only show in Boston.[159]

These festivals, venues, and tours were an exciting part of women's music. Much more was yet to come.

CHAPTER THREE

ORANGE JUICE CANS AND THE BURGEONING NETWORK
Women's Music Continues Through the Seventies

Women's music continued to gain momentum at an amazing pace with new performers and established performers touring even more. Meg Christian was thrilled about this and told the Lesbian Tide *in November 1974 "…there has been an overwhelming response from the feminist community to our music. This is so gratifying because it shows us that what we do is valuable." Women-only concerts were explored, classical music by women became more visible, and festivals attracted enormous numbers, including the Michigan Festival which drew 3,400 women in 1977. More and more fans found women's music on a myriad of labels, including Olivia, Redwood, and many that featured only one or two artists.*

Olivia Keeps Growing

In 1978, Olivia Records had a mailing list of 17,000 people, an amazing feat at a time when there was no Internet and standard promotional outlets like mainstream radio refused to acknowledge them.[160] They developed a system to get records into the hands of fans. At early Olivia shows, collective members asked from the stage who could sell albums in their hometown. If you raised your hand, you were recruited. While some women didn't follow through, many did and started distribution companies to put out catalogs and get the recordings of Olivia and those of others into stores. Terry Grant was one who raised her hand, starting Goldenrod Distribution in 1975. She sold Olivia's albums at a Meg Christian concert in Lansing, Michigan. When she asked about returning the unsold albums after the show, Olivia suggested she sell them to local stores. Laurie Fuchs was also one of those women who answered the call. She started Ladyslipper with Kathy Tomyris (then the North Carolina Olivia distributor). Their catalog was assembled in three days and released in time for the 1977 Michigan Womyn's Music Festival.

That same year Olivia saw the need for a strong lesbian voice to counteract the right-wing backlash that included Anita Bryant, a singer and spokesperson for Florida orange juice. They decided to release a compilation, *Lesbian Concentrate*. It took Olivia only two months from inception to recording, accomplished in a living room on equipment built by engineer Sandy Stone. The eye-catching cover sported a realistic looking orange juice can dotted with condensation and proudly displaying the title. It featured various artists, from musician Mary Watkins singing her original "Don't Pray for Me" to poet Pat Parker reciting her poem "For the Straight Folks Who Don't Mind Gays but Wish They Weren't So Blatant." Most of the artists had already recorded for Olivia or were scheduled for their own releases.

In 1977 and 1978, Olivia grew quickly. The women of Olivia moved out of their communal home and into separate living spaces. They added women to their collective, making it more diverse. Ginny Berson explains, "We didn't want the music to be all white soloists and we didn't want the collective to be a white collective. We thought if we were really modeling feminist values and creating this institution that represents feminism then it needed to be more inclusive."[161] This expansion also made decision-making more complex. Judy Dlugacz says, "Every time someone new came in it increased the time of our meetings. They seemed endless."[162] The collective dealt with difficult issues. "We didn't know when something was racist and when it was not racist," remembers Ginny. "We didn't know how to deal with class differences and at one point we had a fifty-year-old woman with us...she had really different needs."[163] The Olivia collective consisted mostly of women much younger. There was some awareness, though. "We knew for example that you don't ask one African-American woman to be in the collective and think that's it. It wasn't just bodies in the room—it was going to require us to change the culture of the organization."[164] She admits they weren't sure how to do that. There were a lot of "horrible meetings" but "great stuff" too. Olivia was not alone in its struggles. Similar processing went on at other labels and in areas of women's music.

If a mainstream label had experienced the kind of early success that Olivia had, they would have brought Meg and Cris right back into the studio for follow-up albums because they were proven stars who could attract an audience. However, Olivia didn't work within a standard business model. Their goal wasn't to make massive amounts of money. Ginny Berson explains, "We didn't want women's music to be defined as white women and guitar or white women and piano...we weren't into building careers, we were into building a movement so we recorded Linda Tillery, BeBe K'Roche, Mary Watkins, and the poetry of Pat Parker and Judy Grahn."[165] They released Meg Christian's second album, *Face the Music*, in 1977, two years after her first release. Perhaps because of the time interval, it didn't do as well as her first. Olivia had many plans, including buying its own studio in 1977 but that required $150,000. In an interview with KPFT's Diana Moye, collective member Ginny Berson admitted she didn't know where they'd get the money. By the close of 1978 they didn't have enough funds to re-press Cris Williamson's *The Changer and the Changed*, the most profitable record for them up to that point. "We almost went out of business several times," says Ginny Berson.[166] A consultant advised them to cut down the number of collective members and to change their method of payment, currently based on an individual's need rather than her skills or position in the group. Ginny says the way they were structured, "…didn't really work because we were continuing to make political decisions and were running out of money. We could no longer pay everybody."[167] They reduced the number of women in the collective and found a unique way of determining pay scale. "Once we did this reorganizing, it sort of took a lot of the spark out of what we were doing," comments Judy.[168] Despite this difficulty, Ginny maintains that it was an "…amazing experience because we tried to live our principles fully."[169] She laughs when she adds, "We couldn't overthrow capitalism, goddammit."[170]

After these radical changes, it was mostly the original members who stayed. Then, gradually, those women started to leave. When Meg left in 1983, Judy was the only remaining original member.[171] Judy says, "It's funny—at the very beginning, we were in a meeting and decided to officially be a corporation, though we planned to run the business collectively. We said we needed officers, and who wanted to be president? I raised my hand."[172] She was thirty years old when she found herself the last original member.[173] Today the Olivia website lists her as founder and president.

Audience Numbers Increase For Most But Not Everyone

Olivia artists and performers on other labels continued to tour. They needed venues, so more concert production companies were created by women, from intimate coffeehouses to shows in big concert halls. In 1975, the Women on Wheels tour drew huge crowds, mostly lesbians. For their Oakland performance, the *Oakland Tribune* noted the show was sold out days in advance and reported that it was attended by "…primarily young white females, many of whom were outwardly affectionate with each other."[174] Nearly overnight, those artists were playing for as many as 2,000 people.[175] By 1978, Meg Christian's crowds averaged 100 – 1,500.[176] Holly Near regularly drew over 1,000 and in a 1990 show at Boston's Symphony Hall, 1,700 people came to hear her.[177]

For some artists, gigs were inconsistent and musicians like Maxine Feldman found it hard to support themselves doing only women's music performances. Maxine told *Paid My Dues* that some gigs in the seventies paid well; however, some were a percentage of the door and for small venues that wasn't very much. She couldn't afford a touring vehicle. She told *Paid My Dues*, "People said 'Wow! You went cross-country! Far out!' I said, 'Yeah, far out. I took the Greyhound bus. It was fifty dollars.'"[178]

Robin Flower took advantage of the growing women's music network but also found work in folk music. She first put out a self-produced album in 1979, *More Than Friends*. Later albums were on noted folk label Flying Fish and that opened a lot of doors for her. "I always thought that folk music and women's music would be a good marriage. In the early days, it wasn't. There was a lot of fear from straight producers and from lesbians about each other."[179] Often it did work, though, and she loved the concerts. "How lucky we all were to get to be a part of that. There were gigs, there was money, women's centers at universities—we could get gigs from a lot of people."[180] Robin loved touring. "Knowing a lot of people, it felt like the US was my neighborhood—I always had friends to see."[181]

Established Artists Continue to Perform and Record

Holly Near released two albums in the late seventies, including 1978's *Imagine My Surprise*. This exciting album included songs that became classics, including the anthems "Fight Back," "Mountain Song/Kentucky Woman," and "Something About the Women." These original songs, as well as many others in her repertoire, found their way to Take Back the Night marches, peace rallies, and other events, empowering women in many ways. Fan Maxine Israel was especially taken with "Something About the Women" because Holly sang about a beautiful woman. "When Holly sang 'so big and beautiful' I broke down and cried. I was a 'chubby baby,' a 'chunky kid' and then, a 'fat woman.' I'd never heard those words (big and beautiful) used together. From that moment, I realized that I was beautiful."[182] She used the album to inspire her students where she had a job helping women returning to college. During a stressful time, "I brought in my little cassette player and my tape of *Imagine My Surprise*. I played it for them all through finals week. Women would rush in and breathlessly say things like, 'I only have a few minutes before my exam, can you play me one of those songs?' Then they would go off and take their tests, rejuvenated. They would come back and tell me they couldn't have done it without that music."[183]

Alix Dobkin released *Living with Lesbians* in 1976. It included "Amazon ABC," a lesbian-affirming and well-loved song at her concerts. Fan Sheri Snyder first heard it when she was stationed in Germany, at an off-base party where someone put on the LP. "I said 'WHAT? Are you kidding me? That's fantastic!'[184]

Margie Adam released her first album, *Songwriter*, in 1977. Early plans were to record with Olivia, but that fell through when it was clear they intended to record other artists first, delaying Margie's album to an unknown future date. *Songwriter* was recorded on Pleiades Records, a label started by Boo Price and Margie. The album included some of her best-known songs—"Best Friend—the Unicorn Song," "Sweet Friend of Mine," and "Beautiful Soul." The latter was first recorded by Cris Williamson on *The Changer and the Changed*. She was also on Margie's album, adding backing vocals and guitar. Meg Christian, Linda Tillery, Vicki Randle, Kay Gardner, and others added their talents. "Best Friend" was recorded two years later by Peter, Paul, and Mary. "Beautiful Soul" was also recorded by Dusty Springfield.

Kay Gardner continued to perform and compose, further exploring classical music. She wrote her first orchestral piece, "Rain Forest," in 1977 and the next year, conducted it at the National Women's Music Festival. In that audience was noted conductor Antonia Brico. Kay

Margie Adam and Kay Gardner, 1992 National Festival.
Photo by Toni Armstrong Jr.

apprenticed with Antonia in 1977 and 1978. Around that time, she composed a grand oratorio, *Ouroboros*, and co-founded the New England Women's Symphony. Kay's performances often included others. In 1977, a concert tour included her "When We Made the Music," a piece arranged for women's voices. She sent the music ahead and even if there wasn't a chorus in that city, a group of women came together to sing.

Casse Culver recorded *3 Gypsies* in Maine at Noel Paul Stookey's (Peter, Paul and Mary) studio with Margie Adam, Robin Flower, Maxine Feldman, Willie Tyson, and others. It was released in 1976. Maxine remembers, "...we lived in this wonderful old house...and we had a great time...I mean, there were all these musicians in one house...we laughed a lot and sang Broadway tunes, if you can believe that."[185] Afterward, several of the women involved in this project flew directly to the (then new) Michigan Festival. Boo Price recalls, "They all thought we were a little bit nuts for going out and doing this funny thing in a field."[186]

Women's Music an Integral Part of Feminist and LGBTQ Gatherings

Women's music started to be featured at big events. With 20,000 people attending and five million dollars in funding from the US Government, the National Women's Conference in Houston in November 1977 was one of those. An important event for the women's movement, it involved delegates from all over the country, voting on planks ranging from the ERA to lesbian rights. Former and current first ladies Rosalyn Carter, Betty Ford, and Lady Bird Johnson were in attendance, as was lesbian activist Jean O'Leary and feminist Gloria Steinem. Boo Price was tapped by the state department to produce the stage that featured forty-two acts in three days. They asked for feminist acts. Performers included Sweet Honey in the Rock, Malvina Reynolds, and Margie Adam. Jean O'Leary recommended Robin Tyler. A previous member of the comedy duo Harrison and Tyler, Robin had recently struck out on her own. Boo had already booked the stage and told Jean she didn't have room for Robin. When Gloria Steinem called and also requested her, Boo relented and booked Robin, laughing as she commented, "You don't say no to Gloria Steinem."[187] It was Robin's first solo performance before a big crowd.

Boo thought the plenary sessions ending the event should conclude with Margie Adam singing her feminist anthem, "We Shall Go Forth," so the night before she ran it by the conference producer. She said yes. It was eleven p.m. on Saturday and the final session was the next morning. Boo stayed up all night. She called a piano rental company at six a.m. on Sunday. They agreed to have one there by midmorning. "I walked up the stairs and inside like I knew what I was doing, introduced myself and told them I was responsible for the final thing... they took down the information like I was somebody...the truck drove up with the piano and I directed them past all the security...no one questioned me..."[188] Margie sang the song as planned, with thousands of delegates singing along. A recording of that song was put into the Smithsonian for its role at the conference. Boo recalls, "I accomplished a lot of things that seemed impossible and that was the most impossible one. I just didn't allow myself to think how this might not work and somehow, it all did work...and the piano helped (laugh)..."[189]

Boo often looked for feminist events where women's music could be a part. In 1980, she organized a tour of seventeen US cities for the National Women's Political Caucus that included Margie Adam. They would study the local political issues in each town and Margie would incorporate that into her performances. In 1979 and 1980 Boo also arranged for her to do concerts to celebrate the opening of artist Judy Chicago's The Dinner Party in San Francisco and Houston.

There was more visibility for LGBTQ people, too, as witnessed by the local pride events starting up all over the US. The first national march occurred in 1979. Held in Washington, D.C. for an estimated 10,000 people, performers included Meg Christian singing a medley of "My Girl," "Sherry," and "Natural Woman" as well as original songs; Casselberry-DuPreé with several songs including "By the Rivers of Babylon"; Holly Near with her "Mountain Song"; and Maxine Feldman singing her funny "Closet Sale." It was emceed by Robin Tyler.

Women-Only Shows

In the seventies, many aspects of presenting music were explored by feminists and lesbians in the women's music movement, including who would be allowed to come to the shows. One night in 1974, Alix Dobkin and Kay Gardner stood onstage in front of an audience at Brooklyn College in New York City. Through the first three-quarters of the show, Alix felt a sick feeling growing in her stomach as she looked out at her audience. She politely asked the three or four men in the audience to leave. They did so. Feeling better, Alix and Kay finished the show. Alix decided she wanted women-only shows from then on. "They (men) didn't belong there. I wasn't singing to them. It had nothing to do with them. And of course, back in those days and maybe in some places today when a man walked into a room full of women, all the women were thinking about him…one way or the other…either, 'get this prick out of here' or 'I hope he doesn't get his feelings hurt, poor guy'…"[190]

While some wholeheartedly supported her, other women didn't agree, especially mothers of sons. Even her own mother wouldn't attend her shows because her father couldn't come and she didn't want to support what she viewed as discrimination. Alix doesn't regret choosing to do all-women shows, but she would have loved her parents to see some of her greatest accomplishments.

From the start, Lin Daniels wanted to produce women-only shows because she found them empowering. "When men are in the audience there's a different vibe."[191]

One of the things Cris Williamson didn't like about this new women's music movement was the separatism. She told the *Lesbian Tide* (May/June 1980), "Integration is what I want. It seems to me that shutting men out is not the answer."

Others at Olivia didn't agree with her and, in the seventies, were promoting women-only events and experiencing some difficulties. Venues balked. The YMCA was close to suing them. While they thought they'd open shows to men down the line, they felt the time wasn't right yet—that women needed to gather their strength through women-only events. Judy Dlugacz commented, "We couldn't win: when we were doing women-only, there were those who attacked that. When we were doing concerts that were open to everyone, we were…attacked for that by women who felt that we were betraying the separatist view."[192]

At the third National Women's Music Festival, women-only shows were a hot topic. Unlike other venues, this event was held at the University of Illinois where they were required to comply with Title IX regulations. Meg Christian, Ginny Berson and others led workshops about separatism. The men of the festival collective offered their own workshops. Malvina Reynolds, one of the performers that year, handed out a flyer that said in part, "A man who comes to our concert is already half a convert and worth educating…To class all men together is stereotyping, false and unproductive."[193] About a hundred yards away, Holly Near was handing out her own flyer, one that advocated for women-only concerts.

Artists like Evelyn Harris, a member of Sweet Honey in the Rock and part of the arts agency Roadwork, told *HOT WIRE* (March 1986), "I did not know much about the women's community before working with Roadwork. As I got acquainted with it, I admired the fact that there is a sense of family. But at the same time, as a Black woman I found it difficult when men and boy children were excluded. That's not where I was coming from in my culture...I found that in woman-only spaces women still need a lot of work on how they deal with each other." Sisterfire, a Washington D.C.-area festival that Roadwork produced for several years, welcomed both men and women.

Linda Tillery supported space for women but, "I live in a world where there are two kinds of people: men and women. And unless this other half of the population just disappears, I'm going to have to deal with the fact that they're there."[194]

The argument for women-only space wasn't just about the audience, but also who could be onstage. Most early festivals permitted only women musicians. Even woman-fronted bands were not hired if any band members were men. Dianne Davidson was an artist who wasn't too familiar with women's music and women-only events when she recorded her album with Olivia. Before one of Olivia's anniversary concerts, Judy Dlugacz explained to her that the bands would be women-only. Dianne's regular band included her brother as well as her good friend Michael on keyboards. She fought to include them, even considering declining the gig at Carnegie Hall. She argued with Judy, "You're being a hypocrite because you have technicians who are men. Just because women can't see them, that's not fair...Michael is an African-American who grew up in the south. I'll let *you* tell him he's not welcome...We are at a point now where we can run with the big dogs, we should show people that we're not intimidated by male musicians...we're as good as they are."[195]

In the end, Dianne did the show with a trio of women, no one on keyboards. She still doesn't feel right about that decision. "It's interesting that you'd have this whole powerful movement that refused to evolve. If we had evolved then maybe we'd still have some of that beyond the few places that are left."[196]

Later in Alix Dobkin's career, she opened her concerts to everyone. "We can hold our space now. We can have our thing and a guy can walk in...and we don't even think about him. That wasn't true back then."[197] Others came to the same decision until there were few women-only spaces left in the eighties, most of them festivals and the rare smaller venues like Mountain Moving Coffeehouse in Chicago.

A Transgender Woman at Olivia

The issue snapped into even clearer focus in 1976, when Olivia was planning its third album, *BeBe K'Roche*. Since they were based in the Bay Area, they wanted to find an engineer who lived closer than Oregonian Joan Lowe, who had worked on their first releases. Someone recommended Sandy Stone. The interview with her was successful and they thought they'd found the perfect engineer. They were about to go into the studio when Ginny Berson got a call from Boo Price. In the middle of recording Margie Adam's first release, one of the people from their studio, Different Fur, told Boo, "Sandy Stone was a guy engineer from

Santa Cruz who he knew well, who now presents as a woman. I could've dropped dead, I was like '*What*'?"[198] She knew Olivia collective member Ginny Berson and Boo thought, if I was in her shoes, I'd want to know, so she phoned Ginny and told her that Sandy was transsexual.[199] At the time, members of the Olivia collective lived in the same home and had a once-a-week lunch together, a big deal where one member shopped and cooked for everyone. After Ginny got the call she recalls getting out of bed, making the short walk to the office and calmly telling the women there, "I just heard that Sandy is a male-to-female transsexual. I'm going to the grocery store."[200]

Judy remembers calling over collective member Kate Winter to "...ask what a transsexual was. She had a friend who was a transsexual so she was able to describe what it was to the rest of us."[201] They talked with Sandy and it was confirmed. After discussion, they elected to keep working with Sandy because she was an experienced engineer who shared their ideologies. Ginny doesn't remember it as being a huge deal with the collective initially, but as word got out, that changed. "It was not possible at that time to have a good discussion really, it was just a lot of yelling."[202] They stood by Sandy and, "...took a lot of shit."[203] A leaflet from women in the community was circulating, arguing that since Sandy had received her studio training as a man, with all the privilege that entails, that she should not be involved with Olivia. The May/June 1977 *Lesbian Tide* reported a response from Olivia: "Our daily personal and political interactions have confirmed for each of us that she is a woman we can relate to with comfort and with trust." Ginny thought Sandy was very talented, teaching them what she knew and, "... she worked for the same crappy money we all made. She was making a lot of money before."[204]

Sandy maintains that she told the Olivia collective she was transgender when they first talked in 1974.[205] What isn't disputed is that she'd come to them with extensive studio experience, including the prestigious Record Plant in New York City. She'd worked with Jimi Hendrix, Van Morrison, and the Grateful Dead. Sandy was excited to work with this radical feminist collective and engineered several of their albums including *Lesbian Concentrate*.

Alix Dobkin discovered that Sandy was transgender while she was on a West Coast tour in March and April of 1977. She was dismayed that they would hire Sandy and not tell anyone about her. Alix remembered, "There had been this explosive horrible meeting up in Portland, I think, women in the community lambasted them and accused them of all kinds of things...which they were guilty of not knowing their friends from their enemies. Any criticism or any questioning was perceived as enemies of Olivia...they hunkered down. It was just a horrible situation, women were outraged and practically a lynch mob."[206] There were allegations that transsexuals were infiltrating the women's movement. Some thought that Olivia was committing the ultimate betrayal. It was a very difficult period for them. Judy Dlugacz offers, "We're talking about a very young, very angry movement...we'd get both loving feedback and angry feedback...(it was) very exhausting and demoralizing."[207]

More New Artists in the Late Seventies

Therese Edell

Therese always loved to sing. In kindergarten, she sang to the girls waiting in the bathroom line. She went on to play various instruments including the guitar, then later attended the University of Cincinnati, majoring in education. In the seventies, she gained a big following performing in Cincinnati area coffeehouses and bars, sometimes with Betsy Lippitt (violin, guitar, vocals) and Lou Anderson (bass). Therese discovered the National Women's Music Festival when sister musician Annie Dinerman, performing at the event, encouraged her to go. In March of 1977, she met her partner Teresa Boykin. Teresa also became her manager and started booking Therese and side player Betsy

Therese Edell and Adrienne Torf, 1990 Michigan Festival.
Photo by Toni Armstrong Jr.

at gigs outside of Cincinnati, including the second Michigan Festival and many thereafter. At one Michigan Festival, a rainstorm took out all the sound equipment. Therese did her complete set without microphones. She was involved with the festival every year from 1978 to the mid-eighties as an emcee, sound engineer, and musical performer. She also worked several summers in their office, answering phone calls.

Of her 1970 album, *Prophecy's Child*, she joked that it was available only from under her bed. In May 1978 *From Women's Faces* came out on her own label, Sea Friends. Featuring mostly original compositions like the funny "Mama Let Your Children Go" and the folk anthem "Take Back the Guns," it also included the popular ballad "Moonflower," written by Annie Dinerman.[208] Therese toured for several years and ran sound at festivals until multiple sclerosis slowed her down.

Everyone in women's music adored her. "Therese was so kind to me and exuded a tremendous tenderness," recalls jazz guitarist Mimi Fox. "Long before I believed in myself, she was always so supportive of my talent. For this, I am eternally grateful to her."[209] For some of us, she was the first person we'd known who had multiple sclerosis. Alix Dobkin remarks, "She was the first to educate our community about disabilities on a massive scale. So many of us never gave it a thought until she made it personal for us."[210]

Therese was also known for her tremendous sense of humor. Alix adds, "Personally, I will always be grateful to Therese for dubbing me 'Head Lesbian' in the mid-seventies after she first heard (my song) 'A Woman's Love.'"[211]

Teresa Trull

Also starting her professional music life in the seventies was this North Carolina native. She had, "...tons of time alone in the woods with a really overactive imagination. It was a very powerful combination."[212] She liked a variety of music, from gospel to blues to folk. "...I used to take my Joni Mitchell records and my Laura Nyro records down to the basement and play them over and over again..."[213] R&B was another favorite. She lived in a world where "... Sam & Dave were more happening than the Beatles..."[214] Her dynamic vocal style developed while singing in church.

Teresa performed around the area in Durham, N.C., in a duo with another woman. When she was in her teens, she started touring with a rock band, Ed's Bush Band, and performed with them from 1970 to 1974, the only woman in a band of men, all of them several years older. At a young age, she decided to move to New York City to pursue music. Friends told her about Olivia but "I was too nervous. I thought Olivia Records was like a female Warner Brothers. I envisioned them in a twenty-story building with 'Warner Sisters' gleaming over the top. I was afraid I might not be able to take my dog to California because he was male...So, I said no."[215] After playing a radio show, a fan sent a tape to Olivia, unbeknown to Teresa. A year or so later Meg Christian contacted her, asking if she wanted to join her at a concert in Manhattan. It was a wonderful experience and afterward Olivia offered her a job. It couldn't have come at a better time— her apartment was off an alley in a sketchy part of the city and she was tired of scrambling for work. She packed up and moved to California. At first, she worked for Olivia in their A&R (Artists and Repertoire) department, listening to audition tapes. Quickly, she realized that wasn't the job for her. She laughs when she recalls, "I was very young and opinionated."[216] Years later, she could joke with Ferron about how she recommended that Olivia not sign her. Ferron went on to work with other labels.

In 1977, Olivia released her first album, *The Ways a Woman Can Be*. The lyrics for many of its songs like "Woman-Loving Women" were written when she was sixteen to twenty years old. Also included was one of her popular numbers, "I'd Like to Make Love to You," written by Margaret Sloan-Hunter. Supporting musicians included Meg Christian on vocals, June Millington on slide guitar, Mary Watkins on keyboards, and Linda Tillery on drums. Linda also produced the release. Making the album was fun. "I had the best time," Teresa remembers, "it's where I met Vicki Randle and Linda Tillery."[217]

Women's music was a revelation to her. In the rock band, the guys were always trying to get her take the mic off the stand and swivel her hips to appear sexier. She recalls, "I was so turned off by what they wanted me to be…women's music freed me up to be exactly who I wanted to be."[218]

Mary Watkins

Her Olivia recording was also released in the seventies. This composer and pianist was raised in the A.M.E. (African Methodist Episcopal) church. "This music became my lifeline, my connection to God, to the Infinite."[219] Her mother encouraged her to learn the piano and by the time she was eight, she was playing

Mary Watkins, 1982.
Photo by Irene Young ©1982

for the junior choir. When she decided she wanted to become a composer, she didn't know there were other women who did that until she stumbled upon the name Ruth Crawford in an encyclopedia of composers. Crawford was a classical composer known for her work in the twenties through the forties. She was the mother of Pete and Peggy Seeger. Mary majored in music in college and graduated from Howard University in Washington, DC, the only one in her class with a degree in composition. Mary improved her chops gigging around the DC area in jazz combos, musical theater, and working as the musical director for a Black theater group. After moving to the Bay Area in California, one of her first jobs was packing records for Olivia. She recorded "Don't Pray for Me" for *Lesbian Concentrate* before recording her solo album, *Something Moving*, in 1978. It included an ode to a Bay Area breakfast hangout, the funky "Brick Hut," as well as the epic "Witches' Revenge," an almost eight-minute long jazz piece. June Millington produced the album which included musicians Vicki Randle and Linda Tillery. In later years, she recorded and released *Winds of Change* (1982, Palo Alto Jazz), *Spiritsong* (1985,

Redwood), and *The Soul Knows* (1992). Her live shows were largely instrumental and presented in jazz clubs and theaters. She also performed with Holly Near and Teresa Trull. She is well-loved and respected by many in women's music. Bassist Jan Martinelli says, "It was incredible to work with Mary Watkins as producer and bandleader. She is one of my heroes and is very inspirational."[220] Mary told *HOT WIRE* in 1993, "I want to do music that inspires people to be kind to each other; to be kind to themselves, to love each other, to love themselves."

Alive!

The San Francisco Bay Area was home to many women musicians including Alive!, a group of women who met at a jazz workshop in July 1976. Carolyn Brandy (percussion), Rhiannon (vocals and piano), and Susanne Vincenza (bass and cello), were inspired by Cuban, African, and American jazz. They started getting together to jam and eventually, to perform in local coffeehouses and clubs. Their first appearance at a major women's music event was at the National Women's Music Festival in 1977, on the Tuesday main stage. They were so well-received that they were added to the lineup on the Sunday main stage. They followed those performances with a short tour in the Midwest.

In early 1979, they added Barbara Borden on drums and Janet Small on piano, freeing Rhiannon to focus on vocals. Performing originals like Carolyn's "Spirit Healer," they also covered songs by June Millington, Mary Watkins, and Ida Cox. They traveled the US and Canada for several months of each year, playing at women's music and jazz festivals, as well as other venues. Touring was an adventure. Rhiannon recalls, "We didn't have enough money to stop in motels when we had our van and then our RV, so we would start in California and then not stop, except for gas, until we got to the East Coast, or wherever we were playing."[221] They released three albums, *Alive!, Call It Jazz,* and *City Life,* before they disbanded in 1986. "It was the most loving breakup I'd ever been through," comments Rhiannon.[222] They left for various reasons, Carolyn because she wanted to spend more time with her son. Everyone continued to make music. Rhiannon made a solo album, *Toward Home,* in 1991. They had a reunion at the Michigan Festival's fortieth anniversary in 2015 and performed at the National Festival in 2016.

BeBe K'Roche

Another Bay Area band began in 1973 when bass player Peggy Mitchell met guitarist Tiik Pollet at Kate Millet's Sacramento festival. The band changed personnel a few times. Tiik performed with them but didn't stay to record. Their self-titled album was produced by Linda Tillery and released on Olivia in 1976. Their R&B/Latin/jazz sound showcased original songs, most written by keyboard player Virginia Rubino. Probably their most popular piece was

"Kahlua Mama," a love song to a woman. They played locally as well as some touring across the country, including appearances at women's music festivals. Their last performance was at the National Festival in 1977.

Gwen Avery

Also based in the San Francisco area was Gwen Avery. Raised in a juke joint in Pennsylvania by her grandmother, she was entertaining the clientele by the time she was four years old. Influenced by jukebox songs by Etta James, Little Anthony, and Tina Turner, it's no surprise that she would develop a style that made friend Linda Tillery call her "...an authentic blues and gospel singer."[223]

She moved to the Bay Area in 1969 at the age of twenty-five after seeing an article that featured people smoking pot and doing yoga in the streets. She said, "The city was so permissive, there were even openly gay cops. My eyes bulged out of my head onto the page. I was gone."[224] After singing with rock band Full Moon, she did her first women's music gig at a festival in Santa Cruz. Not long after that, in 1975, Gwen recorded two songs for a compilation organized by women from Olivia, *Any Woman's Blues*, to help raise money for a library at San Bruno Women's Prison. In 1977, she recorded "Sugar Mama" for *Lesbian Concentrate*. She modestly called it "just a love song" but audiences loved it. Also, that year Olivia released a forty-five recording featuring that song on one side and Teresa Trull on the other side. In 1978, she was a part of the Varied Voices of Black Women tour. She remembers, "It was so jubilant it was almost riotous... it wasn't the beautiful chants of Meg Christian or Cris Williamson, but it was joyous nonetheless."[225] Also, that year, she sang a song on Mary Watkins's Olivia release.

She didn't always feel a part of women's music, partly because of her stage presentation—"I dressed differently. I would wear satin suits, and platform shoes and an afro, with neckties, beautiful silk shirts. They were wearing plaid shirts and blue jeans..."[226]

Gwen was scheduled to do a full-length album for Olivia but it never materialized. In 2011 she told J. D. Doyle (*Queer Music Heritage*), "I was, I guess, pitched out because I would move my hips, or lick my lips onstage and it was too much for the women's community...it's so insulting when I think of it, to defy my culture, that's what they wanted me to do...to sit there with my legs crossed and my arms folded." After the Varied Voices of Black Women tour, Olivia met to discuss Gwen's album and they decided not to produce her. They didn't make their reasons public.

Woody Simmons

Someone not a part of the San Francisco Bay Area music scene was innovative banjo player and multi-instrumentalist Woody Simmons. She toured in 1975 as part of Cris Williamson's band to support the release of *The Changer*

Woody Simmons, 1989 National Festival.
Photo by Toni Armstrong Jr.

and the Changed. Woody also performed as a solo musician, mostly in the late seventies and early eighties. She learned a frailing banjo technique, a method used in old-time folk, from Mary Wings, then dove further into the instrument, composing unique instrumentals like "Banjo Raga." Her first album, *Oregon Mountains*, was released on her own label in 1977. Accompanying musicians included members of Alive! (Carolyn Brandy, Suzanne Vincenza, and Rhiannon) as well as players from the Berkeley Women's Music Collective (Nancy Vogl, Nancy Henderson). Her second album, *Woody Simmons*, was released in 1980. She's also a recording engineer and album producer.

Trish Nugent

A singer-songwriter, she is best known for the original music she contributed to the landmark documentary *Word is Out*. Her album, *Foxglove Woman*, was released in 1977, the same year as the film.

Ginni Clemmens

Ginni, like Trish Nugent, was also a songwriter but she didn't start out that way. She was a nurse who played the guitar for her patients at a Chicago residential facility for disabled children. Soon, she was playing in Chicago area blues and folk clubs alongside well-known performers Steve Goodman and John Prine. Ida Cox's song "Wild Women Don't Get the Blues" was one of her popular numbers and became an anthem for the women's community. Her warm stage presence, penchant for singalongs, and expressive voice made her a sought-after performer. "She had the kind of voice that made you want to listen to what she had to say," said Jimmy Tomasello, manager of the Old Town School of Folk Music.[227] Ginni took classes at the then fledgling school and in later years, taught there.

Ginni loved finding early blues songs to perform. "I won't sing any song that is sexist, and it's so hard to find non-sexist blues," she told *HOT WIRE* in March 1985, "I've taken to adapting old blues." She changed the lyrics in Bessie Smith's "T'aint Nobody's Business," removing a line about domestic violence and changing it to lyrics that discounted a beauty queen mentality.

Her first album, *Sing a Rainbow and Other Children's Songs*, came out on noted folk label Folkways in 1965. In 1976 *Long Time Friends* was released on Open Door, her own label. Around that time, she came out as a lesbian. In 1981 she offered another release, this one with the Ida Cox tune as the title cut. Also included were folk/ blues numbers like her own "Solid Ground," the album featuring Margie Adam on piano. In 1980,

Ginni Clemmens, 1993 Michigan Festival.
Photo by Toni Armstrong Jr.

Ginni produced *Gay and Straight Together*, a compilation that included a variety of performers, male and female, including Kristen Lems and Paula Walowitz.

Joanna Cazden

Not as well known to women's audiences, her album *Hatching* was released in 1976 and distributed by Olivia. A folksinger, peace activist, and feminist, she toured nationally in the seventies. She released five other solo albums between 1973 and 1997.

Tret Fure

Tret grew up in the Midwest and began playing the piano at age five, copying the songs she heard on the radio, prompting her parents to get her lessons. By the time she was seven, she was writing songs that were so good, her teacher had her playing them for high school students. When she was eleven her brother brought home a guitar. She recalls, "It was like, *mine*. Give me that guitar,"[228] and started teaching herself to play. She devoured every folk album she could find, learning fingerpicking by listening to Judy Collins. Tret remembers, "I put my head to the hi-fi and I'd pick up the needle and put it down until I learned how to Travis pick."[229] (It's a method of playing the guitar often used in folk music.) Later, she expanded her musical knowledge, teaching herself to play the blues from Robert Johnson and Lead Belly recordings.

Her brother was an important part of her early musical development. She laughs when she remembers, "He says 'I taught her her first chords and then she taught me everything I know.'"[230] When she was fourteen, they formed a duo and performed in local venues. The duo broke up when he got married and moved to California. At the tender age of nineteen she started writing her own songs and moved to Los Angeles. There she met June Millington, then a member of rock band Fanny, and two months later moved in with her. Tret remembers, "We just kind of fell in love musically and personally and that was really my first lesbian relationship."[231] Dubbed "Fanny Hill," their house hosted a constant stream of jamming musicians including Crazy Horse (Neil Young's band), Bonnie Raitt, Linda Ronstadt, and Lowell George (Little Feat).

Tret Fure, 1988.
Photo by Irene Young © 1988.

Nikki Barclay, Fanny's keyboard player, suggested to Spencer Davis, a sixties rock performer known for "Gimme Some Lovin," that he look up Tret. He was putting together a new band and even though he was unsure about working with a woman, he contacted her. He loved how she played, especially since he was into acoustic blues then and she had the skills for it. They recorded his album, *Mousetrap*, using her song as the single released from it. She also played guitar and wrote all the songs. Fanny's manager, Roy Silver, saw her perform with Davis in 1972 and signed her to a management deal, enabling her to get a recording contract. Her first album, *Tret Fure*, was released on MCA in 1973. A second album was shelved, lost in the shuffle of label reorganization. She worked hard to get another deal, showcasing all over Los Angeles and going through several managers. A deal was offered in 1978 but she decided against it when they wanted to take the rights to her original songs, have her sing "ridiculous" songs, and dress in leather. Even though she didn't consider herself to be part of women's music, the labels she approached assumed she was with Olivia. It was during this period that she learned to be a studio engineer, one of the first women to do so, and that was what paid the bills.

Tret stayed in touch with June even after they broke up. "She would say you should learn 'Sweet Woman'...June thought I could really do it well and that was my first introduction to Cris (Williamson). (I said) nah, I'm not interested in that song."[232]

Tret co-produced June's first solo album, *Heartsong*, and formed a record company, Fabulous, to put it out on cassette. They toured together. In the eighties and on, Tret would work much more in women's music.

Reel World String Band

Starting in 1977, this acoustic group was one of the first all-lesbian string bands. They started with Appalachian music. "Our first emphasis was on fiddle tunes. We tried to draw vocals from them, but it was difficult to find lyrics to fit our woman's consciousness," said Sharon Ruble, their bass player.[233] Round-

ing out the rest of the band was Sue Massek (mandolin and guitar), Bev Futrell (guitar, mandolin, and harmonica), Belle Jackson (guitar), and Karen Jones (fiddle, mandolin, and guitar). Later, Elise Melrood joined them on piano. Influenced by Texas swing, bluegrass, and old-time folk, they played for a variety of audiences, from miners in Kentucky to Lincoln Center in New York City to the Michigan

Reel World String Band, eighties: Bev Futrell, Sue Massek, Karen Jones, Sharon Ruble. *Private collection, Reel World String Band. Photo by Barbara Dumesil.*

Womyn's Music Festival. Their first album, *Bluegrass Extravaganza*, was released in 1981. To promote it they toured with popular bluegrass band the Osbourne Brothers. They released nine albums and continue to be a favorite at folk and women's music festivals.

The Fabulous Dyketones

Offering something very different from folk, this fun band featured music of the fifties and sixties with slightly skewed lyrics and a theatrical presentation with members sometimes in poodle skirts and bouffant hair, sometimes in leather jackets and ducktails.

Naomi Littlebear Morena and Char Priolo met through the Ursa Minor Choir in Portland, Oregon and after gathering a few others, made their first appearance as the band at a New Year's Eve show in 1977. They knew six songs.

Every member had a stage name, sometimes one butch and one femme. For Char, it was Chukki or Cha-Cha Linguine, later member Yarrow Halstead was Penny Loafer or Buck Naked, and Gloria Cortez was Holly Peno or Louie Luwy. Songs included "My Dyke," (a reworked "My Girl"), "Jenny B. Goode," and "Great Breasts of Fire." Char also had a character called Mother Inferior. As they did more gigs, their repertoire and comedy skits expanded. Performances happened at "Dyke High" and sometimes there was an opportunity to join the F.D.A. (Future Dykes of America). There might be a drawing where the winner could "join" the band. It came complete with their own stage name. Men could win too and be added as a "dicktone." Sometimes they recruited go-go dancers from the audience. Founding member Kristan Aspen says, "It was a challenging group with four Scorpios and too much alcohol as I recall. When we weren't fighting, we did have fun! It was like being a little kid making up theater and stories for all our characters."[234]

The group grew over the years, with a rotating cast of band members including Lisa Koch (Dos Fallopia), Barb Galloway (Baba Yaga), and Lisa Rogers and Maureen McLean (Therapy Sisters). There were eighty-eight different band members.[235] The only constant member was founder Char. She owned the name and took care of band business. In the eighties, they toured and were a popular fixture in Provincetown.

Izquierda and Naomi Littlebear Morena (Martinez)

One of the early members of the Dyketones, Naomi Littlebear Morena didn't stay with the band very long. Already well-known in Portland, Oregon, she'd been putting together all-girl bands since the age of sixteen. After coming out as a lesbian in the seventies, she started spending time at the Santa Ana, California Women's Center where she was introduced to the women's movement and musician Robin Flower. Excited to find another woman who played lead guitar, they formed Sisterhood in 1972, playing mostly covers of favorite folk songs and the other songs Naomi already knew. Around that time she started writing her own music.

Naomi formed Izquierda ("left" in Spanish), a four-piece acoustic band that mostly played her original songs. She described their music this way, "We all were just a group of arty hippies with new age foreshadowing who wanted women to open their hearts to one another, to heal each other, to sing as one… We were more spiritual in our approach to music than political."[236] Their album, *Quiet Thunder*, came out in 1978. It contained her best-known song, "Like a Mountain."

They did their first tour in 1977, including appearances at the Michigan and National Festivals. Because these festivals were attended by women from all over the country, they could make contacts to get enough bookings for several tours.

Original band members included Kristan Aspen on flute and piano, Robin Chilstrom on vocals, Izetta Smith on vocals and percussion, and Naomi on vocals and guitar. The lineup changed after the release of the album. Kristan now did the booking and with all their driving, it helped that she was also an auto mechanic. Kristan remembers: "One year we were going to Michigan, it could've been 1978, and we were driving in a vehicle that Naomi had picked up in Oaxaca, a big '57 Chevy wagon—Sister Elk we called her. We were driving across Idaho and broke an axle in a tiny town. Right there in the pouring rain I replaced the axle…The locals stood around and watched. The local newspaper covered it. This was big news in Kellogg, Idaho."[237]

For the most part, touring was pleasant. Kristan recounts, "It was like a vacation in some ways…meeting new friends…that's what was so amazing about women's culture, you knew them even if you didn't know them."[238]

The band toured until 1980. Often, they would perform with a group of eight to fifteen local women who offered backing vocals on "Like a Mountain." Naomi loved the full sound of their voices—"I feel that by starting these women's pickup choirs we set the foundation for the creation of women's choirs in the future."[239]

Over the years, she's heard from people about "Like a Mountain," the response even prompting a visit to Britain in 1983 to record the song for a compilation album to support the peaceful protests by women at Greenham Common. No surprise, given that in the song she sings that it will "live on and on."

Robin Flower

Robin's musical history didn't start with Naomi and hippie songs. When she was fourteen, a girl in her neighborhood introduced her to the guitar. Not long after that, her parents borrowed money from her brother, who delivered newspapers, and bought her a guitar. She practically slept with it, teaching herself to play and write songs, and then performing around her hometown of Cleveland with her sister and a high school trio. A fan of rock and folk, she learned everything musical she could. At twenty-two, she saw *Easy Rider*, bought herself a motorcycle and set off to see the world, eventually ending up in Oregon where she fell in love with Mary Wings, a potter and banjo player. On a new fiddle, a borrowed mandolin and her guitar, she remembered the mountain songs her family shared. She and Mary played at the Saturday market where Mary sold her pots. A concert promoter heard Robin there and asked if she wanted to tour with Elizabeth

Robin Flower, 1991 Rhythmfest.
Photo by Marcy Hochberg.

Cotten, and old-time folk duo Hazel and Alice. She gave him a big "hell yes." The promoter picked Elizabeth up at the airport. The Muzak in the elevator there was playing "Freight Train," her most popular song.

Robin loved touring with them. She learned a lot, calling the eighty-two-year-old Cotten a total inspiration. "I learned about not being in a hurry. She didn't get famous until her sixties."[240]

Robin's first forays into women's music included playing on Maxine Feldman's 1972 forty-five release. In 1974, she played at the first National Women's Music Festival, in a trio with Mary Wings and Woody Simmons, as the Clinch Mountain Backsteppers. They learned some of their songs on the way in the car. The event was exciting but Robin also found it frustrating because of the politics: "I realized that it was a movement but sometimes for me it was too much. I just wanted to play."[241] A year or two later, Mary Spotswood, Casse Culver's manager, hired her and Mary Wings to play on Casse's first album, which came out in 1976.

Her *More Than Friends* was released in 1979 on her own label. Engineered by Woody Simmons, it included on bass Laurie Lewis, now a mainstay on the American bluegrass circuit, Mary Wings on banjo, Nancy Vogl on acoustic guitar, and Robin on three instruments and vocals. It featured Bonnie Lockhart's (Berkeley Women's Music Collective) folk anthem "I Still Ain't Satisfied" as well as bluegrass standards "Blackberry Blossom" and "Whiskey Before Breakfast." The title cut was a nod to the women who were "more than friends."

Three subsequent albums were released on folk label Flying Fish—*Babies With Glasses, First Dibs,* and *Green Sneakers.* She also played in jazz group Baba Yaga, toured with rock band BeBe K'Roche, and played on many albums including those by Holly Near.

Cathy Winter and Betsy Rose

Like Robin Flower, they also performed at an early National Festival. Cathy and Betsy met at a conference in 1975, played at Boston Women's Music Weekend the fall of that year and at the National Festival in 1976. Known for their harmonies and accomplished guitar work, their songs included the feminist anthem "Glad to Be a Woman." Their album, *Sweet Sorcery*, was released in 1980. They toured for a short while then went on to solo careers.

Baba Yaga

Named for a powerful witch from Russian folk tales, this short-lived jazz band included for a time Robin Flower. She was looking to stretch her musical boundaries and playing with them was the first time she picked up an electric guitar. Their only album, 1978's *On the Edge*, was distributed by Olivia and featured Barb Galloway (guitar), Jan Cornall (drums), Susan Colson (bass), Patti Vincent (sax), Bonnie Kovaleff (trumpet), and Kiera O'Hara (piano) as well as a few side players. Their collection of originals includes the tongue-in-cheek "Monogamy Shbedogyamy." They played in and around their hometown of Portland, Oregon, as well as doing some touring, mostly on the West Coast.

June Millington

While some knew her from the mainstream rock band Fanny, she didn't become known in women's music until her work with Cris Williamson in 1975, when she played on *Changer and the Changed* and also toured with her. The two of them joined forces for later projects, including Cris's children's album *Lumiere*. June and sister Jean played together again—Jean was also in Fanny—for the United Artists album *Ladies on the Stage* in 1977. She also produced albums for others, including Holly Near's

June Millington, 1990 Michigan Festival.
Photo by Toni Armstrong Jr.

Fire in the Rain. Her solo career started in 1981 with *Heartsong*, and continued with *Running* in 1983, and *One World, One Heart* in 1988. She explored a lot of genres, from rock to reggae to blues, in songs that speak to the myriad of human experience. In 1987, she started IMA (Institute for the Musical Arts) with Ann Hackler. There, they teach, record, and support girls and women in music.

Ferron

Not every performer was from the US. Ferron grew up on the west coast of Canada, near Vancouver. At fourteen, she saved up money from a job mowing neighbors' lawns and bought a guitar. Influenced by artists like Kitty Wells and Hank Williams, musicians she heard on the radio, she started writing her own songs, composing over a hundred in a year's time. At fifteen, she left school to work, and inspired by singer-songwriters Bruce Cockburn and Joni Mitchell, she often picked up her guitar. When she was twenty-two, she changed her name to Ferron, based on a dream related to her by a friend.

Ferron, 1989
Photo by Irene Young ©1989

Ferron's intuitive songs come from a life where lessons were learned the hard way. She told CBC Radio (2017): "I needed to hear myself say some things and then there was some kind of grace or gift that came in that allowed my words to kind of bounce on the page. I put two words side by side and I could just see them vibrating, like they're not supposed to go together but they do."

Her first big show was in 1975, a benefit for a women's organization. She continued to play in clubs and coffeehouses around Vancouver while working in restaurants and factories. Her friends persuaded her to record, so in 1977 she released 1,000 copies of a self-titled album, following that up with *Ferron Backed Up* in 1978. Also that year, she met photographer Gayle Scott who became her manager. Together they produced her next release, *Testimony*, using $27,000 lent to her by fans and a credit union. In the first four months, it sold 5,000 copies. By the early eighties, that number had more than tripled. These numbers were tremendous for an independent recording at a time where there was no Internet and radio airplay was difficult if you weren't on a major label. Her well-crafted songs touched many, especially the title cut, a loving anthem to the strength of women. It came from a request—she was asked to write a song for a film, "This Film is About Rape." They gave her a deadline. She struggled with it and finally, inspired by a conversation and her own experience as a rape survivor, she wrote the song the night before it was due. Because it was like a testimonial, she called it "Testimony."

Another popular song on that album was "Ain't Life a Brook," a poetically descriptive song about life after a breakup. She calls "Misty Mountain" a prayer, written when she was staying with her friend Keith: "I think I was suffering PTSD but I only knew that many years later...I don't think they really saw me much for about three weeks. I just slept and didn't give a shit really. Then Keith came down and he said, 'You gotta get up, you've got to care.' The only thing I cared about right then is would he please get the f—k out of my room." It sparked something in her. In the dark, she strummed her guitar and started singing.[242]

Ferron's music is important to many, including fan Karen Escovitz. "There I sat in an audience of women...and dawn started breaking over my thick skull that I was actually a lesbian. The *Testimony* album broke things open for me musically..."[243] Karen went on to discover other women's music as well as her own skills as a musician.

Ferron toured extensively, playing at many well-known venues like The Great American Music Hall in San Francisco, the Bottom Line in New York and the Vancouver Folk Festival. Her fans didn't just come from women's music—she had a huge following from the folk world too. The *Boston Globe* said, "Someday they will call Dylan the Ferron of the sixties." She's been a great inspiration to other performers also. Amy Ray of the Indigo Girls calls her an important early influence.

Carole Etzler

This folkie made two albums in the seventies, *Sometimes I Wish* (1976) and *Womanriver Flowing On* (1978). Her purpose was always clear—it even said "feminist songs" on the cover of her first release. She's known for original songs like "Women Loving Women" and "I'm a Kept Woman in the Bureaucracy." Later, after changing her name to Carole Etzler Eagleheart, she released a recording of spiritual songs, *She Calls to Us*, and two more as a member of the duo Carole and Bren. She presented her songs in a variety of settings from coffeehouses to Unitarian churches.

Sue Fink

Her "Leaping Lesbians," co-written with Joelyn Grippo, was featured on Olivia's *Lesbian Concentrate*. Meg Christian called the song, "One of the great classics of women's music."[244] Solo albums were released later. She has performed with many in women's music including Diane Lindsay, Meg Christian, Margie Adam, and Therese Edell.

She started with piano lessons at the age of ten. Required by her parents to practice four hours a day, she became bored and made up little games at the piano that led to writing songs. At eleven she wrote a musical where the big number was "When Will Will Marry Mary?" She became involved in choral music and then majored in music for her undergraduate and graduate degrees. Sue taught school for six or seven years until the parent of one of her students threatened to get her fired for being a lesbian.

The first women's music event she attended was at a little place in 1975 in Venice, California, a Margie Adam/Vicki Randle concert. She was so taken with that concert and others that she started writing songs for the women's community, eventually organizing a comedy and music show, *Bicentennial Review*, with friend Joelyn Grippo. It was an ambitious effort involving about thirty women. One of the big numbers was "Leaping Lesbians." The crowd loved it. Meg Christian was in the audience and asked if she could perform it. The song became a regular part of Meg's shows. So many fans heard Meg perform it that they thought she'd written it. When it came time to record *Lesbian Concentrate*, Olivia asked Sue if Meg could record it. Sue countered that she should record it. After some discussion, they agreed. Sue remembers, "They gave me no budget for it. They taped the microphone to a lamp...I can't remember whose house it was...it was pretty awful."[245]

Sue had been involved with choruses much of her life. In 1976, she organized the LA Women's Community Chorus. She recalls, "I thought we'd get fifteen or twenty (but) we had seventy-seven people or something like that (at the first rehearsal)...I thought wow, people really want to do this!"[246] She conducted the chorus for ten years. "It was a great community of friends and a great community of music. We got to sing music about women and for women, we had a riot."[247] It was a women's chorus, welcoming gay, straight, and bi women, although Sue jokes, "If they came in feminist, they ended up gay (laughs)...most of them, that wasn't the plan, it kind of worked out that way."[248] They were the second women's chorus to come into existence, the first one started by Cathy Roma on the other side of the country around the same time.

Her solo career developed also and in 1979, she started to tour, including an appearance at an early National Women's Music Festival. Playing the piano wasn't enough so she borrowed $6,000 for a synthesizer and a drum machine, instruments that were unheard of in women's music at the time. "I was possessed. I wanted an orchestra in my living room. I would've sold my soul for it and I did."[249]

In 1983, Holly Near asked her to tour as her pianist. Sue declined and gave her John Bucchino's contact information. She'd been playing in a band with him and knew he was a great musician. That recommendation started a musical partnership lasting many years.

The next year, when Meg called her to play on her farewell tour from women's music Sue said yes, even though, "I don't consider myself a pianist but I play okay and she seemed happy."[250] One of the reasons she agreed was to conquer her tremendous stage fright. Playing in a band with Meg and bassist Diane Lindsay meant she'd have support, and they would perhaps make her less afraid. One night at a big show for two thousand people, Meg asked Sue to take a lead in the middle of a song. "I completely blew the solo. I was shaking and I just wasn't expecting it... I remember her whispering into the mic (as a joke), 'Next keyboardist please' and something happened. I stopped playing. I went out and took a bow and the audience gave me a standing ovation. It changed something and I realized it was okay to be imperfect."[251] Meg gave her time to do a couple of her songs, including "Leaping Lesbians." Sue remembers, "I will always be thankful for that."[252]

On that tour with Meg, Sue passed out a flyer asking people to contribute toward the making of her first album. Twenty thousand dollars arrived in the mail. Diane Lindsay produced it and the techno-pop *Big Promise* was released on the Ladyslipper label in 1985. Diane and Sue toured together the next year, backing each other up with vocals, keyboards, and bass.

She loved festivals. There, she did musical sets and was known for her entertaining emcee work. More than just reading introductions, she engaged the audience in games, songs and fun stories while the stage was readied for the next act. "Those festivals were like going to camp. These are people you'd wait all year to see. We'd all be together and just party and do the concerts. It was so fun and so crazy."[253]

In recent years her songs have been featured in many television productions and in film, and today she continues a successful career as conductor of the famed Angel City Chorale.

Sirani Avedis / Sally Piano

Originally performing under the name Sally Piano, this Armenian-American lesbian and self-proclaimed "hippie dyke revolutionary" started performing in the DC area in the mid-seventies, then toured and released an album, *Tattoos*, in 1980, under the name Sirani Avedis. Her music covered many themes, from racism to loving women, in a pop/rock style. Also a graphic designer, she designed the piano/tree logo used by the Michigan Festival.

Local Performers

Local scenes had their own musicians, some of whom had no connection to women's music, but with a big lesbian following. Others, like the Ohio-based band Moondancer, were inspired by national women's music artists and sometimes covered their songs. In Phoenix, Arizona, singer-songwriter Jane Howard, folk singer Caryl DeGroot, rockers Indavana Blues Band, and acoustic trio Shine were popular. They played at lesbian bar the Habit, coffeehouses, and benefits. Atlanta had singer-songwriters Dede Vogt and Jan Gibson, folk group Anima

Rising, and eclectic band New Era. They sometimes played at Ms. Garbo's, a lesbian bar. In Morgantown, West Virginia, Carla Daruda was a popular blues pianist. Austin, Texas boasted several women performers including singer-songwriter Nancy Scott. Folk band Rosy's Bar and Grill had a big following in Kansas City and elsewhere. Strong feminists, their repertoire included Dory Previn's "Did Jesus Have a Baby Sister?" They performed at a few women's music festivals. Mary Black played around Oklahoma City with Susan Morgan. Influenced by Cris Williamson and Meg Christian, they offered original songs in venues including Herland, a women's space that hosted many events. Guitarist/bassist Mary Reynolds was popular there too, starting in the late seventies. The jazz/rock/folk women's band Iris played around Grand Rapids, Michigan, in the seventies. Birmingham, Alabama also had a women's band, Marathon, which often played at a small straight bar and had many lesbian fans.

Cincinnati's production company, Mound of Venus, featured touring artists as well as homegrown talent singer-songwriter Chris Collier, eclectic acoustic band the Grinders, folk singer Jamie Fota, and guitarist/violinist Betsy Lippitt. Betsy was known to national audiences for her work with Therese Edell, another Cincinnati-based artist. The Grinders also gained some notoriety outside of the area, playing dates in the Midwest including the National Women's Music Festival. Their lighthearted show featured songs like "Whiny White Girl Blues" and "The Cockroach Song," with guitar, percussion, and more.

In the late seventies through the nineties, the place to be in New Orleans was Charlene's, a lesbian club. They featured live music from many including SoftTouch, an all-women's rock band, and Tim Williams, billed as the Creole Nightingale.

River City Womin was a popular four-woman band in Louisville, Kentucky who entertained at the women's bar Mother's Brew in the seventies. Here's how one fan described a performance: "The first time I walked through the doors of the Brew and saw four strong, confident women performing love songs to other women I cried…I stood and listened to those songs as if I had never heard music before. I guess maybe I hadn't, at least not music for me. I returned every time they played."[254]

Haresuite was a folk-rock ensemble from Ohio who played regionally as well as showcases at the National and Michigan festivals in the early eighties. Known for their rich harmonies, they released one album, *Circle of Friends*.

More and more musicians extended their concerts beyond the confines of their local community. The Washington Sisters and Jamie Anderson got their start in hometown feminist and lesbian venues.

Women's Choruses

There were many ways for women to be involved in music. In the seventies, women's choruses began to spring up. In 1975, the Anna Crusis Choir was started in Philadelphia by Catherine Roma. She went on to Cincinnati where she founded another women's chorus, MUSE, in 1984. They do fifteen to twenty shows a year in venues ranging from peace rallies to concert halls. Other choruses started. Many performed songs by Holly Near, Cris Williamson, and others from women's music. The Sister Singers Network began in 1981, presenting conferences where groups could sing and network. Some women's choruses belong to GALA, an organization incorporated in 1983 to serve the needs of the LGBTQ choral movement. They also have regular events for networking and performance. A few women's music festivals—National, Michigan and Campfest—had their own chorus of festival attendees that sometimes performed on stage.

Whether you were a member of a women's chorus, a well-known touring performer, or an audience member, the mid-to-late-seventies were a fertile time for women's music, and it was still just the beginning.

CHAPTER FOUR

••✦✦✦••

A WELL-ESTABLISHED INDUSTRY

The Eighties

Women's music continued to grow at an amazing rate. At the start of the decade distributor Ladyslipper offered five hundred titles, over a hundred of them women's music recordings.[255] The 1987 resource directory *Women's Music Plus* listed over a hundred venues and producers, fourteen women's music festivals, and more than two hundred performers.

New festivals were established including the West Coast Women's Music and Comedy Festival in California, Campfest in Pennsylvania, and the East Coast Lesbian Festival in New England. Established festivals thrived—the Michigan Festival drew thousands, including a record 8,000 in 1982.

Women's music periodical *Paid My Dues* ceased publication in 1980 and *HOT WIRE: The Journal of Women's Music and Culture*, took its place in 1984. Women's music had a prominent place in other feminist publications including *Sojourner* and *off our backs*.

Olivia released over twenty albums,

Michigan Festival night stage, 1985.
Private collection, Lisa Vogel. Photo by Jennifer Campbell.

some from newcomers Deidre McCalla and Lucie Blue Tremblay. They also started subsidiary label Second Wave to showcase musicians with more of an edge, like blues/country belter Dianne Davidson, disco artist Alicia Bridges, and rock/folk singer-songwriter Tret Fure. Icebergg Records put out the first Washington Sisters album in 1987. Established artist Teresa Trull continued to record, moving in a more polished direction. Her *Let It Be Known* was an R&B tour de force. Meg Christian released her third, 1981's *Turning It Over* and fourth, 1984's *From the Heart*. Alix Dobkin put out two albums in the eighties, *XXAlix* (1980) and *These Women/Never Been Better* (1986). Canadian folk artist Ferron released her landmark album *Testimony* on her own Lucy Records in 1980. She followed that with *Shadows on a Dime* in 1984. Classical/folk performer Kay Gardner continued to explore healing music and more with three albums—*A Rainbow Path* (1984), *Avalon* (1989), and *Garden of Ecstasy* (1989). Ronnie Gilbert released four albums in the eighties, including two with Holly Near. Cabaret musician Lynn Lavner honed her chops playing for LGBTQ groups and released her first recording in 1983. Pop rock trio BETTY formed in 1986.

Throughout the eighties Rosetta Records rereleased the music of early jazz and blues women like Bessie Smith, Billie Holiday, Ma Rainey, and the International Sweethearts of Rhythm. Rosetta Reitz started the label with $10,000 borrowed from friends. The label sold thousands of recordings.[256]

The eighties were a challenging time for some women's music performers. Maxine Feldman stopped performing music in the late eighties. Her voice was gone, she had health problems, and she was so destitute she almost ended up homeless. With help from friends and fans, she recovered and emceed at festivals including Michigan and the East Coast Lesbian Festival.

In 1985, for Michigan's tenth anniversary, Therese Edell made her last musical appearance on the main stage, accompanied by friends Deidre McCalla and Betsy Lippitt. Her rich alto voice soared through many favorite tunes, bringing the audience to tears. She continued to emcee at the festival until 1993. Usually backstage for announcements, she came out front that year, her wheelchair pushed by Betsy, to say goodbye.

Other performers—Elaine Townsend, Karen McKay, and more—faded from the scene after one or two albums. At the same time, other musicians were just entering women's music.

Artists New to Women's Music

Washington Sisters

Identical twins Sharon and Sandra Washington released their first album, *Understated*, in 1987 on Icebergg Records. They grew up singing together, putting on shows for family and friends starting at the age of five. Their first women's music performance was in December 1983 at Calico's Coffeehouse in Columbus, Ohio, when they opened for Haresuite. Their first solo gig came a month later at the same venue. They were not strangers to women's music. Both had worked with the Women's Music Union, a production collective in Columbus, and it was around this time when they first attended the Michigan Festival where they became workers for many years afterward.

Sandra recalls for that first solo show Sharon assured her they'd just invite a few friends. Eighty people showed up and had a wonderful time. They did more performances in Columbus and nearby. After sending them an audition tape, the National Women's Music Festival asked them to play there in 1984. Sandra remembers being very comfortable at the event because she knew a lot of the women from her experiences in production. By 1985, they were touring with keyboard player Melanie Monsour.

Their first album, produced by Teresa Trull, included a representation of what they'd been playing on tour, incorporating a variety of styles from a capella to gospel to jazz. Musicians included Linda Tillery and Vicki Randle. Recording for Icebergg Records, they hooked up with owner Karen Gotzler because they all had a history with Girl Scouts. All went well for about a year and a half before it became clear that Icebergg was struggling financially. The sisters had paid for most of the expenses associ-

Washington Sisters and Topp Twins, 1993 Michigan Festival.
Photo by Toni Armstrong Jr.

ated with the recording; however, Icebergg owned the master. When Sandra and Sharon asked about buying it, they were quoted a sum beyond their means and far more than they felt it was worth. Sandra suspects the label was trying to buoy their failing business. It was then that Goldenrod Music, a distribution company, stepped in and without saying anything about a personal connection, asked Icebergg about buying the master. They were quoted a smaller fee. They bought it and sold it to the Washington Sisters for the same amount, one that was much more affordable.

Undaunted, the sisters continued touring, seventy-five to one hundred gigs a year all over the country including big events like the Winnipeg Folk Festival where they met Bonnie Raitt. Over the years they shared the stage with Odetta, the Indigo Girls, and other musicians in women's music. *Take Two*, their second release, came out in 1991, this time on their own label.

They loved being a part of women's music. Sandra expresses a great appreciation for everyone who worked with them, fondly remembering "... feeling like I had a place no matter where I went...there are moments of having coffee or tea or that last drink at night in women's homes all over this country that I will treasure. Sometimes I don't remember their name and I may not exactly remember the city, but I remember the shape of the mug and the feeling. I remember the conversation. That's the stuff I'll remember forever."[257]

Deidre McCalla

Deidre was no stranger to women's music when she recorded her first Olivia release, *Don't Doubt It*, in 1985. She'd been a professional musician long before. Deidre always loved music, starting with a rendition of "Jesus Is My Sunshine" in church at age five or six, and picking up her first guitar at fifteen. During her high school years, she played in a trio and while a theater major at Vassar, paid her dues at coffeehouses. Her first album, *Fur Coats and Blue Jeans*, was released in 1973 on Roulette Records when she was still in her teens. Her uncle was executive vice president but she still had to audition for the Director of A&R before she was awarded a contract. Other label artists included Jimmy Rodgers, and Tommy James and the Shondells. The album was recorded in a professional studio, partly with Lee Holdridge arrangements (John Denver, Neil Diamond), top studio players like Eric Weissberg ("Dueling Banjos") and musicians from the New York Philharmonic. Although the album opened a few doors, it didn't go anywhere because no one knew how to market it. Many radio stations would look at the cover, see a

Deidre McCalla, Michigan Festival, sometime in the eighties. *Photo by Toni Armstrong Jr.*

Black woman and say, "We don't play R&B." Black radio stations wouldn't play her because she wasn't R&B. Deidre says, "I don't play blues. I don't play jazz.

I don't come from Harlem. I want to throw out the stereotypes of what Black women are supposed to do."[258] She learned from the experience. "(It took) the stardust out of my eyes and gave me a sense for how the industry really worked. I saw it was something I wanted to do but with a realistic picture."[259]

Even without a successful recording, she continued to perform. "As more and more women's coffeehouses were flourishing in the mid- to late-seventies, I always wanted to play there and be a part of what was happening," Deidre said to *HOT WIRE* in 1986, "At the same time, I was playing the cocktail lounges and pizza parlors."[260] She also performed at the second National Women's Music Festival. She found out about it through the Deadly Nightshade, a band she helped produce when she was at Vassar. Deidre recalls that at National there were too many performers each night. Even though each act was supposed to play for a half hour, the artist before her went on for an hour and half with the stage manager frantically trying to get her off the stage for the last hour. By the time Deidre came on, she'd whittled her set down to twenty minutes. Still, it was an amazing experience, allowing her to hear performers like Cris Williamson. She also played at an early Michigan Festival.

After a move to Milwaukee in the late seventies to attend the Wisconsin Conservatory of Music, she formed a duo, Gypsy, with Llena dela Madrugada, a musician she'd met through Ginni Clemmens. She also worked with a band, Breakwater. After two and a half years of studying classical and jazz theory, she decided that was enough and needed to see if, "...all my noodling around was worth anything."[261] What better place to do that than one of the entertainment capitals of the US, New York City? It was an expensive place to live so she spent some time in the early eighties working day jobs in addition to playing music.

Photographer Irene Young was her roommate. Irene was doing work for Olivia. Judy Dlugacz would sometimes ask about new musicians Irene could recommend. Deidre told *HOT WIRE* in 1988, that Judy would respond, "'Oh! Not this again! Every time I ask you something, you bring up Deidre.'" Deidre sent demo tapes to Olivia and found out later that they would often get played around their warehouse. This still didn't result in an Olivia contract and by that time, Deidre had decided she needed to do things on her own anyway. Judy gave her advice on finding producers including a recommendation for Teresa Trull. When word got to her that Deidre had hired Trull to produce and arrange *Don't Doubt It*, Judy decided to sign her to Olivia. Around that time, Deidre moved to California, where the label was located. *Don't Doubt It* sold over 11,000 copies in the first three years.

Recording for Olivia changed possibilities for her. In 1986, she told *HOT WIRE* "...I'm with a company that is part of the history of women's music. A lot of times people come to my shows...knowing nothing else about me except that I'm on Olivia."[262] That kind of exposure ensured that she would make a living as a full-time musician for over twenty years. Two more Olivia albums followed, *With A Little Luck* (1987) and *Everyday Heroes and Heroines* (1992).

She played in all kinds of venues, from solo gigs at the well-known Boston area folk venue Club Passim to Carnegie Hall as part of the Olivia fifteenth anniversary tour in 1988—a massive several-city celebration that included performers Cris Williamson, Tret Fure, Dianne Davidson, and others.

Dianne Davidson

Dianne's album, *Breaking All the Rules*, came out on Olivia's subsidiary label

Dianne Davidson, 1988.
Photo by Irene Young, ©1988

Second Wave in 1988. Born in west Tennessee, this blues/country/rock singer had formed her first band at eleven and at seventeen won a recording contract. She recorded three albums for Janus, a major label that also included Cissy Houston and Al Stewart. Many Black radio stations played her. When she was eighteen, she traveled to New York for a showcase that included Howlin' Wolf and Funkadelic. When she told the receptionist who she was, the woman's eyebrows flew up as she exclaimed, "But, you're Black!"[263] In addition to recording her own albums, she sang with Linda Ronstadt, B. B. King, Tammy Wynette, Barry Manilow, Leon Russell, and others. She always identified as a lesbian. In 1976 she told the *Advocate*, "I've had harder knocks because I'm a Southerner. In Nashville you can be gay, straight, a toe sucker…if you don't flaunt it, they're tolerant."

Her introduction to women's music came through Nancy Vogl. She asked Dianne and Tracy Nelson to sing backup on her 1986 Nashville-recorded release *Fight Like the Dancer*. Impressed with Dianne's powerful voice, she told Judy Dlugacz about her and then suggested to Dianne that she send a demo tape to Olivia. Judy liked what she heard. She got on the phone and asked Dianne, "Why haven't I heard of you before?" They talked for three hours. At the time Dianne was taking a break from music and managing an upscale grocery store. She wasn't sure about returning to music. Judy invited her out for a big Bay Area show featuring Olivia artists. Dianne recalls, "I flew out and she met me at the airport. We immediately went to the car wash and I thought, well, this is different, I've never had a label head take me through the car wash before."[264] By the time she left Berkeley, she had a recording contract. The last recording contract she'd signed was over twenty pages. Olivia's was "about three." She had artistic control with this album, recording it with favorite side players. It included the original ballads "Song for My Father," and "Tonight I'll Dream That You Care," as well as the upbeat bluesy Willie Dixon song "Built for Comfort." The latter was one of her most popular numbers because of its positive message about body image and because it was a perfect match for her gospel-influenced voice.

Dianne found the transition from mainstream music to women's music bizarre because it was really about the audience and not a certain genre of music. She wasn't sure what kind of music she performed anyway, jokingly calling it "field and stream." Women's music came with a readymade audience—a plus in her book. Since her lyrics weren't specifically about being a lesbian, she made sure to connect with them by coming out, which fit in well with her conversational style of performance. Audiences liked her stories between songs as well as the music.

She fondly recalls Olivia's multi-artist fifteenth anniversary concert tour in 1988, where "Every night we sang together on something and supported each other. I don't know how you could wish for any more fun than that."[265] They had a wonderful time offstage too. "My band, I always laughed and referred to us as 'the meat eaters' because everyone else was vegetarian. We were also the smokers. Cris (Williamson) would never be around smokers, but invariably she would come to our dressing room, hang out, and have fun. It was all great fun."[266] She laughs when she remembers the sound check at the Carnegie Hall concert on that tour. "This guy comes running down one of the aisles holding up a sound meter and says, 'You've broken state sound levels.' I said, 'I'm sorry.' Cris joked, 'What do you do about something like that? Give them a ticket?' So, we had to turn it down a little bit... then we turned it back up."[267]

Lucie Blue Tremblay, 2007.
Private collection, Lucie Blue Tremblay. Photo by Reva Hutkin.

Lucie Blue Tremblay

Known for her crystalline voice and unique whistling, French Canadian singer-songwriter Lucie Blue was on that anniversary tour. She got her start in her native Quebec, singing and playing the drums for her mother's dance band. Lucie first picked up the guitar in her teens. After briefly studying voice in college she decided she'd rather do her own music and started to tour all over the province. That income was supplemented with day jobs as a data processor, telephone operator, and school bus driver. In 1984, she won three awards at the popular Festival International de la Chanson de Granby in Quebec. It was around this time that she added "Blue" to her name because it's her favorite color and the color of the throat chakra. It was also a way to separate her from the many other Tremblays in Quebec, a name as common as "Smith" in the US. In 1985 she released a forty-five recording and played at a women's festival for the first time, the day stage at the Michigan Festival.

For two years she negotiated with Canadian labels for a full-length album but wouldn't sign a contract because they didn't want her to record "Voix d'Enfant" ("A Child's Voice"), a song about incest. After photographer Irene Young introduced her to the women of Olivia, she realized she could make a recording where she had artistic control. Her self-titled album was released in 1986. With five songs in English and five in French, it included "Voix d'Enfant" as well as "So Lucky," and "Mademoiselle," two of her most popular songs. Also included was a French version of Ferron's "Ain't Life a Brook" ("Nos Belles Annees"). It was important to her to include songs in French. "I'm very conscious of my French roots...I felt that I was really saying who I was."[268] One album side was recorded live at the Great American Music Hall in San Francisco. The *Boston Globe* called it one of the top ten albums of the year.

Lucie toured extensively in Canada and the US, despite being plagued with US visa issues in the eighties. The H1 work visa prevented anyone from coming out as lesbian or gay onstage because it was considered a sexual deviation. She presented her personable show in a variety of venues, from folk coffeehouses to large concert halls. In 1988, she staged a special Valentine's Day concert with over a thousand in attendance, perfect for the woman who says, "My favorite songs to write are love songs."[269] She went on to do two more albums for Olivia, 1989's *Tendresse* and 1992's *Transformations*.

Heather Bishop

Growing up on the prairies of Canada, this singer with the deep vibrato first learned the piano, then the guitar. She became known in her home country, then performed in the US where she played at major women's music festivals. Her first album,

Heather Bishop, National Festival, mid to late eighties.
Photo by Vada Verneé Woods

Grandmother's Song, was released in 1979. Her songs were varied, from the sensuous "Seduced" to Dory Previn's "If Jesus Had a Baby Sister" to Libby Roderick's inspirational "How Could Anyone." Well-known for kids' music, she released four albums for them. It wasn't unusual for her to include those songs at her shows for adults, usually as a singalong. An audience singing "If You Love a Hippopotamus" added to her entertaining performances. A social activist for many years, working for unions, aboriginal rights, and women's rights, in 1975 she helped to found the first lesbian organization in Manitoba.

Hunter Davis

Hunter learned the guitar while in high school. Her first album came out in 1977 when she was in college. After making another album, she then found women's music. *Harmony* was released in 1986 on Redwood. Her 1988 album,

Torn, was produced by Teresa Trull, with Cris Williamson singing a duet with her on "Arm and a Leg." Publicity for the album included a quote from author Rita Mae Brown: "The lyrics snap, crackle and pop. What fun."[270] In later years, she worked as a staff writer for Famous Music/Paramount. She's written songs recorded by Kim Carnes, Willie Nelson, and Clay Aiken.

Edwina Lee Tyler

Edwina grew up in New York City in a family of musicians. From the age of three she found rhythm banging on anything she could. At nine, she received her first drum. Edwina performed with her parents, in church

Edwina Lee Tyler, National Festival.
Photo by Vada Verneé Woods.

and at local concerts. There were no female African drummers for this young musician to learn from and the male musicians she encountered were not always supportive because the djembe and other drums were not considered women's instruments.

By the time she was in her twenties, she was making a name for herself as a musician, playing a variety of drums and hand percussion and becoming an inspiration to others. Throughout the eighties, she worked in theater, performed in concerts, and composed. She started her band, A Piece of the World, in 1979 and played at many women's music festivals including Sisterfire, NEWMR, West Coast, and Michigan. Michigan holds a special place in her heart—she played there starting in 1981 and every year for several years. "Being on the land is letting your mind be free, because you are not in the city. I do women's festivals because I like the energy."[271] She toured Europe with the band and elsewhere with others including dance group Urban Bush Women. *Drum Drama!*, a recording released in 1987, was distributed by Ladyslipper. It was common in her performances to see her moving around the crowd yelling out "I love you!" as throngs of dancing, happy women swirled around her. Edwina inspired many women to play the drums, including those well-known in women's music.

BETTY

Starting in 1986, this pop rock trio includes Alyson Palmer, and sisters Elizabeth and Amy Ziff. Their fun and edgy songs feature tight harmonies with bass, guitar, and cello. They started recording on their own label, The Man from

BETTY, 1995 National Festival.
Photo by Toni Armstrong Jr.

B.E.T.T.Y., in the nineties, releasing a total of nine albums. They are ardent supporters of women's rights, a cure for breast cancer, an end to sexual violence, and sometimes stuff that's just for fun— like "...everybody's inalienable right to safely dance naked in the streets."[272] At shows they could burst into a bouncy "I'm a Girl Watcher" or rip into original rap tune "Wolf-woman." The *New York Times* called them "...clever, off center and charming."[273] Bridging the gap between women's music and mainstream, they performed at women's festivals like Michigan and Sisterfire, as well as Carnegie Hall, Mardi Gras in Australia and all over the world. They've appeared on CNN, Showtime, and NPR. Their songs have been featured in films and TV shows including the popular *The L Word*.

Yer Girlfriend

A much different band started in Louisville, Kentucky in the late eighties. Embracing a folk-rock style, this refreshingly-out band had a huge following in their hometown, regularly performing at their city's lesbian bar the Carriage House. Two of their members told *HOT WIRE* in 1991, "We made sure to say the word 'lesbian' at least fifty times a night, until the audiences got used to hearing it." They also did some touring and played at Midwest and Southern women's music festivals. Laura Shine, Carol Kraemer, Patty O Veranda, Kathy Weisbach, and Phyllis Free joined forces with vocals, keyboards, drums, bass, and guitars to crank out original songs like "Get Over It" as well as songs by others, like Maxine Feldman's "Angry Atthis." Staunch supporters of women's music, they were thrilled when one of their fans became interested in Lucie Blue Tremblay or Deidre McCalla because they heard the band do their songs. They released three albums, including the first in 1989, *We Won't Be Silent*. Their second album *L-Word Spoken Here* came out in 1992, several years before the TV show of a similar name. A third album was released before they disbanded in 1996.

Therapy Sisters

This band from Austin, Texas started in 1987 as a "musical self-help effort." Describing what they do as folk-a-billy swing, they've played all over the US and overseas. They've performed in a variety of venues, from political events to coffeehouses to women's festivals. Their lineup varies but always includes guitarist/ukulele player Lisa Rogers and bass player Maurine McLean. Featuring tight harmonies, their material often has a lighthearted approach. They released nine recordings and have logged over 400,000 miles on two vans.

Phranc

At the tender age of seventeen, Phranc met Alix Dobkin and their meeting changed her life. Afterward she made a beeline to a barber shop, got a buzz cut, and changed her

Phranc, 1996 Michigan Festival.
Photo by Toni Armstrong Jr.

name from Suzy to Phranc, using an unusual spelling suggested by a friend. In California she joined a band, Nervous Gender, even though she could barely play the guitar. "Nobody was a musician then; people couldn't play their instruments, which is one great aspect of punk."[274] She moved on to other bands including Catholic Discipline and Castration Squad. In 1981, she put down her electric guitar and picked up an acoustic. Her first album, *Folksinger*, was released on Rhino Records in 1985. Songs ranged from the fun "Female Mud Wrestling" to the serious "Handicapped." She self-produced her second release, *I Enjoy Being a Girl*, containing one of her best-loved songs, "M-A-R-T-I-N-A," her ode to Martina Navratilova. Island Records picked it up in 1989.

Despite the atypical acoustic guitar, she continued to play for punk audiences, gaining a name for herself as an opener for bands like The Smiths. She came out at every show. Crowds didn't always love her. Sometimes she could win them over with sheer bravado and sometimes with humor, like tossing out tampons during her performance of "I Enjoy Being a Girl" from the 1950's musical *Flower Drum Song*. During one difficult show in Toronto opening for the Pogues, she endured twenty minutes of taunts from the audience. She stopped and said, "Let's talk a little bit about tolerance and acceptance here now," and dove into "Take Off Your Swastika." She dedicated it to the crowd and sang it like it was the last song on earth. They quieted and cheered madly afterward. She told *People* magazine in 1989, "I enjoy playing for an audience that would never hear the word lesbian in a positive context." She also played for women's music audiences, including festivals. They were a mixed bag for her, perhaps because she was so different from other artists on the circuit. Still, she remembers that, "… some women-only shows have given me a great deal of energy and amazing happiness."[275]

Casselberry-DuPreé, 1989 Michigan Festival.
Photo by Toni Armstrong Jr.

Casselberry-DuPreé

Both Jacque DuPreé and Judith Casselberry grew up in musical households—Jacque sang gospel, and Judith heard everything from Nina Simone to Bob Dylan. Jacque first met Judith in Los Angeles when both were in high school. She told *HOT WIRE* in 1985, "I was playing my chromo harp during lunch period at East Flatbush High School one afternoon when this tall youth with a major afro, a trench coat, and a guitar case came up to me. She was J. Casselberry. We clicked from the beginning."

Judith Casselberry moved to the Bay Area in the seventies where she was first introduced to women's music through a women of color group that offered political and social activities. There, she met Vicki Randle, Gwen Avery, Mary Watkins, and Linda Tillery. When Jacque DuPreé moved up from Los Angeles, they formed Casselberry-DuPreé and in 1979 or 1980 did their first gig together at San Francisco's Artemis Café. Performing their avant-garde African-American folk, they toured until 1994. They released a tape in 1984 and then two albums, *City Down* and *Hot Corn in the Fire*. Their first festival performance was at Michigan in 1980. Other festival appearances included National, Ohio Lesbian Festival, Rhythmfest, NEWMR, and more. Their powerful voices covered everything from Toshi Reagon's "Foolish Attitudes" to the Eagles' hit "Take It to the Limit." Judith offers, "We like to call attention to specifics, like South Africa or the role of women in Christianity or love, but we try in the end to sum it all up; we all have to rise to our full potential."[276] After the duo split in the nineties, Judith Casselberry played with Toshi Reagon's band, BIGLovely, and with her own band, JUCA. She was also a long-time worker at the Michigan Womyn's Music Festival.

Lynn Lavner

Cabaret performer Lynn Lavner first came on the scene in the eighties, performing in venues as varied as the National Women's Music Festival and the International Mr. Leather contest and releasing four solo albums with material that dealt mostly with LGBTQ themes. She knew early on that she was a lesbian, joking, "They gave me a dollhouse and I did the electric."[277] She learned to play the piano as a child and in 1978 when she was in her twenties, started to work in a piano bar. Most of her audiences were gay men. "They had the money to come in and have a nice dinner, and they were the ones who love the same music that I grew up loving—Broadway show songs, Gershwin, Porter, Kern, and Berlin…"[278] By 1982, she was adding original songs to her repertoire of covers. Her first paying gig was at the popular Duplex in New York City. Club owners from Provincetown and Fire Island heard her there and started to book her. She first played in San Francisco late in 1984 where another cabaret performer, Sharon McKnight, took her under her wing, giving her a ten-minute spot in the middle of her act. Lynn was well-loved at Robin Tyler's festivals where she started performing in 1986. She was on the road for thirteen years.

While gay men were always dedicated supporters, Lynn played for women's audiences later in her career. Performing for women, for her, was different. She quips, "I think that was probably in the years when a lesbian act was a woman with a guitar singing about her dead pony. And that was just never my thing…I'm not a folkie."[279] Some lesbians didn't like that she wore leather on stage. She considered it a political statement. "There's always been an evolution politically of what's correct...and I thought, well, who are the two groups who are most despised in our community by outsiders and some in our community? They are, of course, the drag queens and leather people...I grew up trying to avoid what drag queens wore, so that was eliminated immediately."[280] She visited a Christopher Street leather store and ordered clothing, joking that "...it's not easy to get handcuffs in a girl's size twelve."[281] (She's a small woman at five foot tall.) Popular songs included "Such Fine Young Men"—perhaps the first song any woman did about AIDS—"(I Like) Older Women" and "A Lesbian Too Long." No matter what she was singing, it was always important for her to be out. "Being in the closet is a...life sentence of being fearful and vulnerable and frightened...and creating a barrier between ourselves and other people."[282] Many remember her saying something that's appeared in many places over the years—"There are six admonitions in the Bible concerning homosexuality, but our enemies don't want us to remember that there are 362 admonitions in the Bible concerning heterosexuality. It's not that God doesn't love straight people, it's just that they seem to require a lot of supervision."[283]

Toshi Reagon

Toshi Reagon, 1995 Michigan Festival.
Photo by Toni Armstrong Jr.

Born in Atlanta and raised in Washington, D.C., Toshi is the daughter of Sweet Honey in the Rock founder Bernice Johnson Reagon. Not only was Sweet Honey a big part of her growing up but also, her family was close to Toshi Seeger and Pete Seeger. June Millington was an enormous influence too. "I used to follow June Millington around and beg her to show me everything about playing the guitar."[284] In 1983, she performed at Sisterfire with her new band the Agitones, and in 1984, she played on the day stage at the Michigan Festival as well as many times after that, often on the night stage. She incorporated a lot of styles—rock, reggae, funk, R&B, and new wave—as a solo performer and with a band at women's music festivals, colleges, and folk events. Her first recording, *Demonstration*, was released on cassette. In 1990, she put out *Justice* on folk label Flying Fish and followed that with ten albums on various labels. She's worked with a wide variety of musicians, from Ani DiFranco to Lenny Kravitz. Toshi appreciates the various audiences who enjoy her music and there's a special place in her heart for women's music. In 1989, she told *HOT WIRE*, "I love the women's community. And it treats me very, very well."

Laura Love

Laura Love, 1991 Michigan Festival.
Photo by Toni Armstrong Jr.

Also known for a style that encompasses several genres, bassist/songwriter/vocalist Laura Love grew up with a mother who was a jazz band singer and a father who was a sax player known for his work in the Count Basie Orchestra and with his own band. She was raised solely by her mother, a woman who struggled with a multitude of mental health issues. At the age of sixteen Laura struck out on her own, renting her own apartment with her sister and paying the bills with a job at a fast-food restaurant. They lost that apartment three months later because the landlady was uncomfortable renting to someone "colored." That same year, she was reunited with her estranged father. She sang with his band, her first experience performing outside of a few school events. They never grew close. Her relationship with her mother was tumultuous. Her early years are chronicled in her memoir, *You Ain't Got No Easter Clothes*.

Later, she moved to the Seattle area, playing with various bands and then releasing her first solo effort, *Menstrual Hut*, in 1989, followed by many others on several different labels including her own label, world music label Putumayo, and two releases for Mercury. She was also a member of the band Venus Envy, appearing on their two albums. She describes her style as "folk-funk, afro-Celtic and Hip-Alacian," music that is, "...both joyous and melancholy..."[285]

Her memorable melodies and upbeat stage presentation make her a favorite at women's music and folk festivals all over North America, Australia, and Europe.

Barbara Higbie

Barbara spent her youth in Indiana studying classical piano until her family moved to West Africa when she was thirteen. In the two years they lived there she became interested in all kinds of African music. Moving back to the States, this time to Southern California, was a culture shock. It was there she became interested in country music and learning to play the fiddle. She moved to France at eighteen to attend the Sorbonne and then dropped out after less than a year and became a street musician in Paris. It was around this time that she decided to become serious about music. She studied classical and jazz piano and played in many bands. Eventually she found her way to the jazz/new age label Windham Hill, where she was their first female artist. In 1983, she teamed with Teresa Trull for *Unexpected*, and a few years later for *Playtime*. Their energetic chemistry shone on many stages in the eighties and later, all of the major women's music festivals. Songs ranged from earthy upbeat fiddle tunes to soulful pop ballads. Barbara's international upbringing influenced her writing and playing, from African rhythms in some of her piano pieces, to more rootsy music that shine with a hint of country. Barbara also has released five solo recordings and has performed with many artists including Holly Near, Ferron, Vicki Randle, Bonnie Raitt, and Amy Ray. For two years, she played in Robin Flower's band.

Ruth Barrett

From a music-making family, Ruth first became aware of women's music in the seventies. She'd been collecting songs since she was twelve years old and was especially interested in old folk songs where women had the upper hand and also stories of otherworld beings. In the early seventies, folksinger Frankie Armstrong became her mentor. Ruth recalls, "She didn't sing high and pretty. She taught me the power of singing in a low powerful way."[286] Singing a capella and accompanying herself on the fretted dulcimer, she teamed up with Cyntia Smith and in the eighties and nineties released five recordings of original and traditional songs. She became a leader in the Goddess Spirituality movement. Her performances include women's music festivals, dulcimer festivals, and spiritual gatherings.

Ann Reed

This Minneapolis/St. Paul folksinger started her career in a duo with another woman, playing bars and coffeehouses. She remembers an especially odd audition: "I was rather skinny with long, heavy, wavy hair and NO sense of fashion and

Judy was a taller, larger woman. We showed up to the audition and we were getting our guitars out of their cases when the manager walks in, takes a look at us and says 'Uh…yeah. You're not really what we were looking for.'"[287]

They never got a chance to play. Three weeks later, they went to see who he did hire—a woman in a low-cut dress with an average voice who barely knew how to play the guitar.

Most of Ann's performance experiences were more positive than that. She became a popular solo performer around Minnesota. She also did some touring and played at the National Women's Music Festival. Known for intricate guitar work and personable stage presence, Ann started releasing albums in 1981. On those twenty-two albums are favorite songs including a parody of "Diamonds Are a Girl's Best Friend" called "Power Tools Are a Girl's Best Friend," as well as serious inspirational numbers like "Every Long Journey" and "Heroes."

Melanie DeMore

Melanie started piano at the age of five, sang in her church choir, and taught herself to play the flute and bass. After earning a degree in music, she joined a convent where she taught music and did community work. She continued her music after leaving the convent. Her rich alto voice can be heard on her first recording, *Come Follow Me*, released in 1986. Later recordings include *Share My Song* (1993) and *In the Mother House* (2012). She's worked with many in women's music including Mary Watkins, Ronnie Gilbert, and Linda Tillery. Performing all

Pam Hall, Margie Adam, Melanie DeMore, and Alix Dobkin, 1992 East Coast Lesbian Festival. *Photo by Toni Armstrong Jr.*

over the world, a great deal of her later work has been with choirs. She's performed in many different venues including the National Women's Music Festival. Continuing as an educator, she offers workshops in voice, Gullah stick pounding, and more.

Debbie Fier

This musician wears many hats, from fronting her own band to tuning pianos. After discovering women's music in the seventies, she released her first album in 1982, *In Your Hands*, produced by Susann Shanbaum. Her next recording, 1986's *Firelight*, was produced by Mary Watkins. Proficient on drums, piano, and vocals, she played at all the major women's music festivals from 1982 to 1995. As a side player, she appeared with many in women's music including Linda Tillery and Melanie DeMore.

Altazor

This exciting four-woman group recorded two albums for Redwood and played at women's festivals as well as other venues. Dulce Arguelles, Lichi Fuentes, Jackeline Rago, and Vanessa Whang sang and played a variety of Latin instruments including tiple, charango, and more, as well as flute, guitar, mandolin, and piano. Concerts offered original music as well as songs by others.

Judy Fjell

A singer-songwriter who started recording in 1980, Judy is known mostly on the west coast and in Montana, her home. She's sung in a variety of settings, from the Michigan Festival to peace marches. Judy has released eighteen albums and runs three women's music camps. Different from the women's festivals, these camps are interactive settings with workshops and jams where women play music together.

Mosa (aka Mimi Baczewska)

This multi-instrumentalist and songwriter released her first recording, *Mimi*, in 1985. "My intention for my music is to lighten your heart, inspire your mind and soothe your spirit."[288] She released five more albums and, in the nineties, performed at the National Women's Music Festival, Gulf Coast Festival, and others. She's also a craftswoman who offers her crochet work, fabric art, and more at events.

Jamie Anderson

Inspired by the nationally touring artists she loved, this Arizona-based singer-songwriter made her first recording in 1986, a tape financed by a woman who'd heard her at a women's festival open mic. Jamie started touring in 1987 and sold two hundred of the amateur recording. Her first professional album, *Closer to Home*, was released in 1989 and she went on to release ten more, selling thousands. Jamie has appeared in forty-seven US states and at most women's music festivals. Known for humorous songs like the country-flavored "Wedding Song," ("Sure I'll come to your wedding / But I'll dance with the bride") she's also recognized for serious songs such as "Dark Chocolate," a bluesy love song to a woman.

Jamie Anderson, 1986.
Photo by C. Elliot.

Other Artists

Folk performer Susan Graetz released her album, *Somewhere Between*, in the eighties. There are two photos of her on the cover, one featuring her in a femme outfit smelling a flower and the other with a decidedly butch look, making it clear she took a lighthearted look at life in some of her songs. Kay Gardner also appeared on the release.

In the same decade, another folk musician, Gerri Gribi, released her third album, *Womansong*. With her focus on traditional folk songs by and about women, she was popular at colleges.

Political musician and cantor Linda Hirschhorn released her first album, *Skies Ablaze*, in the mid-eighties. Appearing on her album were women's music favorites Nancy Vogl, Laurie Lewis, and Carolyn Brandy.

Gayle Marie's second album, *Double Talk*, also featured musicians from women's music—bassist Jan Martinelli, and pianist/producer Mary Watkins. Known for her powerful voice and charming stage presence, she performed her pop/jazz music at festivals and other venues in the eighties.

Performing in an old-time folk style on fiddle, banjo, and guitar was Karen MacKay. She released two albums during this decade, including *West Virginia Woman*, a collection of traditional songs, and *Annie Oakley Rides Again*, an album of all-original music about lesbian relationships, world peace, and reincarnation.

Judy Reagan was inspired by a Holly Near performance at DC Gay Pride in 1979 or 1980. "My world rocked when Holly showed me that I could write and sing about things that were important to me and there would be people who wanted to listen."[289] Judy released her LP *Old Friends* in 1983. It included original songs "Hollywood Haircut," an ode to the older lesbians who came before, and "Rose Covered Radical," a funny tune about an activist who changed her priorities after meeting a woman at a "Tupperware party in the suburbs." Judy performed at women's music venues and more. Maxine Feldman invited Judy to share a stage with her in Provincetown and at the National Women's Music Festival.

Bobbi Carmitchell was a Pennsylvania-based singer-songwriter with a folky style. After playing in a trio called Wind and Wood, she branched off as a solo with her first album *Crossing the Line*. She did some touring with her own music and as a side player with Lucie Blue Tremblay.

Alaskan Libby Roderick is best known for her life-affirming song "How Could Anyone," which appeared on her first recording in 1990, *If You See a Dream*. Known in peace and social justice circles, she also performed songs from her six albums in women's music venues. Fan Barbara Swahlen discovered her in the late eighties. "She sang about love, politics, and human rights—the things that were in my heart and it changed my life."[290]

Classical flute and guitar duo Musica Femina did their first national tour in 1984. Janna MacAuslan and Kristan Aspen's shows included original compositions as well as work by other women. They released four recordings and played at colleges and women's music festivals.

Pop singer-songwriter Kay Weaver released at least two albums. She is best known for her film *One Fine Day*, a celebration of women through history. With her original song providing the soundtrack, it featured photos of Amelia Earhart, Emily Dickinson, Sojourner Truth and many more, plus video footage of suffragettes and others. It has opened the National Women's Music Festival for years and always elicits cheers.

Also known for her pop music was Nancy Day. Based in the Midwest, she performed at clubs, coffeehouses, and festivals including Michigan, National, and NEWMR.

Singer-songwriter Alice DiMicele started releasing albums in the eighties. Her passionate songs about the environment and more span several genres, from rock to folk. Known mostly on the west coast, she's released fourteen albums, all on her own label.

DC area folk/rock band Lifeline applied feminist principles to songs about the labor movement as well as other issues. They performed regionally and made a 1986 appearance at the National Festival.

Established Artists Continue to Record and Perform

Ronnie Gilbert

Although she became known to women's music audiences in the early eighties, Ronnie Gilbert had been a performing musician for a long time. She was a member of the Weavers, from the 1940s through the 1960s. This legendary folk group was best known for classics like "Goodnight Irene," which sold almost two million copies, making it one of the best-selling records of 1950. They also supported progressive causes, something noticed by the House Un-American Activities Committee in 1951. Because it was written by Lead Belly, a Black man who'd been a convict, even "Goodnight Irene" was suspect. They lost their Decca recording contract, a TV show offer, and many gigs. After a sabbatical they made

a comeback in 1955, with a sold-out concert at Carnegie Hall. They toured sporadically for the next eight years, did a fifteenth anniversary show at Carnegie Hall in 1963 and broke up that same year.

Ronnie's career didn't start with the Weavers. Born in 1926, she moved around a lot as her Jewish immigrant family searched for jobs, but they always found money for her dance and music lessons. Her parents worked in garment factories and her mother helped to organize the

Ronnie Gilbert and Holly Near, 1983.
Photo by Irene Young © 1983.

International Ladies Garment Workers Union. During World War II, while still in her teens, Ronnie joined a folk group specializing in songs of social protest, the Priority Ramblers. Later, she did a variety of work, including union organizing.

After the Weavers broke up, she released three solo albums, achieved a degree in clinical psychology and opened a therapy practice. She also worked in theater, setting aside her music for a few years except for a 1980 sold-out reunion show with the Weavers at Carnegie Hall. She connected with Holly Near around then because Holly had dedicated an album to her. Ronnie recalls: "I heard the record, and I thought, this is one of the best things I've ever heard. And I cried the whole time. I remember I was vacuuming the house, and I put this record on, and I could not do another thing. I just listened to it over and over and over again. The songs went straight to my heart..."[291] One of the reasons for that was the subject matter. "...what drew me to her above everything else was that her songs were not only filled with her identification as a progressive, but as a progressive *woman*."[292]

A movie about the Weavers was made and Ronnie insisted that Holly be a part of it. "...she represented what was new, what was coming into our lives rather than we who were going out of people's lives."[293] It was for that film that they sang together for the first time. That short clip excited Near and Gilbert fans. The phone at Redwood Records started ringing off the wall with requests for concerts together. Aside from the Weavers show, Ronnie hadn't been onstage as a singer for twenty years but that didn't stop her. She loved singing with Holly and connecting with audiences. "Maybe they took me into their bosom as warmly as they did because they assumed I was a lesbian…it didn't trouble me that I was a hetero-oriented woman…I felt very honored to be trusted and accepted by the community."[294] Ronnie also loved that they stayed in community housing—another way to get to know the wonderful fans.

In 1984, she recorded her first album with Holly Near, *Lifeline*. She went on to release three albums on Redwood—*The Spirit is Free*, *H.A.R.P.* (with Holly Near, Arlo Guthrie and Pete Seeger), and *Singing with You* (with Holly Near). *Love Will Find a Way* was released on her own label, Abbe Alice, in 1989.

She chose her songs carefully. "When I consider any song, the major issue for me is: how will this song impact on women; how does it speak to women's sensibilities, women's lives?"[295] She tried to do that when she sang with the Weavers for their 1980 show and although they embraced peace and social justice issues, their songs didn't always support women. She uses their "Wasn't That a Time" as an example. "…the first verse starts, 'Our fathers bled at Valley Forge…' and ends, 'their faith was brotherhood.' How can I sing that song today, when I know in my heart and my brain that a culture where women are not important enough even to be mentioned is a culture where the ideal of social justice for everyone can never be a reality?…What's the foundation of all the oppression in the world, where does it start? On women…"[296]

Acting continued to be a big part of her life, including appearances in the films *Running on Empty* (1987) and *Crossing Delancey* (1988). She worked in theater also, including her one-woman play about Mother Jones. Somehow, she found time for almost yearly solo tours as well as concerts with Odetta, and for two tours of Australia, with Judy Small. In addition to performances at women's music festivals, she appeared at well-known Canadian festivals—the Vancouver Folk Festival and the Winnipeg Folk Festival. In 1985, she became partners in love and work with Donna Korones. She credits women's music in her coming out as a lesbian partly because Donna was a women's music fan.

Holly Near

Holly was very active in the eighties. In addition to recording and touring with Ronnie Gilbert, she released seven of her own albums, including one with Chilean Latin music ensemble Inti-Illimani and one with American folk group Trapezoid. She worked for social justice in many areas including a tour to help save college women's studies programs, a fifty-city anti-nuke tour, and much more. She recorded and toured with Pete Seeger, Arlo Guthrie as well as Ronnie Gilbert. Their *H.A.R.P.* album was released in 1984. Holly received a plethora of awards including a nomination from *Ms.* for 1985's Woman of the Year and in 1987, the Award of Distinction from the National March on Washington for Lesbian and Gay Rights. San Francisco Mayor Art Agnos declared July 7, 1989 as Holly Near Day.

Holly continued to gain new followers. It was in the eighties that fan Cris Soluna first heard her. "I was transfixed...I had recently come out and was forever changed."[297] Gay male musician Ron Romanovsky was first introduced to women's music and Holly in the eighties by a lesbian friend. It was "music that really spoke to our lives as gay and lesbian people," Ron recalls. "I listened a lot to Holly in those days. Meg Christian, Cris Williamson, Margie Adam, they were all songwriters whom I admired very much."[298]

Margie Adam

Margie continued to perform and record. *Naked Keys*, an all-instrumental album, was released in 1980 on Pleiades Records. Other albums were released in this decade, including a collection of love songs, *Here is a Love Song*, and an album of a live performance, *We Shall Go Forth*. In 1984, she took a "radical's sabbatical" and took time off from performing.

Ferron

This poetic folksinger continued to perform, gaining a large following in Canada and the US, playing venues in women's music and on the folk scene. Her 1984 release, *Shadows on a Dime*, was heralded as one of the best of that year by the *Boston Globe*. *Rolling Stone* gave it four stars out of five—an unusually high rating for an indie recording in a publication that mostly covered mainstream artists. The title cut came from a dream about the price of lessons throughout your life, using the metaphor of riding on a train. She released eleven more recordings, including two for Warner Brothers and later, releases with indie musician Bitch. Bitch also produced, along with Billie Jo Cavallaro, a documentary about Ferron, *Thunder*.

Sweet Honey in the Rock

They continued to perform their a cappella blues/R&B/African/gospel offerings with a changing lineup that included over twenty different women. They gained more visibility with concerts all over the world, including an appearance at 1979's MUSE (Musicians United for Safe Energy) concert that also featured Bonnie Raitt and Jackson Browne. Their "A Woman" appears on the soundtrack. Over the years they've also performed in Japan, Africa, Australia, Russia, and Europe. They've appeared on PBS several times, including two documentaries about them, *Gotta Make This Journey* and *Sweet Honey in the Rock: Raise Your Voice*. Individually and as a group they are great advocates for many groups and causes, including the Free South Africa movement and the deaf/hard of hearing community. In 2014 and 2015 they celebrated their fortieth anniversary with appearances in many cities including the Old Towne School of Folk Music in Chicago and the US Embassy in Addis Ababa, Ethiopia.

Teresa Trull

The three years after her first Olivia release were a busy time. "I toured extensively and learned a lot more stage technique."[299]

Let It Be Known was released on Olivia in 1980.

In 1980, she started writing songs with Ray Obiedo. She first met him when she was painting her apartment one Sunday morning and singing to music on a gospel radio show. She recalls, "I look out the window and this guy goes 'Hey who's singing in there?' I said, 'It's me,' and he said, 'Nah get outta here! We're having a barbecue, come on over.' I thought, oh, okay. I went over and who's there but Herbie Hancock, Sheila E, and Ray Obiedo."[300] Not long after, she and Ray decided to write songs for her next album and to license them to other artists. She did this for several reasons; one, to supplement her income; and two, to put songs with meaning on the radio. "A song that has any kind of

Barbara Higbie and Teresa Trull, 1998 Michigan Festival.
Photo by Toni Armstrong Jr.

positive image about women, relationships, or love is very helpful...I know there were songs I clung to when I was growing up like Aretha's 'Natural Woman' and like 'Sweet Inspiration'...Songs that didn't politically shake the world...but it was a lot better than hearing the Commodores sing 'She's a brick house...'"[301] She and Obiedo had success in 1984, placing two songs with R&B group the Whispers on an album that went gold. She and Ray worked together for over ten years. Some of their songs are featured on Trull's *A Step Away*. Linda Tillery recorded their work as well.

During this decade, she performed with a ten-piece band that included Vicki Randle on vocals. They opened at jazz festivals for artists like Stanley Clarke and Earl Klugh.

In July of 1982 she met pianist/violinist Barbara Higbie at the Reno gay rodeo where they were both performing, Barbara with Robin Flower's band. By August, they did their first gig, at photographer Irene Young's book launch (*For the Record*) where they received a standing ovation. Teresa remembers, "I never had so much fun performing onstage with anybody ever."[302] They'd only been playing together for eight months when they started writing songs for their first release. It was an interesting combination of talent—both had experience in folk music but Teresa had moved in a more R&B direction while Barbara had been playing jazz and bluegrass. *Unexpected* was released in 1983. They toured extensively, then took a break in 1985 because they were each involved in so many other musical projects.

Teresa's next solo effort, *A Step Away*, was released in 1986 on Redwood Records. She'd scoured the liner notes of albums by Bonnie Raitt and Aretha Franklin and contacted some of those musicians, never expecting to hear from these high-powered studio players. To her surprise, they replied and said yes, they'd join her. Using the studio where Michael Jackson recorded *Thriller*, they recorded the rhythm tracks in two days—unheard of in an era where just that part of an album could take weeks. It was an exciting project for her where she learned a great deal about producing. One of the most popular songs, "Rosalie," was written by friend Bonnie Hayes, an unabashed love song fueled with an infectious keyboard riff.

In 1989, Teresa produced and performed with Cris Williamson on *Country Blessed*. The *Oakland Tribune* gushed, "If only Waylon and Willie could make albums this good and heartfelt."[303]

Teresa phased into producing when she was penning songs with Ray Obiedo. Because they were writing R&B and pop, they needed demos where potential artists and record labels could hear a fully-produced version of the song—unlike more acoustic genres like folk where a simple guitar was all that was required. She went on to produce many albums including those by Lucie Blue Tremblay, Deidre McCalla, The Washington Sisters, and gay male duo Romanovsky and Phillips. Ron Romanovsky exclaims, "God bless Teresa Trull...It was an absolutely stunning experience in the studio with her...she created one of our most popular albums (*Trouble in Paradise*)."[304]

Kay Gardner

Her music was employed in films and TV in the eighties. A documentary, *Invisible Women*, featured music from her album *A Rainbow Path*. Part of *Moods and Rituals* was used for an art film, *One Hundred Women*. TV show *Nova* also licensed her songs. Kay's work was used in other ways too. The Yale School of Medicine asked her for advice regarding the role of music in relaxation. They planned to try it with anesthesia during surgery. The connection between healing and music was always important to her and the reason she formed Healing through the Arts in 1980. It was through this organization that she raised money for her groundbreaking work *A Rainbow Path*, released in 1984 on the Ladyslipper label. Each cut on this album focused on a chakra. Eight recordings followed, until the last in 2000. She also composed orchestral and choral works during the eighties.

Nancy Vogl

After the break-up of the Berkeley Women's Music Collective in 1979, Nancy continued, touring with friends Robin Flower and Suzanne Shanbaum, and doing solo work. *Something to Go On* was released in 1984 on Redwood Records. Mostly an acoustic album, it

Nancy Vogl, 1988 Olivia celebration, Carnegie Hall.
Photo by Toni Armstrong Jr.

featured songs with vocals on one side and instrumentals on the other, really showing her virtuosity on the guitar. Meg Christian admired her technique. "I love to hear Nancy Vogl play the guitar…her clean, sure technique, her warm musicality, versatility and the energy and ease in her playing."[305] *Fight Like the Dancer*, released in 1986 on Olivia, had more of a country sound. Dianne Davidson sang backup.

Therese Edell

This charismatic singer-songwriter quit touring when multiple sclerosis affected her hands and voice. At one of her last performances, in 1983 at the National Festival, she joked that she got used to saying "lesbian" at her concerts and now it was time for the same for "multiple sclerosis." She was known to many as the Voice of Michigan, the main stage emcee whose melodious voice would advise women about everything from requests for kitchen volunteers to taking flash photos (don't do it or you will be "tackled to the ground"). In 1989, she flew to Mississippi to work at the first Gulf Coast Women's Music Festival where she joked that she was "Visiting Professor." She also assisted with sound, and "told lawyer jokes."

Cris Williamson and Tret Fure

In the late seventies, June Millington asked Tret to engineer Cris's children's album, *Lumiere*. Tret and Cris hit it off and it wasn't long before they were personal and musical partners. Soon, they were touring together. It came at a time when Tret was disheartened by the LA scene, a place where your career was dead when you turned thirty. "I was struggling in LA. All the money I made engineering went into my bands and doing showcases…you didn't get paid to do them, you paid for it. The first show I did with Cris there were thousands of hungry women in the audience so it was a great transition."[306] Although her entry to women's music was mostly positive, she was faced with a crowd more used to softer singer-songwriters. "They would say 'We want Cris!'…and 'You're too loud, get off the stage.'"[307]

Soon, they grew accustomed to this singer-songwriter who played an electric guitar. She would open for Cris who would play on her set, then she'd accompany Cris on her set. Tret recalls: "Our music became more and more closely aligned. We started writing more together. I was…going less rock, more folk and she was going from folk to a little more

Cris Williamson and Tret Fure, 1984.
Private collection of Tret Fure. Photo by Jill Cruse.

rock. So, it was a nice blending of styles and talent. Our voices were so beautifully matched that sometimes you couldn't tell one from another. That was something that people loved and we loved."[308]

Through Cris she was introduced to Judy Dlugacz who worked out a deal for them to release June Millington's *Heartsong* on Olivia in 1981. Tret's first solo album with them, *Terminal Hold*, was released in 1984 on their new subsidiary label, Second Wave. Included was one of her most popular songs, "That Side of the Moon." Not only was she excited to be working for women's music audiences, but she could have total creative control on her albums, something she wasn't offered in the mainstream. "My songs are all very personal. They come from different places in my life and different places I've been."[309] She recorded two more albums for Olivia, *Edges of the Heart* (1986) and *Time Turns the Moon* (1990). Cris and Tret were performing a lot together and some of their lovely vocal harmonies appeared on these releases. Cris also co-produced the two earlier albums. Tret played an integral part in six Cris Williamson albums—*Blue Rider* (1982), *Portrait* (1983), *Prairie Fire* (1984), *Snow Angel* (1985), *Wolf Moon* (1987) and *Circle of Friends* (1991).

Women continued to find and embrace these artists, as well as others on Olivia. In 1982 Katrina Rosa was the mother of three small children and trapped in an unhappy marriage with a man when her cousin sent her a tape of Cris Williamson, Meg Christian, and others. "I played that tape daily and cried. I wondered when I would find my life."[310] Later, she gathered the courage to leave her marriage and live openly as a lesbian.

Big Celebrations and Changes for Olivia

Olivia celebrated its tenth anniversary in November 1982 with two concerts featuring Meg Christian and Cris Williamson at Carnegie Hall. Three months in advance they'd almost sold out both shows, 5,400 women and 200 men. Women came from almost every state and several countries, some arriving in limos and dressed in tuxes and gowns, some dressed in jeans and traveling in taxis, and others on motorcycles. Judy Dlugacz told the excited audiences, "When we didn't have money to promote the albums, you hand carried them from person to person. When we didn't have money to do publicity for our events, you brought your friends. When we didn't have money for distribution, you demanded that the stores put the records in their bins."[311] Decked out in satin Olivia jackets for the first set and, for the second set, in tails, they performed new songs such as "Anniversary," Betsy Rose's "Glad to Be a Woman," and a medley of older favorites including Cris's "Joanna" and Meg's "Ode to a Gym Teacher." Their all-star backup band included Tret Fure on guitar, Vicki Randle, and Linda Tillery on backing vocals, Diane Lindsay on bass plus more. Both shows were recorded. Tret Fure, also the Associate Producer and Mix Engineer, remembers it as a highlight of her career. While she was busy running back and forth between the recording truck and the stage, she recalls peeking out at the vast audience before the show and being blown away. Panic set in when she realized that several songs from the first show couldn't be used for the album because of feedback from the monitors. Fortunately, the same songs in the second show turned out well. The celebrated album *Meg/Cris at Carnegie Hall* was released in 1983 on Olivia's Second Wave label.

Many of the band members from that show toured together for about a year afterward. Tret recalls, "We traveled with a great group of women and...played great places across the country—huge theaters. Those days I'll never forget."[312]

Meg released her third album, *Turning It Over*, in 1981. In 1983, she left the Olivia collective although in 1984 she recorded her last Olivia album of new material, *From the Heart*. The latter contained songs about her spiritual transformation, "Living in the Moment" and "Darshan," as well as other songs of personal growth. Meg's departure from Olivia left Judy Dlugacz as the only original collective member. Meg had grown weary of near-constant touring and had started a journey of spiritual discovery, becoming a follower of Siddha Yoga, a discipline led by Gurumayi Chidvilasananda. She had been skeptical at first: "I was all nervous that it was some kind of weird religion, in that I was going to go in and have to start worshipping something with twenty-three arms and forty-two legs, and snakes coming out of their ears. It's not that at all. It's a way to teach you to get in touch with what you've already got inside."[313]

In 1986 Meg put out *The Fire of My Love for You: Songs for Gurumayi Chidvilasananda* under her new name Shambhavi Christian. Meg sometimes traveled with the charismatic guru and fans came to appearances. Some embraced Gurumayi's teachings while others were confused at Meg's new direction. Meg no longer performs at women's music concerts except for a few big Olivia events.

Meg was well-liked by a great many in women's music. Tret Fure offers this: "I loved Meg. She was a brilliant writer and guitarist, very generous, tender, and funny...one of the people I love the most. I have tremendous respect for her that she would leave her career to follow her spiritual path."[314]

Original collective member Ginny Berson had left in 1980. She weathered many storms during her time with Olivia but, "...it became clear to me we were going out of business if we didn't start acting like a business and I wasn't interested in having a business. I was interested in building a movement."[315] She went on to work at community radio station KPFA in Berkeley for many years, some of it as Director of Women's Programming, "...a great way to continue movement building in the women's community."[316]

Growing Pains for Established Festivals

The National Festival almost ended in 1980 when it left the University of Illinois at Champaign-Urbana where it had been held since its inception. There'd been growing tension between organizers and the university. An official festival history notes, "In short, the university has had enough of uppity women trying to use a male space." Jewel Echelbarger, a festival board member, organized a meeting of women in Bloomington, Indiana. They met for several months, decided to have the festival at the university there and applied for grants. In 1981, just a few months before the event was to happen, with no grant money coming in, they canceled. Spirits were low and for a while, it looked like the festival would cease.

Mary Byrne, a nightclub owner from Indianapolis, stepped in, and using $10,000 of her own money, produced the festival in 1982 at Indiana University in Bloomington. Mary was well-acquainted with women's music. She'd come back from attending her first National Festival knowing that she wanted to produce concerts and that was why she'd bought the nightclub, Labyris. She'd never produced a festival. Robin Tyler, who produced the 1980 festival, met with her for several hours, helping her to learn the ropes.

The group had a tough time at first. Meetings were long and it was a struggle to make decisions because everyone had a hand in everything. Mary changed that, assigning each of them specific tasks. In the end, Mary produced the main stage and Jewel did everything else with the help of a group of volunteers. The event included musicians who'd supported them in the early years, including Margie Adam, Kay Gardner, Alive!, Robin Tyler, Ginni Clemmens, and Mary Watkins.

The festival received support from the lesbian community in Bloomington. Soon, when local businesses realized how much they'd benefit, support from other quarters grew. In 1984 the mayor appeared on stage, thanking the women for attending. Also, in the audience was a city council member.

Women in the Arts was formed as a non-profit to put on the festival not long after the move to Bloomington. Mary stepped away for a few years then came back in 1985 when the organization ran into problems and again, there was talk about the festival ceasing. Mary remembers, "I was so pissed and said I'll do it if you stay out of my hair and they did."[317] She found ways to empower the workers. Many of them came back year after year.

Mary Byrne and Doralyn Folce, 1991 National Festival.
Photo by Toni Armstrong Jr.

She went to as many other festivals as she could, including NEWMR (New England Women's Music Retreat), Campfest, Sisterspace, and twenty-four Michigan festivals, scouting talent and keeping her ear to the ground for possible issues. Mary says this about Michigan, "It was always the hotbed—the festival that had all the political angst...the problems happened at Michigan and before the next National we figured how we were going to deal with it."[318] Interestingly, she doesn't remember getting together with the other festival organizers to support each other in a more formal way, only that she attended the festivals.

Some who attended National liked that it was held indoors, perfect for attendees who didn't want to camp and for performers who appreciated a nice hall. Comic Kate Clinton called it the "festival for the rustically challenged."

Women continued to find women's music and culture through festivals, including National. Fan Theresa Thompson first attended in 1985. "I'll never forget how I felt when I first saw the music video by Kay Weaver and Martha Wheelock, *One Fine Day*. I felt like I had finally come home and with my tribe. From that point on I fell in love with all kinds of women's music and it's been an incredible journey of music and life."[319]

While other festivals offered networking opportunities for producers, bookers, musicians, and others, it was National that provided a special workshop series that covered the business of music. Later, AWMAC (Association of Women's Music and Culture) started there. It was this networking that also encouraged Mary Byrne to stay connected—"I knew that's where the women's music industry happened...all the producers coming together figuring out, 'What do you mean by marketing?'" She laughs and adds, "...without National the whole women's music industry would implode."[320]

National featured many workshops over the years and brought in speakers like Geraldine Ferraro, Judy Chicago, and Anita Hill. Their 1980 program lists over sixty workshops. Their 1990 flyer noted, "Although music is an important part of this festival, its emphasis is on the broad spectrum of women's culture through workshops, special conferences, networking, and seminars." The 1990 festival featured a performer and producer series, as well as special workshops for women of color, writers, older women, about women and money, and a spirituality series. The performer and producer series were especially extensive, with workshops about writing a business plan, learning about publicity, fighting racism, booking yourself, performing with men, home recording, and much more. In 1996, they presented over three hundred workshops.

Performers loved this festival. Sandra Washington (Washington Sisters) fondly remembers a time at a Bloomington National festival with her sister Sharon, Linda Tillery, Judith Casselberry, Jan Martinelli, and Carrie Barton. They started singing in the lobby of one of the dorms. "Then we got hungry and went to Mama Bear's (the pizza place) and sang for two or three hours over there. At one point, these local guys came by and said, 'Do you know 'Proud to be an American'? [a patriotic song by country artist Toby Keith] or something like that and we went, 'Yeah, sure,' and we sang that and something else. These guys were weeping. We were having a blast and it was so cool, a magical night."[321]

Mary Byrne produced the festival until 1999. She loved the work. She told a festival crowd, "(I have) the most wonderful job in the world. You wouldn't have to pay me for this job but I'm glad you do."[322] The festival is currently held in Madison, Wisconsin. In 2015 they celebrated their fortieth anniversary.

The Michigan Festival went through changes too. After the first festival in 1976, Boo Price met with Lisa Vogel and offered, "If you want, I'll come back next year, bring my production crew and produce this properly."[323] Lisa agreed, and the next year Boo produced the main stage with sound engineer Margot McFedries, lighting designer Leni Schwendinger, and stage manager Jennifer James. The same crew worked the first few years, training other women to do the jobs. Boo produced the main stage every year except one until 1994, as well as initiating and improving areas of the festival. In 1983, she came on board as co-producer of the festival.

Feedback from festival attendees and volunteers for all the festivals was always important. With their input organizers developed these notable events. For the Michigan Festival, that meant establishing and improving the Womb (health care), the Community Center (area for socializing, open mics and workshops), the Women of Color Tent, DART (Disabled Access Resource Team), the Lois Lane Run, the Acoustic Stage, dances, films, and intensive workshops (three- to six-hour workshops with some held daily for the week).

After the first Michigan Festival, Lisa was sure there wouldn't be another one because it was a huge financial risk and a tremendous amount of work. "There were only a few years that I was absolutely sure there would be another fest," Lisa remembered.[324] It continued for forty years, averaging 2,500 to 3,000 women each year, with a high of 8,000 in 1982 and 1995 (their twentieth anniversary). Musicians have included those well-known in women's music as well as newcomers. Mainstream artists Tracy Chapman, Sia, Laura Nyro, Lorraine Segato, and the Indigo Girls have also performed.

New Festivals

National and Michigan weren't the only Midwest festivals. In 1989, the Ohio Lesbian Festival started as a one-day event in September on rented land near Columbus. In recent years one stage starts in the afternoon and runs until late at night. It's drawn as many as two thousand women. There's a lot going on, with workshops, a crafts area, drumming, and sports. One year, they advertised water balloon fights. With a commitment to Ohio performers, they've presented Jamie Fota, Betsy Lippitt, and the Columbus Women's Chorus, as well as touring artists from outside the state—The Washington Sisters, Teresa Trull, and Ferron.

The Midwest festivals were popular but the locations made it hard for women outside of the region to attend. It was good news for them when producer Robin Tyler started the West Coast Women's Music and Cultural Festival in 1980 with Torie Osborne as director. It was the first time the area had seen a large-scale festival and the first festival to put "cultural" and later, "comedy" in its title, acknowledging in a prominent way that there was much more than music at these festivals. Other festivals offered a variety of entertainment also but did not make it part of their name. Started with an $18,000 settlement received by Robin Tyler from an auto accident, it was held in a beautiful wooded setting near Yosemite, California and in the end, cost $100,000. Robin put the remainder of the expenses on credit cards. Two thousand women showed up, enabling them to break even. That first festival featured music from Alive!, Gwen Avery, Alix Dobkin, and more, as well as workshops from writers Margaret Sloan-Hunter and Charlotte Bunch, and wiccan priestess Z Budapest.

Another reason for starting the festival came out of an experience Robin had emceeing at the Michigan Festival. She recalls, "(Organizer) Lisa Vogel told me

I was too slick...So, I said okay, rather than fight with Michigan, I'll just start my own festival." She laughs and adds, "...knowing nothing about it."[325]

Like the other festivals, hers would be women-only but "I didn't want a separatist festival. I wanted a feminist festival which meant that our festival sponsored

Robin Tyler.
Private collection, Robin Tyler.

a lot of feminist speakers (because) I came out of politics and the women's movement and not out of music."[326] This festival and others she produced featured authors Rita Mae Brown and Kate Millett, activist Flo Kennedy, and others. (The National Festival also brought in authors and activists.) Sometimes it made for an interesting meeting of cultures when someone not familiar with a women's music festival was invited to participate. Robin remembers feminist activist Ellie Smeal showing up in heels. Robin gave her some sneakers. Singer/actress Nell Carter was nervous about staying in a cabin in the woods. The festival audience enjoyed her performance but didn't realize she was a Tony award winner and an actress known for the popular TV show *Gimme a Break!*. At the end of her show she looked out at the crowd and stated, "*I'm* Nell Carter." Robin Tyler laughs when she remembers, "It was really funny watching people not know who this star was."[327]

It was also important to Robin Tyler to feature comedy at her festival, something she felt was almost ignored at other festivals where music was the focus. She declared, "I'm not going to hide the comics behind guitar strings."[328] Beer was available for sale, also setting it apart from most festivals. Even though she'd been sober for years, it was important to her to give attendees a choice. AA meetings were also offered.

Robin thought her events should feature all kinds of music. In addition to performers well-known in women's music, she also booked big band Maiden Voyage, jazz performer Kellie Greene, and rocker Carol MacDonald.

Writer Ellen Elias reported on the audience diversity of the 1985 West Coast festival: "...there are the Berkeley Birkenstockers, the stylish Southern

Californians, the hardcore vegetarians…and the hardcore leather queens…we are crystal planters and flannel shirt wearers. We are exotic and ordinary, and probably ninety-five percent lesbian."[329]

In 1986, the festival happened again, this time with 3,500 attending. In 1987, the festival was canceled because of area fires. Many people, including Robin, lost money. She expressed her frustration to *HOT WIRE* in March 1988, "We pre-spent for food and for the land [money] which we haven't gotten back, and people have asked for so much back in refunds that we're almost out of money…I'm very disappointed. On the other hand, craftswomen—who lost money because they were going to sell up there—have been wonderful to us. A lot of craftswomen have made donations back…" She managed to keep the festival going for twelve years. The festival ended in 1992 when attendance had dropped to one thousand.

Buoyed by the success of the West Coast festivals and because there was no festival in the South, Robin started the Southern Women's Music and Comedy Festival in 1983 in Georgia with partner Lisa Ulrich. Robin comments, "We were in the middle of some of the most red-necked, Ku Klux Klan country… this county made *Deliverance* look liberal."[330] Concern was so high they posted armed guards at the perimeter. Two thousand women enjoyed the event. Safety was threatened again at a subsequent festival when a local paper, the *Gainesville Times*, ran an article with the headline, "Radical feminist nudists invade Southern camp."[331]

Southern women weren't prepared for some of the aspects already common to festivals in other parts of the country, like vegetarian food, women's spirituality, and a direct way of speaking that is considered impolite there. Writer Jorjet Harper wrote about the 1990 festival in *HOT WIRE*, commenting that it wasn't as political as other festivals, despite speakers like LGBTQ activist Urvashi Vaid, and Pat Ireland, then the vice president of NOW. She wrote, "Things happened at Southern that I'd never expect to see at Michigan. Sitting in a workshop, for example, I noted to my shock that I was surrounded by women wearing mascara *in the middle of the woods.*" There were cabins with flush toilets and meals included hot dogs and barbecued chicken—a far cry from the vegetarian fare offered at Michigan. She noted the presence of S/M dykes and conversely, two lesbians who carried their Bibles with them. The festival continued for several years, nine of them at a Jewish camp near Atlanta until a new director asked them to leave in 1991.

Many of the women attending Southern had never been to a women's music festival before, including Wanda and Brenda Henson from Mississippi. Wanda commented, "It was an immense amount of culture shock, but it was *my* culture, it was *my* people, it was *my* home. My whole life is different now."[332] She and Brenda opened a women's bookstore, the first in their state, and started the Gulf Coast Women's Festival in 1989. At first, they held it on rented land, then received a grant to buy their own. After four years, they purchased a former pig farm near Ovett, Mississippi, a rural area about a hundred miles southeast of Jackson. The locals weren't sure what to make of this group of women and many of them were angry. There were nasty letters, volatile town meetings, a dead puppy draped over their mailbox, and threats that were taken so seriously, the perimeter was guarded. The Hensons appealed to authorities for help and at first were told that no crime had been committed. After they received a death threat in the mail, a federal offense, the FBI took notice. It became big news, with appearances on *Oprah*, *20/20*, and mention in the *Village Voice*, *TIME*, and *Newsweek*. The Hensons persevered. With the help of LGBTQ organizations, activists Suzanne Pharr and Robin Tyler, and others, they would establish their festival and gain the trust of locals.

Campfest began in 1984 in New Jersey, then moved to southeastern Pennsylvania. Drawing as many as a thousand, it was advertised as the comfortable festival because women could stay in cabins and swim in the Olympic-sized pool. Concerts were held outdoors but could be moved inside to Radclyffe Hall in inclement weather. First produced by Lee Glanton and Geri Sweeney plus a host of volunteers, it was organized by Lee in later years. It was important to her to present entertainers with a specifically lesbian and feminist focus. Over the years that included The Washington Sisters, The Fabulous Dyketones, Alix Dobkin, Suede, Jamie Anderson, Dianne Davidson, and Lucie Blue Tremblay.

Sisterfire started in 1982 in Washington, DC. Presented by the arts organization Roadwork, it had a strong multicultural commitment. It offered a great deal of variety, from a women's film festival to the Deaf Community Stage. There was a special area, the Hearth, for kids, which included entertainment and activities just for them. Sisterfire later moved to Maryland. Open to women and men, it drew several thousand each year. Volunteers, men and women, were called Sistersparks, but only women were allowed on stage. In 1987 5,000 people heard music on five stages. Musician Debbie Fier played there one year, in a trio with Nydia Mata and Jean Fineberg. She recalls, "It had a great vibe—lots of vitality and diversity."[333] Debbie remembers the excitement of meeting Laura Nyro, also booked at the festival. Over the years audiences enjoyed many others—Margie Adam, Mercedes Sosa, Elizabeth Cotten, Tracy Chapman, Alice Walker, Sweet Honey in the Rock, Urban Bush Women, Ronnie Gilbert with Holly Near, Meg Christian, and many more. Their last festival was in 1988.

The East Coast Lesbian Festival was the earliest to have "lesbian" in the title. First produced in 1989, and organized by Lin Daniels and Myriam Fougere, they wanted an event explicitly for lesbians. They told *HOT WIRE* in 1990, "We believe that to a very large degree, womyn's culture is lesbian culture. We thought it was high time to call a celebration of that culture by its proper name." The first festival took place in Massachusetts for a thousand women. In subsequent years attendance averaged four hundred to one thousand. Not only was there a commitment to hire only lesbian performers (other festivals only specified that they be women) but they also sought out lesbian staff, and craftswomen. They offered activities similar to most other festivals—workshops, lesbians of color tent, a crafts area and more, as well as areas not seen at other festivals, such as a separatist tent. Entertainment ranged from the techno-pop of Sue Fink to dub poet Lillian Allen.

NEWMR (North East Women's Musical Retreat) was held in various locations on Labor Day weekend. The organizers had been to the Michigan Festival and wanted a similar event closer to home. In 1980 over a thousand women attended the first festival at a ski resort in Connecticut. It was a lovely place but problematic, with almost no level land. Other locations in New England were used in later years. Numbers never matched that first year; however, they drew several hundred each year.

Drawing an audience mostly from the southwest, WIMINFest had its main stage in the KiMo Theatre in Albuquerque. Other events were scattered around the city including some in a city park. Beginning in 1985 and held over Memorial Day weekend, it also offered dances, and one year a "dyke dog" contest.

There were many other festivals, some that only happened a time or two, such as the Lone Star Festival in Texas, a small event in Arizona, one in Hawaii, a Southern Women's Music Festival not run by Robin Tyler, one in Alaska, and in later years, the Iowa Women's Music Festival. Related festivals offered music but had a different focus, such as a women's motorcycle festival, and several spiritually-oriented festivals.

CHAPTER FIVE

••◦✦◦••

TROUBLE IN PARADISE

Facing Many Challenges

The women's music network had set out to create something different from mainstream music. It was successful on many levels but there were times when the love was lost. There were arguments about privilege and professionalism, and worries that women's music had become too much like the mainstream. There were financial concerns, issues with accessibility, and other problems at festivals. While the issues were sometimes created and sustained from outside women's music, there were constant accusations of racism, classism, and homophobia. Sometimes the issues were worked out. Sometimes they weren't. Sometimes it was just sex, drugs, and rock n roll.

Festival Issues

It was challenging for all the festivals to find and keep land. NEWMR was held in several locations and even after they received a large amount of money from an estate, couldn't find suitable land to purchase. The National Festival was held at seven different Midwest sites over the years. Robin Tyler had difficulty with her festivals. She talked to *HOT WIRE* in 1988 about the West Coast Festival: "The county tried to not give us a permit to hold the festival, saying that because it was women-only we discriminated against men." With the aid of attorneys, she was finally able to convince them to give her the permit just a week before the deadline.

In 1982 the Michigan Festival moved from rented land near Hesperia to land in Oceana County, close to the town of Hart. The farmer who owned the land offered to sell it to them; however, the purchase required a $50,000 down payment. Given the festival's struggle with money that kind of payment seemed unreachable. Boo Price recalls, "I came up with the idea of lifetime memberships and I said we're going to sell these for a thousand dollars each... it'd be like $10,000 (each) today...we made up a list of anyone who might have the money."[334] Lisa Vogel and Boo called women on the list, telling each one that if they contributed $1,000, they'd have a lifetime pass to the festival. They also announced it at worker meetings and from the stage. Some women combined their money to get one membership. The festival sold fifty lifetime memberships, enough to buy the land.

The festival had developed a good relationship with people around the old land and wanted to do the same in this new location. Lisa Vogel and her sister approached the sheriff a few weeks before the festival. Lisa remembers, "We went in and said, 'Hi, we're organizing this music festival...We just want to check in with you and see what you need us to do...We want to make sure we do everything right.' He says, 'We know everything about you.'"[335] He threw a newspaper on the desk. The front page headline screamed 'Two Thousand Lesbians Converge on Oceana County.' The sheriff was quoted all through the article, warning people that these women were bad influences, they ran around naked and they beat up men, even using knives on them." Lisa says, "I went ballistic (and told him) 'Do you understand that you just threw (down) a gauntlet for every man who might want to kick some lesbian ass...?'"[336] The festival responded with a letter printed in the local paper, telling the community that they came in peace and didn't intend to harm anyone. The story was picked up by the national press and heard about all over the country. One day, as organizers were building a stage in preparation for the festival, the state police made a visit to inform them the FBI had learned a biker gang, the Devil's Disciples, and another group were planning to disrupt the festival. Lisa informed the sheriff, "You created this. What we need you to do is place squad cars on all roads and stop anyone a mile away and they did that...combined with the fact that we were steady and we brought all this money into the county, we ended up being friends."[337] In later years, Lisa was on a first-name basis with the sheriff and a lot of the people on the force.

Festivals had issues with accessibility. Because the Michigan Festival only had a few weeks to prepare for the 1982 event, some areas were not up to par, including accessibility for women with disabilities. In subsequent years DART developed further, offering deaf and hard of hearing women, and women with limited mobility, a way to attend and enjoy the festival.[338] Other festivals also struggled with accessibility. At the first East Coast Lesbian Festival in 1989, protesters blocked the front gate because the land wasn't accessible for every woman. They moved to more accessible land for subsequent festivals. It was especially difficult for outdoor festivals since most camps available for rent could not be navigated easily by women with mobility limitations. Even the National Festival, held indoors and usually on a college campus, has had issues obtaining rooms that were truly accessible and getting shuttles that could carry everyone who needed rides to the various venues. Mary Byrne, the producer for many years, recalls this of Indiana University in Bloomington, "Because of us...curb cuts started. We were the forum that pushed them into making that campus accessible. I'm sure they didn't think we were doing them a favor (laughs)."[339]

Festivals also experienced periodic financial problems. Unlike mainstream festivals that have corporate sponsors, women's festivals were supported solely from ticket sales, vendor space rental, festival merchandise sales, and raffle sales. The National Women's Music Festival formed as a non-profit in 1982 and because of that could raise money with donors and an annual auction. Women's festivals haven't sought major corporate sponsorship. Unlike other alternative-type festivals, no women's festival ever changed its name to reflect major sponsorship. (For example, the Newport Folk Festival used various corporate sponsors in its name over the years including Ben and Jerry's, and ATO Records.)

Weather has always been an issue for festivals. Michigan had umbrella-bending rains in 1977 and a tornado in 1978. During one East Coast Lesbian Festival, it rained so much that performances were delayed again and again, moved indoors and then back outdoors. At Campfest they had access to a huge indoor space. The acoustics weren't good, but it provided a dry place for concerts if the weather turned nasty. A gust of wind blew down heavy stage lights at the West Coast Festival in 1983, narrowly missing musicians on stage. A direct hit could have caused injury or even death. Festivals held indoors were not spared from weather problems. At the National Festival tornado warnings delayed performances and participants were herded into safe spaces. Mary Byrne laughs when she remembers, "We had people from all over the country and with the west coast people you didn't want to say the 'T' word (tornado) so we would call them electrical storms. Once there was one in the middle of Adrienne Torf's concert...you could hear the sound system crackle...I had to go out and stop her performance and tell everyone 'We're experiencing an electrical storm and everyone has to go down to the basement.'"[340]

The audience dutifully trooped down to the basement, then made it fun and sang until they got the all clear announcement and could return to the show. The concert picked up where it had left off.

Health issues were a concern also. In 1988, Michigan had an outbreak of a mysterious illness that affected ten to twenty-five percent of the women attending, even putting some in the hospital with stomach cramps and severe diarrhea. Later it was determined to be shigella, a bacterial infection easily spread in large gatherings. The festival took precautions in later years, with hand washing setups and more. No more outbreaks occurred.

Festivals meant different things to different women. To the S&M community, it meant they could meet and have parties without constraints except those they set for themselves. Some festie-goers had difficulty with their presence. Starting in the late eighties and lasting for a few festivals S&M supporters staged protests at the Michigan Festival. They even dropped flyers from an airplane in 1990. In 1985, NEWMR also had protesters because their program explicitly prohibited S&M activities. The Gulf Coast Women's Festival had a similar ban. Robin Tyler didn't have an issue with S&M women at her festivals: "Whether I practice something or not, it's not up to me to be judgmental."[341] It was a group of S&M women who organized some of the breakfasts at her festivals. She remembers, "… it was on time and good…I don't know if they got up that early or maybe they were already up (laughs)."[342]

At an early festival produced by Robin Tyler, some festival attendees misheard one of the musicians, insisting that she had sung "Beat me in the woods." They approached Robin, wanting to talk to the musician. Robin said no. She wasn't at the performance but was prepared to support the musician. The protesting group threatened to boycott the performer. Robin doesn't remember if the women followed through, but she does recall that the musician was Melissa Etheridge and she hadn't sung what the protesters had feared.

Transgender women weren't very visible at festivals through much of the seventies and eighties. On the crew of the West Coast Festival Captain Michelle worked as the fire captain, a position required due to the high fire danger. This was important, especially because the eighth festival was canceled due to an immense fire. Producer Robin Tyler says, "We not only did not have any backlash accepting her on the crew, but we were grateful because without her, we would not have been able to have the festival."[343] Robin also says transgender women attended her festivals. "My focus was women. If people were coming on and identifying as a woman, that's fine."[344] Michigan Festival producer Lisa Vogel says that awareness came gradually and some women were misidentified. "…when we began the festival in 1976, there really wasn't much of a presence of the trans community, but there was, for the first time, an interracial community of dykes living together at Michigan. It was womyn-only and we, as producers and organizers…would have womyn come up to us and say, 'There's a man on the land,' and we'd go over and it would be a bearded womon… or often it would be a butch black womon. And white womyn were not used to being around a diversity of black womyn. So much so that when I was approached, my first question would be, 'what is the person's skin color?' and then if they said black, I wouldn't even bother taking it any further, I'd just say, 'sister you know, I think you need to check yourself."[345]

Racism

Despite efforts to create a safe space for all women, racism has been an issue in women's music. To better understand, educate, and to create community, many festivals had Women of Color tents or tables. Amoja Three Rivers co-founded the Womyn of Color tent at the Michigan Festival and did the same at NEWMR. Festivals also featured workshops around identifying and combating racism. Still, it was difficult for women of color performers because it was assumed that women's music was the domain of white singer-songwriters. Many took issue with that, including Toni Armstrong Jr.: "The stereotype is racist; it minimizes or just plain erases most of the contributions which women of color *always* made to women's music. The musical styles of women of color frequently require ensemble or band instrumentation; between the economic difficulties of touring and the racism inherent in the white-dominated women's music circuit, these groups have usually not gotten the widespread recognition they deserve. *That doesn't mean they haven't existed.*"[346]

After Casselberry-DuPreé did their first gig in San Francisco, they decided to branch out but knew there would be barriers. Judith Casselberry recalls "…it was definitely a mixed response because the structure that was being built at the time was being forged primarily by white women."[347] She found hope, though, especially through the festivals that, "…created a space where, even though we weren't always where we wanted to be, it showed us what was possible."[348]

At the second West Coast Women's Music and Comedy Festival in 1981, there were protests when it was alleged that women of color who worked in the kitchen were paid less. A group of two hundred chanting women interrupted a night stage performance of Maiden Voyage and then between acts, producer Robin Tyler appeared on stage with comic/activist Flo Kennedy for a heated talk, partly with each other, about the volatile issue. Many audience members left that night to join a discussion and protest. Others stayed to hear Meg Christian, who came on after them without an emcee introduction. At first, she wasn't her usual talkative self between songs, but toward the end she warmed up. Aside from a vague reference to getting along, she didn't directly address what had happened, perhaps because she didn't know the details.

It was a difficult period for Robin Tyler. She was accused of hiring all Black women for the kitchen work. She recalls: "We had hired two African-American coordinators, and they had hired all their friends because the kitchen was the best-paid position on the land, $500. But they said I was just a rich Jew trying to get rich off the backs of the women's community. They told me I had to give them one third of the business or they would organize a march against the festival."[349] ("They" refers to the protesters, a group including women of color and white women.)

The next year, the festival was boycotted and she lost $50,000. After the 1983 festival, one of the performers, Margie Adam, returned her fee to help. Activists and friends Margaret Sloan-Hunter and Flo Kennedy stood by Robin but initially she did not receive a great deal of support from other prominent women of color. She lost money for three years, finally breaking even with the fifth festival, an event that featured white musicians Cris Williamson, Alix Dobkin and Ferron as well as African-American performers Casselberry-DuPreé, Toshi Reagon and Deidre McCalla. Looking back on that period, Robin comments, "It amazed me that people thought I was making a fortune with two thousand women near Yosemite because it's very expensive to produce in California, when Michigan, with 10,000 women, was never accused of it. That is why I know beyond a doubt that the issue was anti-Semitism."[350] (The Michigan festival has never drawn 10,000 women but it's come close. Overall, it was the biggest festival in terms of attendance.) Sometimes the controversies seemed like that adage about six people seeing the same accident but telling six different stories. In her *Songs in Black and Lavender*, Eileen M. Hayes says, "Among other things, the incident that

Tyler recounts demonstrates the interplay of fact, rumor, good intentions, and misunderstanding in women's music festival culture."[351]

The issue of racism also came to a head at the Michigan Festival in 1989. White Southern musician Dianne Davidson performed on the night stage and introduced one of her songs, a tribute to Hattie, the Black woman who raised her, in a way that upset some audience members. No one said anything to her after her set. The following day there was a meeting of approximately two hundred women. Alix Dobkin had been active in anti-racist work prior to this so she made sure to attend the gathering. She remembers it being attended mostly by white women and the consensus was that they felt Dianne didn't recognize her caregiver as someone with her own life, which for many Black women meant they had to leave their own families behind to care for white families. The group came up with a list of demands and because Alix was emceeing that night, asked her to read them. Dianne was staying at a hotel in town but she spent the day after her performance at the festival. Alix was busy working. Others were looking for Dianne and didn't find her until just before the start of that evening's entertainment. Alix recalls, "We surrounded her and said 'Please, just say that you acknowledge this woman [Hattie].' She felt totally under attack. We were pleading and it was getting dark and the show was going to start."[352] Dianne answered, "No comment," because she didn't have all the information and wasn't sure what Alix was talking about. Her response added fuel to the fire. Some women thought she wasn't taking responsibility for her actions. Alix read a statement from the stage. Later she realized she hadn't run it by the producers, Boo and Lisa, as required by festival guidelines. Ordinarily, it was rare that any political statements be made from stage. Most emcee work involved asking for volunteers, reiterating guidelines, announcing raffle winners, and introducing musicians. The producers were sidetracked by another emergency—S&M women threatening action in the downtown area where the Community Center was located, and rumor was they were going to take down a tent. Their action had nothing to do with racism or the incident with Dianne. Alix says with a smile in her voice, "You can imagine what kind of night that was."[353]

Dianne was baffled by the charges of racism. She asked a group of African-American musicians popular at the festival, and who knew her, if they thought she was racist and their response was no. Later, she told her long-time friend and keyboard player, Michael, an African-American, about the women calling her racist and he laughed because he thought she was making a joke.

Over the rest of the festival, meetings were held to work through the anger and reach some clarity. Later, Dianne apologized even though she felt she was misunderstood. "I would never dishonor the memory of Hattie that way."[354] That incident followed her around for a while. One writer claimed she had left a message on Dianne's voice mail and never received a return call; she assumed Dianne didn't want to talk with her. Misguided white women told Dianne they were angry at the Black women who protested, and Dianne had to set them straight about who was involved and why their assumption was wrong that it was only Black women.

Protests like this and about other issues were disturbing to festival producer Robin Tyler. She saw these kinds of actions as battering. "We don't have the right to batter other women in the name of political correctness. I know because I was attacked (at the 1981 West Coast Festival) and it took me twenty years to recover. I went through therapy and they dealt with me like a rape victim."[355] As a result, she made a point to hire Dianne, Carol MacDonald, and others whom she thought were victimized at other events "...because if you're a victim and you don't recover you become a perpetrator...then you have this horizontal hostility, beating each other up in the movement."[356]

Carol MacDonald was accused of being anti-Semitic and of advocating violence when she appeared on stage with leather-clad women. Margie Adam commented, "While our beloved radical feminist community has been the most earnest, sincere and rigorous about addressing all these issues of any community (faith-based, political or otherwise) anywhere... we have also been the most unsparing and unforgiving critics along the way."[357]

Looking back on the Michigan Festival incident with Dianne, Alix Dobkin says, "It was well-intentioned and not well-intentioned...We didn't have all that much experience with this issue."[358] Because of her visibility as a performer she was seen as a spokesperson about racism and got flak from white southern feminists who thought she was regionally bigoted. At a Gulf Coast Women's Festival in Mississippi a year or two later, she offered a workshop about these issues.

Alix recalls, "It was so intense and emotional. There were all these white women who'd been raised by Black women and never really thought about what that meant. There were women crying. I explained as best I could, my situation and my point of view. They talked about how they never talked about it. It reminded me of when I went to Germany and mentioned I was Jewish at all my concerts. Women would hand notes to me, 'I wasn't born yet, don't blame me.' Women were so moved because it was never discussed before. It was the same kind of deal. It had been unspoken and there was this big guilt thing that women had grown up with, whether they were conscious of it or not. It all came out around this song."[359]

She noticed that in the fourteen years of Michigan worker meetings she attended that the issue of racism, as well as other concerns, came up again and again but "...how we dealt with each other changed. We learned a whole lot in those years about listening to each other, about not being so inflexible."[360] It was a lesson learned in other areas of women's music and outside of the Michigan Festival. Women's culture provided the vehicle for important work.

In other years at Michigan there were incidences that set off a firestorm of dialogue about racism at the festival and later in publications like the *Lesbian Connection*. One year an anti-racist march through the crafts area resulted in some craftswomen being charged with cultural appropriation. In 1993, a white woman entered the Woman of Color tent looking for drugs.

It was a complex issue. Although women's music was viewed by some as mostly white singer-songwriters, an effort was made by organizers and performers to include a variety of styles and cultures. Boo Price comments, "There were more white women than women of color but from the very beginning there were a number of women of color who were very prominent."[361] She went on to name several women of color who were there from the start, including Linda Tillery, Mary Watkins, June Millington, Vicki Randle, and Gwen Avery. Techno-pop artist Sue Fink says, "People were trying to reach out in a positive way to people of all races and not have it a white movement. They got to hear music of all different kinds—I thought that was really cool—whether it was classical or R&B."[362] Kay Gardner expressed her hopefulness to *HOT WIRE* in 1986, "I'm really glad that the Black performers are coming to the forefront now. For too long it's been a middle-class white feminist phenomenon. I'm terrifically inspired by Mary Watkins's music and by the magical performances of Edwina Tyler and A Piece of the World."

While more and more women of color appeared on women's music stages, most of the women behind the scenes were white. Judith Casselberry recalls, "… in some production companies, there were one or two women of color involved, one of the exceptions was Sandy Gonzales in Albuquerque, New Mexico."[363] Sandy was a member of WIMIN, a group that produced local women's music events as well as WIMINFest.

Linda Tillery wanted a diverse audience. In a meeting of women's industry professionals, she challenged the mostly white crowd to find her audience. She told *Sojourner* in 1983, "…it feels wonderful to look out into the audience and see other people who look like me, because a lot of times it isn't like that…it's real important to have people in the audience who have a historical grasp on what it is that you are about. Otherwise you're performing in this 'void'; this is the first time in their lives they've ever heard rhythm and blues, or blues, and they're thinking, 'Boy this is a new discovery.' This stuff has been around for a long time. I'm just a new messenger."[364]

Linda Tillery was raised on gospel, jazz, and R&B, a different background than some of the white singer-songwriters. A story about her early days working in the Olivia office illustrates this. "I brought down some records that I wanted to listen to. I put on an album by the Commodores. There was a woman there who got very uncomfortable. I said, 'What's wrong with you?' She said, "That music really makes me uptight; it's cock rock.'"[365] Linda explained that among other things, it wasn't rock. "She objected to it because it's speaking to my cultural experience, if not to my experience as a woman…I need to hear stuff by other people like me."[366] She told *Sojourner*, "I'm a woman who is dedicated to working with other women and getting out messages about our struggles, and also about our cultural struggles as Black women." Linda cited the limited involvement of Black women in women's music. "Very few Black feminists have been recorded, which doesn't mean that there are not Black women making music. That's exclusive of Casselberry-DuPreé, Edwina Lee Tyler and A Piece of the World, Women of the Calabash, Toshi Reagon…These women are out there and because of lack of money it's harder in the beginning for us to be noticed…"[367] That was one of the reasons that Karen Gotzler of Icebergg Records decided to record Casselberry-DuPreé. "We felt strongly that the work of Black women has not been recorded enough in women's music, and a lot of the reason for that is their access to resources."[368] There are parallels between this and history as a whole. Linda Tillery comments, "It's impossible to discuss contemporary American music without naming...thousands of Black performers since the late 1800s."[369] When asked about her influences, she names Bessie Smith. "(She) was like two cannons going off at one time. She put the blues on the map with her style of singing."[370]

African-American comic Karen Williams emceed at many women's music festivals. She didn't mince words when it came to racism and often talked about it in her routines. At a 1989 National Festival, she looked around the room and quipped, "Aren't you white women bored with each other?"[371]

Some concert producers didn't want to bring in Black performers because they didn't think they'd draw as well as white singer-songwriters. Mary Watkins comments, "...due to lingering racism in the women's community they 'unfortunately' could not afford the financial risk. That was hard to listen to but fortunately I always had my eye out for opportunities to put my music out into the world, not just the women's community, knowing there was and is more than enough racism to go around and that I could not afford to think in narrow terms about who should or should not hear and receive what I had to give. It has been my experience that people of all races happen to respond to good music, and I've always tried to deliver it."[372]

Many concert producers made outreach to the Black community when they produced African-American performers but didn't always get a huge response from that community. This angered Sandra Washington so much, she almost left women's music in the mid-eighties. Both she and her sister Sharon recognized that racism was obvious in women's music, just like it was in mainstream music, and that wouldn't change unless there was a solid foundation of trust. Sharon told *HOT WIRE* in 1987, "...ladies, it's going to take more than a few efforts. A whole network of trust and mutual satisfaction must be built, and mutual satisfaction will not occur if decision making is still in the hands of white women only— until tokens are the exception and not the rule." Deidre McCalla offered, "There are some Black student unions and Third World women's coalitions that get together and bring me in, but they wouldn't do that for everyone."[373] Invitation also depended on the genre of music. Deidre adds, "I do not have—musically— the same audience that Linda Tillery does. I grew up listening to Motown, but my guitar learning was the folk scene...I think the vast majority of Black women are more akin to the music that Linda does."[374]

Other factors played into getting women of color on women's music stages. Judith Casselberry mentions several bands and adds "...they were incredible bands but it was very hard for them to get any kind of touring support because it was very expensive to put them on the road."[375] Producing a solo folk/pop singer-songwriter in concert was fairly simple; however, some styles such as salsa and R&B require a full band. That meant getting a bigger stage, paying more musicians, hauling in more equipment, and other challenges.

When asked about who ran the women's music movement, Gwen Avery told J. D. Doyle in a 2011 *Queer Music Heritage* interview, "...when I started doing it I knew damn well that I was a token person because most of the people that we performed for certainly didn't know a lot of Black women and certainly weren't into Black women singing the blues until Teresa Trull did the Ma Rainey tune ("Prove It on Me Blues")."[376] She told the *San Francisco Gate* in 2002, "...the same issues of race and classism that confounded the early feminist and gay rights movements also infected the women's music scene."

Performers weren't always sure where they stood. Deidre McCalla states, "My music is not typical of what people expect a Black woman to be doing...I was never clear with the women's music audience if they booked me because they liked my music or because I was Black."[377] Sandra Washington (Washington Sisters) maintains they didn't come up against a whole lot of racism, probably because their music "...wasn't so different than what was women's music."[378] It changed a bit, though, when they started singing "Lift Every Voice and Sing," widely known as the Black American National Anthem. They got advice from other African-Americans too. Sandra thinks that maybe it was Linda Tillery who advised them, "'Never ask for less than full asking price for anything in January, February, or March, from King's birthday through March'...we always went full price and universities willingly paid it. That's a cheap way to not feel guilty anymore."[379] (February is Black History Month and March, Women's History Month.)

Many of the women's music festivals had difficulty attracting women of color. African-American musician Melanie DeMore told *HOT WIRE* in 1993, "I want to see more diversification at the festivals. A lot of the performers are women of color, but we need more sisters in the audience."

Naomi Littlebear Morena experienced frustration at the pressure put on her because of her ethnicity: "I didn't like putting my 'oppression' on stage or being criticized for not." (For her email interview, she is the one who put quote marks around "oppression.") "I got a lot of flak for playing with white women, for not being angry enough, for being too angry, for not playing songs in Spanish, for not playing salsa. It was ridiculous and crazy making but worse, it took my focus off my art."[380]

Naomi felt her culture was just one part of who she was as a musician. Although she spent her early years in a barrio with grandparents who didn't speak English, she later lived with her mother in a white community. "It was there that I lost myself to teaching myself to play music, inspired by the Beatles, Buffy St. Marie, Joan Baez and heaven forbid, the Rolling Stones."[381] She recalled a painful experience when a radio producer in San Francisco would not play her band's album because there were no other Latinas in the group.

French Canadian Lucie Blue Tremblay felt cultural considerations were important. She sang and recorded in French and English. She told *HOT WIRE* in 1986, "Going into western Canada or the United States with half your songs in French is scary when you're used to traveling in places where five years ago you would go with a Quebec license plate and get three flat tires...It's very important that I not lose my identity as a Francophone." Lucie was thrilled when audience members spoke to her in French, even if it was rudimentary, because it showed they respected her culture. Women loved her songs in French, even if they didn't understand the language.

Anti-Semitism

Alix Dobkin told the July/August 1977 *Lesbian Tide*, "Anti-Semitism exists in the women's movement just because it's so institutionalized. It's subtle." She talked about being Jewish on stage, sometimes offering a song in Yiddish. When she toured Germany in the seventies she told the audience she was Jewish, angering some. Robin Tyler experienced resentment from some because she was Jewish, especially around the events at the 1981 West Coast Festival. Also, because she was a festival producer, women assumed she had lots of money, playing into that stereotype.

Anti-Semitism came from outside of women's music too. It was one of the reasons the Gulf Coast Women's Festival lost land they were renting—the owner objected to a Shabbat dinner.

Jewish women found support and connection at festivals with Shabbat celebrations and more. Some of the festivals had a table or booth where Jewish women could meet.

Money and Class

At first, finances weren't a high priority. One of the early Michigan Festival organizers, Kristie Vogel, recalls, "...even though we should probably have had a better business model (or any!) our primary goal was never to make money, but to have a successful celebratory gathering of womyn."[382] Margie Adam adds, "Early women's music was not set up to make money. Money was at the bottom of the list. Sisterhood was at the top of the list...The definition of success began to change and include monetary compensation."[383] Still, it was difficult to make money, even for a well-attended festival like Robin Tyler's West Coast Festival. She recalls, "We didn't even make any salaries, not a cent, until the *fifth year*."[384] While some festivals could pay a few women, it wasn't much and, mostly, these large events ran on volunteer help. It wasn't unusual to hear a request from the stage that twenty women were needed at the kitchen, *now*. Not only did they gain satisfaction helping the festival to run, but sometimes it came with other perks. Alix Dobkin serenaded security workers at the Michigan Festival gate several different years—concerts couldn't be heard from there and she thought they should enjoy some live music. She also did special performances in the Belly Bowl (worker area) because many workers couldn't attend shows. At the 1981 Michigan Festival, the emcee told the audience that one hundred and fifty women were needed to do overnight security shifts. As an incentive, Teresa Trull offered to hug every volunteer. Meg Christian promised private concerts. Both followed through. Meg worked into the wee hours, even though she'd already entertained onstage earlier that evening.[385]

Early women's music events had low ticket prices. As admission prices rose, some women thought that meant artists and producers were making a lot of money. Holly Near made it clear that wasn't the case in an interview with the *Lesbian Tide* (September/October 1979). After detailing how all the costs associated with a concert had gone up (hall rental, insurance, travel, etc.) she said, "Somehow, within the women's community we're real offended by concert prices going up like everything else."

Sometimes finances determined how events were done—how big the venue, how much promotion, and what performers were booked. Events producer and editor/publisher Toni Armstrong Jr. has always created and supported women-only events but grappled with the realities. In *HOT WIRE* (Sept. 1989) she wrote: "...our founders did/do not come from the ruling class...Everything we have built has come through intense effort and sacrifice...In our projects, economic realities often dictate who gets hired..." While some separatists demanded that events, records, and more be women-only, the reality was that it wasn't often possible. Toni says, "The choice is simply not between women-only and mixed; the choice comes down to mixed or no event at all."[386] In places like San Francisco, there was a large reservoir of women musicians and technicians from which to draw. For someone in Des Moines, Iowa, the reality was much different.

Artists worked hard to raise money for albums. Kay Gardner put together a flyer asking for funding that she presented at gigs. Linda Tillery raised money in the same way. She told *HOT WIRE* in 1985 that she needed thousands for her next release, *Secrets*. "There won't be many times in my life when I'll see $30,000 flash before my face." She also noted that it was a small percentage of what major labels spent on an album.

After releasing *A Step Away* on Redwood Records in the eighties, Teresa Trull thought about another album with them but, "Someone like Redwood can't afford to put out $26,000 for the record and then another $20,000 to promote it...basically they end with a $75,000 budget including the artwork and promotion and everything."[387] The average studio budget for a mainstream LP in 1988 was $80,000 to $100,000 and that *only* covered recording.[388] Adding graphic design, duplication, promotion, and more made for a hefty price tag.

Ferron and her business partner Gayle Scott went into the studio to record 1984's *Shadows on a Dime* knowing they hadn't raised enough money to leave with the tape. Two fans were there to watch the recording and heard Gayle telling the studio rep that they were short. One fan had just received a school loan of $5,000 and offered them half. The other fan had just gotten a $1,000 car loan, decided she could take the bus for another year, and lent them the money.

While some women had to raise money to record or produce shows, others had connections to get funding or had family money. Often it was covert or they'd be attacked for being a part of the privileged class, regardless of what they achieved with their wealth. Liza Cowan, for a time Alix Dobkin's lover, told the

Lesbian Tide (July/August 1977) "I would like to see lesbians stop attacking me because I have money. We heard a rumor (that) some woman said 'any woman who has control of more than $10,000 is immoral.'" Alix continued the dialogue, "...being poverty-stricken seems to have been exaggerated into some kind of holy purpose...as though somehow that's going to make you less responsible for the exploitation in the world. As if we're responsible!" (It should be noted that Liza did not fund Alix's recordings. Alix raised the money herself.)

Sometimes it wasn't about the money. Sharon Washington confided to *HOT WIRE* in 1987, "...we will never get rich in women's music. The mainstream music industry may give you wider exposure, but the connection with women's energy is what drew us to this industry and continues to fuel us emotionally."

It wasn't necessarily about fame, either. Teresa Trull wanted success but she was modest in her expectations—"'Successful' to me was not just successful in the women's community, or successful in terms of the music industry. For me, success meant not having to worry about paying my rent, and not having to worry whether or not people would show up if I gave a show...I've made a living which is more than a lot of people do, and I can be thankful for that."[389]

Accountability, Community Building, and Professionalism

Women's music performers looked for ways to stay accountable to women's community. Alix Dobkin asked concert producers to offer community potlucks the day after shows. She recalled, "After eating we'd sit in a circle (like for consciousness-raising groups). I asked that we each state our age, when we came out (or didn't), what we wanted/needed from our community, and what we could contribute to it. Women learned new things about each other, made new connections, discussed local issues, and made plans. It was uniformly inspirational for all!"[390]

In the early years Olivia collective members Ginny Berson and Meg Christian also met with the community before or after a show. The results were not always satisfying. Ginny remembers, "We didn't know how to do these very well and they were very brutal (with questions like) how dare Meg charge $2 for a ticket?"[391] Ginny recalls a particularly ugly confrontation in Seattle where a group of lesbians "...picketed a concert that Meg did because she had romantic love songs. They had a flyer with 'man' in 'romance' capitalized to let everyone know that this was very patriarchal and male."[392] More issues came up right after Olivia relocated to the Bay Area. To celebrate the move, they presented a big concert featuring Teresa Trull and Linda Tillery each doing a set. Some audience members were enraged that a woman, Linda, played drums because they thought that was a male instrument. They also felt that women's music shouldn't include electric guitars. Members of Olivia met with audience members. Ginny says, "We took abuse for several hours. One of the Olivia collective actually had a nervous breakdown because of it."[393] Among themselves Olivia members took to calling that event "Slimy Sunday."

Ginny Berson also remembers one year at the Michigan Festival when there were "…four different flyers circulating about Olivia—one that said we were too separatist, one that said we were not separatist enough, one that said we were acting like a bunch of socialists, and one that said we were too capitalist."[394] Even though Olivia published its financial statement in *Paid My Dues* and held workshops that outlined where the money came from and where it went, the negative feedback felt endless. Ginny says, "There got to be a point where it was not productive and too painful."[395] They quit doing the feedback sessions. Judy Dlugacz told *HOT WIRE*, "For several years in the early eighties I was not very accessible…I couldn't hear one more criticism. Over the years, I have felt extremely misunderstood."[396] Despite the difficulties Ginny comments there was also, "…a tremendous amount of love and kindness, generosity and support."[397]

While "business" was a dirty word for some in women's music, producer Robin Tyler had a different view. "I was always upfront that I was starting my festivals as a business. You're not supposed to say that…you aren't supposed to run them as a business."[398] Olivia president Judy Dlugacz told *HOT WIRE* in 1989, "I wish I had come to Olivia with more of a background in business, and I wish I hadn't had to grow up doing the job."

In the eighties, venues expanded. Women's music went from church basements to Carnegie Hall, from new performers accustomed to small coffeehouses to polished musicians who played for big crowds. Margie Adam says, "Women's music was my love, my romance, it was fuel for my deepest intentions. It was a container for me to pour my heart into and find a friendly place to stretch and become the most articulate I could be and stretch to present the finest version of my artistry."[399]

Boo Price produced concerts and remembers this from mid-seventies shows in the bay area of San Francisco: "Other than Full Moon Coffeehouse, it was church basements. I decided to produce this big Women on Wheels tour at Oakland Auditorium. I took tremendous flak for taking it over ground…lesbians were just beginning to find each other and identify as a group. Maybe there was fear involved. Also, that newness of wanting to keep it all to ourselves…I understood why people wanted to keep it small and closed. Anyone who wanted to do that could continue to do it, but I felt like it was time to make it as big and public as possible. I weathered that. I did take some criticism for it, but it didn't last long."[400]

Margie Adam was one of those arguing for venues with higher visibility. "There was some resistance from women in women's music because it smacked of show business. They were nervous we'd lose the community feel."[401] Performers also raised their fees and extended their contracts, asking for better sound and light along with professionals to run them.

Kay Gardner contemplated what this new level of professionalism meant for women's music. She told *HOT WIRE* in 1986, "Women's music has changed a lot since the early days. We all have become a lot more professional…In the process, though, we have lost a lot of the 'joie de vivre' and enthusiasm we had at the beginning."

Musician Betsy Rose wondered about the bigger halls and sophisticated presentations after she attended a 1986 show. "What we call women's music is no longer a secret underground code, an 'I know you know' wink...It was exhilarating. But afterward was a kind of hollow depression, similar to a post-caffeine or sugar rush. A cultural form which had once felt like a breakthrough, a moment of historic shift, now felt a little rote, as if nostalgia, not raw hunger, was bringing us together."[402]

While this level of professionalism often made for a better presentation, it also created a higher risk for concert producers. Nancy Vogl comments, "We brought some of the same requirements and expectations to a system that wasn't ready to support it. If you take a subculture of a subculture—so you're taking the feminists and the lesbians from the women's movement—and imposing the requirements of the dominant culture professional music person (then) you're taxing a system that isn't developed yet."[403] Some venues and concert production companies were already on precarious financial ground and one show where expenses exceeded income would mean their demise. More than one concert producer spent money from her own pocket to cover losses incurred from an event. Sometimes it was the performer who cut the producer a break, taking less than the guarantee outlined in the contract and hoping to make up the loss at subsequent engagements. Teresa Trull sometimes gave money back if ticket sales weren't high enough to meet her guarantee. "Nothing bummed me out more than thinking that I possibly put someone in a financial bind," she recalled. "I've been in a financial bind, I know what that's like."[404]

Sandra Washington thought a professional presentation did not have to mean a high budget. "I am not wanting to build a network of yuppie dykes that excludes the not-for-profit companies or the community groups."[405]

The Big Cheeses, Support Between Performers, and Mainstream Musicians

The financial risk involved in organizing a show meant that some concert producers weren't as interested in lesser known performers because they needed the bigger audience to cover expenses. Race and class played into this. Margie Adam remembers, "White middle- and upper-middle class women produced the concerts because they had the financial resources. When there were more choices some producers gave themselves the out—'I'm only going to produce women who sell at this level.'"[406] And for many of them, those women were Margie Adam, Meg Christian, Holly Near, and Cris Williamson. They became known in some circles as the Big Hamburgers or the Big Cheeses. It was said with a laugh but everyone knew if you wanted a big crowd, bring in one of these four. "The producers might have had all the political savvy in the world," says Margie, "but the audiences didn't come when they brought someone else...I felt very strongly that any audience of mine should be willing to show up for a sister artist of mine, not just the favorites. Early on they actually did. It was a commitment to a generalized vision of a woman-identified culture."[407]

It was a frustrating situation for anyone who wasn't a "big cheese." Even for well-known performers like Kay Gardner, it was an issue. She was once booked for an October concert but was told in August they had to cancel because they were bringing in one of the big four and they didn't have the finances or the energy to do her show too. "My feelings were badly hurt," Kay confides, "but when sharing the story with other non-cheese performers, I found that each of them had a similar sad tale to tell."[408]

Lesbian singer-songwriter Ann Reed was one of those "non-cheeses." She was very popular in the Midwest, especially in her hometown of Minneapolis—even beating out Prince as the favorite performer in the area for one poll. "I was really trying to get into some of the women's music festivals, labels, venues and found it a pretty frustrating exercise."[409] During the eighties, only half of the venues she played were women's music events.

Sometimes it was just a matter of musicians and producers finding each other. While there were directories published over the years, most notably *Women's Music Plus*, it was nearly impossible to keep up with the shifting landscape. Staying current with venues was mind-boggling as it seemed they came and went like quick summer storms. Established venues and artists changed phone numbers and addresses, making them difficult to contact. There was no Internet then so finding someone was much more complicated than a simple online search.

A reliable way for a musician to find places to play was to get contacts from a more experienced performer. Kay Gardner carried around a list of contacts. Margie Adam remembers Kay sharing these with her. Margie reciprocated. When Sue Fink was starting out, she tried to get venue contacts and advice. Margie Adam sat down with her for three hours and shared her contact list. Sue wasn't so lucky with others. She remembers, "Performers were very reluctant to share information. In fact, one of them invited me and a couple of other people over and tried to talk us out of doing women's music. She said the market was too small and competitive and that I'd never make it."[410] The pendulum swung the other way too, with musicians generously sharing contacts and sometimes a stage with new performers, as Maxine Howard did at an early Michigan festival with (then) newcomer Tracy Chapman. Alix Dobkin was so impressed with then-unknown Lucie Blue Tremblay in 1986 that she took her on tour with her. Alix learned some French and they performed songs together. Some artists encouraged opening acts on their tours. Sue Fink was one of those. "I've had a million people that I don't think are very good opening for me, but I think opening acts are still a good idea. I know it helps bring in audience. I think it's good for the community, especially when it's somebody from the local community who performs."[411]

Even if musicians and agents knew who to call, they might not get the gig. Producers had mountains of press kits and phone messages from eager musicians wanting a booking. Self-booking singer-songwriter Erica Wheeler recalls finally getting up the courage to phone Robin Tyler to ask for a spot at one of her festivals only to find out she'd phoned at a tough time. "Robin said, 'Oh hello, a tree just fell on my house.'"[412] Eventually she played at Robin's West Coast Festival, presumably booking it at a time when greenery didn't interfere.

Sandra Washington did all the booking for the Washington Sisters and while she didn't find anyone who'd share a lot of resources, a few would give her a couple. Then she'd use the contacts she'd acquired as a producer. "I didn't mind fishing for gigs and I didn't mind asking people 'Do you produce or do you know the producer in your town?' I built my own Rolodex."[413] Sandra shared her resources with other musicians.

Actually, it was Jane Ann Greeley, Sandra's alter-ego, who booked. She found it easier to book if she pretended to be someone else. She remembers with a laugh, "There are people who would say 'Oh my gosh, Jane was so lovely today when I spoke with her'...it was great."[414] There were times when the Sisters had someone else book for them, but it didn't always go well. One booking agent got them a fair number of gigs, but Sandra and Sharon realized she had an A line of artists who were getting the best gigs. The Washington Sisters were on the B list.

While everyone in women's music tried to be fair and different from the mainstream, dysfunction and personality were still thrown into the mix. Robin Flower remembers: "It became who you know and who you slept with...there were a number of times when I got shit on by women's music people. I don't know if it was because I wasn't on Olivia or Redwood. It was disappointing... you'd hope that lesbians would act differently. Most producers were great, but once in a while you'd hit something where you'd say '*what?*'"[415]

Producer Robin Tyler laughs about the year women complained about the lack of "big cheeses" at her Southern Festival. It was the same year she booked Melissa Etheridge, who at the time didn't have a national reputation. In fact, Robin booked her three times for her festival in California and once for the Southern Festival. Melissa told *HOT WIRE*'s Toni Armstrong Jr. in 1989, "A friend of a friend brought Robin Tyler to hear me. She heard a good rockin' set and asked me if I played at women's music festivals...I didn't know what a women's music festival was."

She wasn't the only mainstream artist to play women's festivals. The National Festival booked several over the years including Odetta, Janis Ian, and Tracy Chapman. Ian was well-received in 1995 at National. On stage she quipped, "I was really worried about playing a women's festival because I don't really have any singalongs...I thought about doing 'Kumbaya' but my partner threatened to leave me."[416] Later in the show she admitted again she'd been terrified to do this gig. The audience responded with loud applause. Someone yelled out "Welcome home!" and she responded, "Thank you."[417] Chapman gave up an engagement opening for James Taylor to appear on the day stage at the National Festival in 1986. She told the audience that unlike other festival performers, she didn't have a recording but they could call her up and ask her to perform in their hometown. Her first album, on a mainstream label, came out in 1988. Presumably, her phone number had changed by then.

Ageism Less of an Issue

Early women's music audiences and organizers were primarily young women. There were older women at events, although Ronnie Gilbert recalled this about her first visit to a women's music festival: "It did not look like a very welcoming place for older women, if I had stopped to think about that. And maybe that was part of the reason why I didn't stay a second day."[418] Later, festivals became savvier about including older women and began offering special camping areas for women over forty or fifty as well as workshops for them. Also, as women's music continued through the years, audiences grew gradually older until the issue reversed. The National Festival, wanting to draw younger women, started the late-night SheRocks! series where they featured alt-rock bands and others that might be of interest to women in their teens and twenties. While the series got some attention, it never really caught on. Michigan was more successful in drawing younger women, perhaps because of the artists they included on regular stages, from punkers The Butchies to glam pop Leslie and the Lys. In later years, the day stage was almost entirely devoted to these acts.

Ronnie Gilbert always felt accepted in women's music, regardless of her age, because of her long music career and association with Holly Near. However, she wondered about the lack of inclusion of other older performers, including folksinger Faith Petric who applied to play at the Michigan Festival for a couple of years and wasn't chosen despite her experience and popularity. Ronnie muses, "I don't know whether that's ageism or there's simply not enough room for everybody who applies. But it would seem to me that a woman her age applying for a place in a summer's program should be welcomed in."[419]

Six Beds of Separation, a Star System and Acting Badly

Women met and fell in love at women's music events—audience members, musicians and others alike. It sometimes worked and sometimes, not. Robin Tyler quips, "All of us knew each other via six beds of separation."[420] Ginny Berson learned a lot about the music industry when she met Meg Christian, became her lover, and started booking her. Even after their five-year relationship ended, Ginny continued to book her, sometimes at events that also included Meg's new partner. Boo Price and Lisa Vogel were lovers for about five years while they co-produced the Michigan Festival. Even after they broke up, they continued to produce the event for six more years. Boo remembers, "We quit living together but we chose a place for her to live that was within a mile of my house. We were very bonded. We each had other lovers and they came to the festival…The only issue was that our lovers would feel like we (Lisa and Boo) were closer to each other than to them."[421] When the professional breakup happened in 1994 and Boo left the festival, it was catastrophic, with some friends and festival workers siding with one side or the other. Some performers and staff never worked at the festival again.

A star system developed , completely opposite from the beginning years where almost anyone could perform. Margie Adam remembers, "We as a community were saying out loud, we don't have celebrities but what other model did we have? I really give us respect for trying...The pull toward the star system was irresistible..."[422] In a 1976 interview with the *Lesbian Tide*, Holly Near insisted, "I haven't become a star. It's just that things we're all working towards together are becoming more understood by numbers of people. And that should be a positive thing..."[423] There's no doubt that it's great to be acknowledged by fans. Cris Williamson says, "When you are recognized and people handle it well, then it's really nice being famous. If I'm in a museum somewhere...and someone comes up and says, 'I loved your concert,' and they then just go away—it's so sweet."[424]

They didn't always leave the performers alone. Kay Gardner wasn't exempt from fan adulation and she found a unique way to deal with one woman. "In some cases, drastic measures are needed. I found the following solution quite by accident. One of the organizers of a women's music festival was giving me the starry-eyed worshipful looks I've grown to loathe. It was as if she expected me to float from place to place while exuding the essence of white lilacs, nodding benedictions to everyone along the way...I asked this woman if I might use her bathroom. When I finished, the essence I left was much more earthy than the scent of lilacs. When the woman caught the essence, I could see the starriness drain from her eyes immediately. From then on she treated me as she'd treat anyone else."[425]

She also had a more persistent fan, one with mental health issues, who stalked her for eight years. The misguided fan followed her to gigs and camped on her doorstep, even causing Kay to be evicted from one home. While dealing with her was difficult, Kay could laugh at something that happened when she was living in an isolated cabin in February. "I looked out my kitchen window to see an unwelcome apparition happily strolling along the dirt road, wearing a wool blanket toga and no shoes, and carrying a ribbon-wrapped scroll. There was a knock on the door. All I could think was, Beware of Greeks bearing gifts. I answered the door and took the gift, but did not invite her in. With an I-found-you smirk on her face, she went down the hill, singing gaily, and when she reached the bottom, she ran into my landlord who was working in the woods...'Where are you from?' he said, eyeing her strange winter attire. 'I'm from the moon,' she answered. 'Oh, then you must be a friend of Kay Gardner's.'"[426]

Most women's music enthusiasts weren't unpredictable or dangerous, just passionate. Michigan festival worker Tess Wiseheart remembers one fan. "A young woman kept trying to get past security, back into the worker/performer area. She kept getting stopped. I finally went over to her. She was shaking like a leaf. I asked her what was up, and, teary-eyed and stammering, clutching three albums in her hands, she told me she wanted to get autographs from three performers. She loved them so much and she had worn their records out."[427]

The fan was only three days sober and was working hard to maintain that. Tess looked for the performers and after a short while found two of them. She told them about the fan. Robin Flower and Margie Adam met the woman and autographed their albums.

Tess continues, "I was struck by the fact that when I was growing up, I wanted the Beatles' etc., autographs, but here was a new generation, revering womyn's music. I got busy for a few minutes, and I turned around to see if she was still there. She was, and she was sitting in a chair, and Robin Flower was sitting right beside her, talking to her. It probably went on for twenty minutes or so. I'm guessing it was the biggest thrill of her life, and I have loved Robin for it forever. And that young woman came up and thanked me every year thereafter."[428]

Ferron has such a devoted following that it reached cult status. She told *Queer Music Heritage* in 2006, "…there's a whole bunch of people, thousands of people, who hold me in this incredible esteem and I am not able to match it…(they) use some of the songs to actually make it from point A to point B without offing themselves. You know, in some ways, so did I—I had to make meaning out of a meaningless life."

Fans could be hard on artists, wanting them to cover every topic important to them. This frustrated Teresa Trull. "I can only most accurately portray my personal experience or something that affected me deeply personally."[429] Political topics were not of the utmost importance in her work although she recognizes and validates that it was for other artists in women's music.

Some fans didn't know how to act with women's music artists—should they give them warm hugs, treat them like aloof stars or see them as a savior? In 1976, Holly Near told the *Lesbian Tide*, "Right now, people are reacting off a system that…perpetuated stars. The other extreme is to think that every musician you ever heard should be your best friend and if they don't come over for coffee then they're a star. Neither of those things are good."[430] Artists received letters from followers who poured out their hearts, relating how a song or performance saved them. Holly Near talked about how difficult it was to answer a letter like that—she would "…mainly just encourage her to find a community to work with because I can't be that community for her."[431]

In her book *My Red Blood*, Alix Dobkin talks about how nasty some audience members could be: "…(my) steadfast commitment and loyalty to women and women-only space has gotten me picketed, boycotted, trashed, and blacklisted by lesbians. Uncharacteristic as they have been, these instances, although hurtful to my feelings and pocketbook, provided excellent song material…They are also the exception that proves the rule of ongoing, resolute support and sustenance from my community."

While there was adulation for performers, it didn't usually reach the mania that existed in mainstream music. Deidre McCalla recalls going to an event that included Debbie Gibson and Suzanne Vega. Audience members were, "…hanging over the balcony screaming, 'Debbie! *Debbie!* DEBBIE!' We were like, God, women would never be that blatant at a Cris Williamson concert! It was kind of a shock. Our audiences are a lot cooler than that."[432]

At many festivals and concerts, an effort was made to offer a restful place for musicians where there wouldn't be distraction from fans. The Michigan Festival created a restricted worker area, later named the Belly Bowl. At first, it wasn't well received by all festival attendees, with some women complaining of classism. The 1979 festival program explained this separate space: "We're trying to break down the 'star' dynamic at this festival, and performers are struggling to make themselves accessible to womyn attending. Please be sensitive and do not abuse this accessibility…it puts an incredible strain on the performer and makes natural interaction impossible."

Cris Williamson, like many performers, was concerned about getting private space before a show. She told the *Lesbian Tide* (May/June 1980), "They used to say, 'What do you need a dressing room for?' Everyone was worried that someone was being elitist. I have my friends protecting me now."

On the flip side of the coin Teresa Trull witnessed bad behavior from artists when she toured as a member of a mainstream performer's band. It really opened her eyes. "…I came to the conclusion that if you get famous enough, it doesn't matter how good a person you are, it will still make you into a jerk. You just can't have…that many people wanting to do things for you, and not have it corrupt you."[433] Perhaps a similar thing occurred occasionally with some women's music artists. With a laugh, Margie Adam offers, "Some of us suffered from a messianic urge."[434] Misbehaving women's music artists didn't destroy hotel rooms, but they could be short with fans and stage personnel. At one festival, there were issues with a metal stage that created a vibration and a buzz through the speakers that couldn't be fixed. Nonetheless, one artist complained so much that the stage crew attached a toy bee to an offending speaker. The artist made it clear that she didn't think that was funny. Sue Fink remembers a concert produced by some nice women who did an excellent job. They weren't treated well by the other performer on the bill, though. "They treated the producers like dirt…they had a dinner for all of us afterwards with the other musician and her friends making fun of the dinner and the people putting it on…these were the people who took the time to put on these concerts."[435] These producers never did another event.

Michigan Festival worker Tess Wiseheart remembers one particularly badly acting member of a band who "…thought she was Janis Joplin, slugging off a big bottle of whiskey the whole week and pushing to the front of every line. The day she was supposed to go, all of the others in her van were there and loaded in. They all had different flight times, and I had to pay attention to the one with the earliest flight. The whiskey bottle had the latest time so she just wandered around. I told her over and over again to get in the van. She cussed me out, drank some more and went in to get something to eat. I looked at my watch, and I knew that they had to go or performer number one would miss her flight. So, I went over to the driver and said, 'Go' and she did. The last I saw of the drunk was her running down the path behind the van, dragging her instrument and yelling 'Wait for me.' Not one iota of guilt on my part."[436]

Producer Robin Tyler fondly recalls the professionals who "…did their jobs and it wasn't emotional."[437] She cited Cris Williamson, noting she is fun and "… has a great personality."[438]

Occasionally, it was the venue operators who behaved badly. Sue Fink recalls a club gig in the eighties that started with the woman who picked her up at the airport. She had a shotgun in the backseat, noting, "Well you know at the club it can be pretty rowdy so I pull that out and the rowdy people leave."[439] Sue had sent posters ahead, using a photo that was a couple of years old. "I didn't look exactly like that person. I'd grown my hair and probably put on fifteen pounds. Their booker took one look at me, pointed at the poster and said, 'I booked *that* and not *this*,' pointing at me."[440] Because of a big football game, the bar decided to have her show three hours early. Sue jokes that she wasn't going to argue with a woman with a gun so she did the concert at the earlier time. Hardly anyone was there. Afterwards, a late arriver complained she hadn't heard any music and would pay Sue ten dollars to sing her a song. Sue declined. "That was quite a day," Sue recalls, laughing.[441]

Jamie Anderson remembers a bar gig where the owner remarked, as Jamie was doing her sound check, that the sound equipment had better be good because it "cost more than she did." Like many performers, she remembers gigs where no one picked her up at the airport, and community housing where she was expected to sleep in a bed with sandy sheets.[442]

Alcohol and Drugs

As in mainstream music, alcohol and drugs played a part in the women's music scene. Ginny Berson remembers her first National Women's Music Festival in the seventies. She noticed a lot of drinking and drugs (mostly marijuana) with the audience and performers—"That was the norm pretty much then."[443] She saw that at other events, too. Robin Flower played with rock band BeBe K'Roche for a time. They were living the rock life including, "…a lot of drugs and crazy times. We went on the road and played locally. It was like a rock fantasy. We stayed up all night and drank."[444] Lighting designer Cindi Zuby recalls working with one performer for three different concerts and at every one, she was drunk.

Worker Sherry Cmiel remembers an encounter with BeBe K'Roche at the National Women's Music Festival. She laughs about it now but at the time it wasn't so funny. She was asked to go up to the balcony and ask the band there to stop drinking because it was against university rules (where the festival was held). "I was so shy and they were so, well, BeBe K'Roche. I don't think my request was successful. I think a sneer was involved."[445]

Meg Christian was open about her battle with alcoholism. At a 1984 concert in Birmingham she told the audience that 1976 had been her last year of drinking, joking that she'd done a lot of shows and "remembered one or two."[446] She also alluded to "wrapping her car around a tree." In 1983, she told radio station KPFT's *Breakthrough*, "When I hit bottom, it was a few months before we did the *Face the Music* album, in 1977, and thank God there was a women's alcoholism recovery program in Los Angeles…I found out that I…needed help, and this was the place I got it." Holly Near recalls in her memoir, "…in 1976 many of the participants in women's music were using drugs or were alcoholics and/or co-dependents." Margie Adam says her reaction to the sometimes blistering criticism she got was to drink and added, "…some of us used drugs, some retreated and some developed a style of communication of 'stay away.'"[447]

As in mainstream music, there were a variety of views about this topic. The *Lesbian Tide* (May/June 1980) asked Cris Williamson about drug use. "I don't think it's a crime to get high…It is a tool to be used carefully. There is an old tradition in various cultures of dreamers using drugs to help them get places."

Over the years, there were musicians rumored to have a problem with cocaine. One even had it mailed to her when she was on the road. One well-known Midwest concert producer was known to offer musicians drugs after their shows, from pot to cocaine. For a few years there was an area at one of the festivals where it was easy to purchase illegal drugs and many knew how to find the "store." Sometimes drug use depended on your circle of colleagues and friends. Alix Dobkin recalls sharing marijuana but not being offered other drugs.

In the mid-eighties, it was alleged that a distribution company and label was partly funded by drug money. Karen Gotzler and Patricia Reddemann, owners of Midwest Women's Music Distribution and Icebergg Records, were never charged, but Karen's brother, Steven, was convicted of conspiracy to distribute several thousand pounds of marijuana and of cheating the IRS. The indictment states that Steven and his wife approached Karen and asked about giving money to the company, then getting it returned to them in the form of wages. Karen maintains she never knew it was drug money and that Steven and his wife were legitimate employees. Steven spent several years in prison. Karen testified before a grand jury, telling them she thought the investment came from one of his many businesses, including a recording studio and record label.[448]

Defining Our Music and Our Audience; Including Men in Performances

Sometimes the issue was the style of music. Woody Simmons's 1980 album was criticized by some for being too pop. One writer even took exception to the photo on the cover, featuring Woody in a casual sitting pose with her knees open. Teresa Trull's 1980 album, *Let It Be Known*, received similar criticism. With a full band including Jerene Jackson's electric guitar and Julie Homi's keyboards popping through the speakers, it was more polished than her first release. Some loved the presentation while others thought it was not feminist and too slick. Teresa told *HOT WIRE* in March 1988, "…it had three lesbian songs on it—and people still yelled at me all day about how it wasn't 'as woman identified.'" She recognized the difficulty of selling what she did—"…folk definitely sells better in the women's music scene. Now me, I don't *want* to do a folk record."

Some artists came under fire because their lyrics lacked a clear political view. Writer Cindy Rizzo said in *Gay Community News* in 1981: "I have gradually become less and less of a women's music devotee—going to fewer concerts and buying fewer records. This all began when Cris Williamson's *Strange Paradise* was released and was promoted by her first major national tour in years. Musically her songs were of the highest quality…lyrically, they were nowhere. Cris's songs were becoming increasingly devoid of feminist, much less lesbian, content. And her concert raps were worse."

Rizzo continued, explaining how she felt that women's music in general was falling into the same trap. Naomi Littlebear Morena agreed with Rizzo. She told *Out and About* in 1984, "It (women's music) has gotten into what is more commercial, more mainstream, and less feminist oriented."[449] Cris Williamson countered that point of view when she talked with the *Lesbian Tide* (May/June 1980). "I am trying to speak as a poet in the personal sense and have it applied in some general way." Some still saw the positive aspects of women's music. Nancy Vogl told *HOT WIRE* in 1988, "As a group, we might not speak the overt messages of ten years ago across the board, but the music is non-oppressive, non-sexist, and non-male-identified."

For artists like Margie Adam, it wasn't just about the words but also the presentation. "We saw the refining of our art as a political act as itself. There was an expectation that it would be propaganda in the key of C…there were those of us who from the beginning had our eye on the prize—right to the *New York Times* and right to Carnegie Hall—this is how fine our artistry is. *That* was revolutionary."[450]

Teresa Trull never chose songs because they were lesbian although "Rosalie," an upbeat song written by Bonnie Hayes, is clearly a love song to a woman. (It was originally written for Huey Lewis to perform, as was "A Step Away," but he turned both down.) Teresa said to *HOT WIRE* in 1988, "…whenever I've chosen a song—whether it is clearly lesbian or not—it has never been for me, *ever*, a political choice. It has always been an emotional choice."

Kay Gardner expressed her disappointment at what she perceived was a watered-down presentation in some women's music. "Women's music is extremely diverse, and yet we still go for the commercial appeal—just like the boys do."[451] She cites Motown as an example of trailblazing, "….(they) didn't compromise their art to please the current music scene. They didn't assimilate. They offered something new, stuck with it, and now everyone is imitating them."[452]

Similar thinking fueled the view that even music without lyrics could be women's music. Margie Adam was dismayed when she first played her instrumentals in concert. "The audience would take that as a toilet break. Women's music was specifically defined as something with lyrics. Very few of us were also instrumentalists."[453] In 1980, after releasing the all-instrumental *Naked Keys*, she was approached by the Windham Hill label. The New Age genre that started in the eighties was led by this influential label but at the time, they were a small folk label. They were intrigued by Margie's instrumentals and asked her to sign with them. She decided to stay in women's music. Margie didn't consider herself a New Age artist but her work was like that of pianist George Winston, a popular artist on Windham Hill. Barbara Higbie also recorded for them.

Meg Christian had this view about instrumental work: "(Women's music is) music that comes out of a consciousness of who I am as a woman in this world. That can be an instrumental piece. The difference is the intent."[454] Toni Armstrong Jr. adds, "Even if there's not one word spoken in the performance set, there are many ways performers can cooperate and put forth effort to contribute to the bigger picture of women's music."[455] She notes that could include using women musicians, engineers, and more whenever possible. It's also important what the artist says between songs: "Robin Flower usually makes a point of somehow including the lesbian aspect in her raps, and Adrienne Torf always seems to find an appropriate way to bring it up from the stage—even though her music is totally instrumental."[456]

Trumpet player Ellen Seeling acknowledges the importance of lyrics and believes instrumental music can also have a positive impact, "…an audience of feminists can get a real charge out of listening to a woman play her ass off… To me, the greatest turn-on is seeing a woman handle her instrument and the performance situation with ease and assurance…communicating irrefutably that women artists are as strong, skilled, and creative as any male counterpart."[457] Performance partner Jean Fineberg adds, "Since our band DEUCE is instrumental, it might be a bit of a stretch for a political movement to embrace. But we feel that just the existence of women playing non-traditional instruments in a jazz setting is its own political statement."[458]

Kay Gardner thought the music itself could be woman-identified. She told HOT WIRE in March 1986, "…just as women need a new language to express ourselves, so do women musicians…we need a new musical language." She went on to express her anger at using a musical lexicon invented only three hundred years ago by the Roman Catholic Church. "Thank goodness for the influx of Asian and African peoples into our country, or our music would be totally boring." Kay points out that European-based music only uses sixty-five scales while in South India, there are thousands. Her research revealed women-identified scales from two cultures, Greek and Hindu. "These scales were invented by women and speak to women and to men who aren't afraid of their female sensibilities. This is probably why so many say that my music is evocative, haunting, etc. An ancient memory has been stirred just by listening to these women's scales."[459] Dulcimer player Ruth Barrett agrees with this view. "(There are) certain modes and scales that were outlawed in certain times of history. The dulcimer is a modal instrument…Kay told me there were certain modes outlawed because they were considered too female…naming it as too female, well I'm going to play in those tunings."[460] Mary Watkins agrees that women's music does not have to have lyrics and that a modal structure could identify it.[461]

The characteristics that define women's music also depended on performance and communication. Mary Watkins comments, "…the approach to performance can be and often is very different in men and women."[462] Jeanette Muzima, a member of Latin jazz band Bougainvillea, echoed that. She told Sojourner in 1983, "I can feel the difference, and I can hear the difference…I don't feel comfortable playing with men. There's no communication." Linda Tillery had a different opinion about performance and sometimes had men in her band, "I don't think that women play an F-major-flat-five any better than anybody else."[463] Drummer

Michaelle Goerlitz enjoys playing and doesn't feel a difference, "...music is something men and women can do well together."[464]

Whomever they performed with in the eighties, female musicians were seen more and more in mainstream music. Big band Maiden Voyage was on the *Tonight Show*, Cris Williamson toured with Jackson Browne, Holly Near appeared on *Sesame Street*, and Teresa Trull sang with Bonnie Hayes's band when they toured with Huey Lewis and the News. Some fans celebrated this increased visibility while others believed performers were selling out. At the same time rumors abounded about mainstream musicians who might be lesbian but weren't out. Melissa Etheridge, who made her major label debut in 1988 but remained closeted for several years, finally came out in 1993 at an inaugural ball for Bill Clinton. The Indigo Girls also had a lot of lesbian fans but didn't come out until later. Amy Ray first fell in love with a woman in the eighties. She discovered Cris Williamson and Ferron early on and while she cites them as influences, she and musical partner Emily Saliers decided not to become a part of the women's music scene. They preferred what they called a more diverse network. Amy remembers, "We spent most of our time playing in clubs that we would consider to be like the post punk clubs...what we were looking for was the most diverse scene as possible."[465]

Recognition from the mainstream of artists in women's music was slow. Some press praised individual performers but wrote negatively of women's music. In 1980 the *NY Daily News* talked about Deidre McCalla: "...although she's definitely a feminist, records for a label which was launched to give women musicians a voice, and has been active in women's music events, what she plays is by no means just gender philosophy with a beat." That was one of the huge misconceptions about women's music. Deidre told *HOT WIRE* in March 1986, "Because of the stereotype that has been imposed on women's music, people avoid it based on what they think it is. For the most part they go, 'Well the quality isn't very good, the production isn't very good, and it's just songs about hating men.' I really have to strain to find one album out of the hundreds that bothers to write songs about hating men. It's the male perception."

Still, there were glimmers of hope that the mainstream music industry was coming around—this recognition was important because it meant more people would hear about women's music. One way this was illustrated was through awards. In 1985, Deidre McCalla was nominated in two categories for the New York Music Awards; other nominees included Cyndi Lauper and Whitney Houston. Teresa Trull won for Best Producer. *Frets*, a popular magazine for acoustic music fans, voted Robin Flower "Best New Artist." Sweet Honey in the Rock received a Grammy for their participation in an album honoring Woody Guthrie and Lead Belly. Over the years many women's music artists were nominated and some won Bay Area Music Awards—these high-profile awards included mainstream artists Neil Young and the Grateful Dead as finalists.

Some outside of women's music were anxious to learn about us. Arts activist Amy Horowitz fondly recalls the time that Pete and Toshi Seeger came to Sisterfire, a women's music festival that she helped produce, because they wanted to learn. She recalled it was "...probably one of the most powerful days of my life...to sit with him to see Sisterfire through his eyes. He was larger than life for me."[466]

Dianne Davidson came from mainstream music. She had these views: "I want to take women's music back to the mainstream. I'm happy about who I am...I want (audiences) to listen with open hearts...I hope I can sell some records and bring financial resources to other women musicians."[467]

Alix Dobkin saw it this way: "I always visualized my future within the lesbian/feminist community, and had no interest in using women's music as a stepping stone to a more mainstream career...I had (and have) nothing against that road and think it's a valid function of our culture, but I did (and do) have something against a performer taking away from her audience and not giving back a perspective that they couldn't get from many other places."[468] Kay Gardner saw the issue in this manner, "We in women's music have been so successful with our cross-over and outreach that we've been assimilated into mainstream...So long as we don't compromise who we are in the process, there's nothing necessarily wrong with the move; we are doing important work, *and* we are beginning to survive economically.[469] Rhiannon, a member of the jazz ensemble Alive!, went on to perform with Voicestra, a mixed-gender group led by Bobby McFerrin. She found that her time in women's music was a tremendous benefit. "I would not be doing what I am doing now had it not been for the women's movement and for women's music."[470]

While performers like Rhiannon continued to honor women's music after they joined the mainstream, there were some who used the women's music circuit as just another way to get work. Publisher/editor Toni Armstrong Jr. says, "Considering the women's music circuit as 'just one more set of gigs' is an insult and a rip-off to all of us who work countless hours to create a space *where lesbian and feminist content can exist.*"[471] Jamie Anderson remembers a meeting of women at a Folk Alliance conference in the nineties where the straight performers complained about not getting booked at women's music festivals. Folksinger and labor activist Anne Feeney, who's straight, firmly told them, "Lesbians have so little space, let them have their festivals."

There was a worry that "lesbian" was heard less from the stage. Lesbians rejoiced after Holly Near released *Imagine My Surprise* in 1978 and came out as a lesbian. Later, when it was rumored that she was seeing a man, some fans felt defeated. In 1979 when she donated money from her concerts to the anti-nuke movement and spoke about the issue on stage, some lesbians saw that as further proof that she had abandoned them. In the *Lesbian Tide* (September/October 1979) she countered, "I am not in any way at all leaving the women's and lesbian movement. But if we don't stop this thing (nuclear industry) there won't be anyone around to do women's music..." Sandra Washington remembers hearing her perform around this time at a National Women's Music Festival. "She basically did performance art, singing from her diary...she basically said, 'How dare you question my ability to love women if I love a man?'...she was so classy... we all got schooled."[472]

While Teresa Trull loved her lesbian fans, she enjoyed playing for diverse audiences: "Some of the most rewarding experiences we have are when people who have to be there (janitors, waitresses, and sound technicians) come up to us and say, 'Hey that was a really great show!' I know we change people's ideas. We've been told that before the show, these people thought that it would be 'nothing' because it was 'just' women. Next time they're around all women their attitudes will be more positive. It may seem like a small accomplishment, but these things have a way of growing."[473]

In an interview with an Oakland, CA paper, Robin Flower stated she was a musician first and a lesbian second. She received angry responses because that didn't sit well with some fans of women's music. In a September 1989 interview with *HOT WIRE*, Cris Williamson said: "I've worked with audiences for years to get them to not shout at me, to not jump up in the middle and seize the energy... The things people have yelled—your jaw just drops." Audiences are important to her but that's not the only reason she is a musician. "I please me first. I write for me, to feel better, to express myself, to make something pretty. And it goes out like a child, it toddles into the world. And then people say, 'Well, I don't know why it's dressed like that.'"

Some musicians believed that if you weren't specific about lesbian relationships, people would assume you were straight, making you less of an advocate for lesbians. Alix Dobkin has always been out in her songs and presentation. "If you don't write specifically you'll be swept away in the mass belief that every romance is boy/girl and unless you're really clear, you're contributing to it. I can't do that."[474]

In a 1989 interview with *HOT WIRE*, Cris Williamson maintained that "... my music is not gender music...To me, I don't care *who* you love in this world— it's *that* you love." In that same interview, she surmised no one really knew if she was a lesbian. A flurry of responses from fans caused her to clarify with a letter in the next edition. She explained that she has always been private about her personal life and that her response was a kneejerk reaction. "It was a puzzle to me after fifteen years of singing to lesbians, defending lesbians, and being a lesbian that I found myself responding so defensively." She ended her letter with, "...I am a lesbian and I remain proud."[475]

Toni Armstrong Jr. offers that "Woman-identified is not synonymous with 'lesbian,' but women should be important in some way in the artist's act..."[476] There are many songs about women who are not lesbians, including "Lodestar," Cris Williamson's homage to Judy Collins, and Meg Christian's "Song to My Mama."

Although most in women's music were lesbian, the importance of heterosexual women can't be overlooked. Musician/festival organizer Kristen Lems is straight. In the early part of her career, so was Ronnie Gilbert. Musician Ruth Barrett cited two straight feminist musicians as influences—folksingers Frankie Armstrong and Peggy Seeger. (Peggy later partnered with a woman.) While Armstrong and Seeger were not known well in women's music circles, other women covered their songs. Willie Tyson's version of Seeger's engineer song was so popular, audiences thought Tyson had written it. While Holly Near had a relationship with a woman, she also had a long-term relationship with a man. She told the *Advocate* in 2013: "When I was with a man, I did not think of myself as straight or bisexual. I thought of myself as woman-identified and monogamous...I find words to be very tricky...But regardless, I have been very much a part of the lesbian community since the early seventies. I can't imagine myself without the lesbian community."

The Washington Sisters offered a show that was the same, no matter the type of audience. Sandra commented, "The fact of our sexual orientation is not the prime focus of our lives or our music. We don't always 'come out' at gigs, but we do always sing the same material...I'm not much of a romantic-love songwriter, so singing pronoun-specific love songs isn't usually an issue."[477]

Some audience members needed women's music performers to be out because they wanted a role model. Until the nineties there were few out artists in the mainstream. Many celebrated when the Indigo Girls came out. Emily Saliers told *HOT WIRE* in September 1991, "My only problem with the issue is when it becomes a focus—when you start thinking about k. d. lang, for example, and you don't think about her music, you think about her sexuality."

Some performers embraced the term "feminist" while others preferred something else. Bernice Johnson Reagon, in a 1989 interview with *HOT WIRE*, stated: "I am a radical Black woman living in these times, and therefore a part of the overall movement of women organizing to redefine the space we have to live in. Many of these women—but not all—call themselves 'feminist.' As far as I'm concerned, you have to be a radical woman...I don't see 'feminism' necessarily, as the term that's big enough to cover all of the radical women I see..."

Ginni Clemmens sometimes came under fire for singing songs written by men, like "Let the Woman in You Shine Through," by Peter Alsop. "I think it's possible for a man to be a feminist. I'm into coalition and building bridges. Growth is pointless if it just puts you into another closet."[478]

Ronnie Gilbert wondered about singing with men: "...were Holly's songs 'women's music' when they were sung by me and three men (the Weavers)? I'd hate to think that working with men takes me and the songs I sing out of the realm of women's music, but I have heard arguments from some quarters that would support that idea. Personally, I think we can really divert ourselves out of business with that kind of hair splitting and I'd rather not do it."[479]

She, too, says men can be feminists, saying that Si Kahn's song "Woman to Woman" is one she wishes she'd written. He was also the co-collaborator for her one-woman play about Mother Jones.

Toshi Reagon got some flak for performing songs written by men. "If you find a good song by a man, you make it your song and put it in a positive way. If I like a good R&B song, by the Temptations for example, why should I deny my culture?"[480]

Casse Culver formed bands that included women only, but she also had a band with three men. She started a Boston-area show with three solo songs, then brought the band on. A small group of women left. It didn't dampen

Casse's performance and she played her heart out for the still-packed house. The protesters returned and complained to Casse about the men in the band. She angrily responded, "You can buy anybody's records you want. You can go to anybody's concerts you want. You don't have to come to mine. That's your choice. But I'm not going to change what I believe I need to do for myself and my audience just because you're upset."[481] It was at a point in her career where she felt differently about men. "I decided to add men to my band because I wasn't angry at men anymore...So, I moved from anger to forgiveness to love. When I did that, when I opened myself up to that, I found that men had a lot to offer me, in terms of a different vantage point, a different view. I was strong enough now where they couldn't control me."[482]

While most women's music recordings featured only women's voices, The Washington Sisters included male backup singers on their album *Understated*. Sandra commented, "(We) are not forgetting who the majority of our audience is. The material we perform is meant to be felt and understood by all people who can accept diversity and welcome coalition building. It was especially important to have male voices heard on "Say No!," a song about apartheid in South Africa and the United States."[483] There was such a strong opinion about male vocals in women's music in general that the Michigan Festival even prohibited women from playing taped music that featured male vocals anywhere on the land, even at their campsites.

Occasionally, male musicians appeared in concert with women's music artists, although not at festivals until much later. National allowed it on a limited basis for their SheRocks! series. Some audiences thought that having men on stage was acceptable because they took a supporting role to the women who were in charge. Linda Tillery told *Sojourner*, "...there just aren't a lot of women around who are capable of doing the kind of music I do."[484] She went on to praise bassist Joy Julks but noted that if Joy wasn't available and the next best bass player was male, she wouldn't hesitate to hire him. Holly Near regularly performed with male pianists—in the early days, with Jeff Langley and later, with John Bucchino. She was viewed differently by most, perhaps because she came from the anti-war movement and had often performed with men. Still, some audience members grumbled about men on stage, and at rare shows, yelled out comments or threw things at the performers.

Some artists focused on shows where most of the audience was lesbian. Others played occasionally for these audiences, often at women's festivals, but played for others too. Nancy Vogl performed for a variety of crowds. With out-lesbian songs, she saw herself as a bridge. "It pleases me to play straight folk clubs and have men and straight couples hear things that they wouldn't otherwise hear. I will always support women-only concerts and events, and I am who I am because of the women's movement. But I also am who I am because of the labor, civil rights, and anti-war movements..."[485] She also saw no issue with changing a little of her presentation, especially with important political issues, "If I wear a little makeup and put on a dress to maximize my effectiveness at a church group to raise money for radical political work, that's not a compromise of my integrity, that's a reordering of my priorities."[486]

Holly Near had also always played for all kinds of audiences. A 1976 *Lesbian Tide* article stated, "Near wants her music to reach all different kinds of people and so she might perform at a nightclub, an all-women's concert, a United Farm Workers' rally, or even a men's consciousness raising group 'If they thought they could learn something from it.'" In 1987, she put out *Don't Hold Back*, a collection of love songs on Chameleon, a label not associated with women's music, in an attempt to reach a mainstream audience. Side players included Bonnie Raitt and Kenny Loggins. Of that experience Holly said: "It ended up being…the wrong use of money and energy and time, but we had to try it, we had to find out whether it made sense. And I realized at the end of it that I'm really not the kind of person that wanted to go out and do the kind of compromising that's required in order to be in the mainstream, and that I worked much better being a social change activist artist and staying in the alternative communities."[487]

Homophobia and an Anti-Woman Backlash

Some artists lost jobs because they were associated with women's music or were thought to be lesbian. Drummer Phyllis Free recalls a couple of times in the seventies when the trio she played with, Jan Riley and Friends, lost hotel club gigs. "We were notified by our agent that the hotel had canceled the second (upcoming) week of our contract…(it) came the day after the three of us had gone out dancing at a local gay bar after our gig the night before. We were never given a (real) reason for the cancellation."[488] Free also remembers an instance where they could work something out with the club. "We were informed by our (very supportive) agent Doug West, that the manager of a club on Hilton Head Island, where we had developed quite a following, had canceled our upcoming engagement as a result of complaints by the (female) servers that they were uncomfortable with the fact that we were drawing a 'lesbian crowd'"[489] They drew an audience that included softball teams and tennis pros because it's a resort area, but not all were lesbian. The venue manager even praised them for bringing in a bigger crowd. "With the support of our agent, I followed up the news of our cancellation by requesting a one-on-one meeting with the manager, who then admitted that she had gone against her conscience…our contract was reinstated and we were hired back again."[490]

Jamie Anderson lost a gig at a straight bar when the owner told her his straight patrons would be huddled in the bathroom in fear if she came and sang lesbian songs. A folk organization in Washington State refused to hire her because there would be mothers and children in the audience. A member of their group angrily told them that she was a lesbian mother and she wanted to hear Jamie. They still refused to book her, even as an opening act. Another folk group in Connecticut only booked her after a lesbian in the community made a tremendous effort to promote her. They reluctantly scheduled the concert and she played for a sold-out crowd. Even after repeated attempts to follow up this successful show, they would not book her again, perhaps because the lesbian who advocated for her the first time had moved out of town.

Carol Kraemer, of Yer Girlfriend, worried how safe the band was when they went on tour. "I had huge internalized homophobia and fear, like will we get kicked out of this Cracker Barrel because people are being too out? Do we look too dykey? For me, it was part of my own personal process of figuring that out. I had a lot of fear in those moments of thinking whether it would be OK for…us fairly dykey looking women to go in."[491]

Women performers also had trouble in other areas—in the nineties the a cappella group The Rhythm Method contracted with a cassette duplication firm, Just Like the Master. After the band invested time in negotiations, the company refused to work with them because they were lesbians. Folk duo Justina and Joyce sold over 10,000 recordings and played in a variety of women's music and straight folk venues and still they could not get a booking agent or signed by a folk label because they were an out lesbian couple.

In 1990 Ladyslipper ran into trouble when the back of their catalog featured the cover of Ruth Barrett's recording *Parthenogenesis*. Album artwork by Sudie Rakusin included a mermaid with bare breasts. Ladyslipper had already invested hours of time with design

Ladyslipper catalog 1991, "tits."
Used with permission, Laurie Fuchs and Ladyslipper Inc. Artwork on Ruth Barrett's album cover ©1989 Sudie Rakusin.

Ladyslipper catalog 1991, "no tits."
Used with permission, Laurie Fuchs and Ladyslipper Inc. Artwork on Ruth Barrett's album cover © 1989 Sudie Rakusin

and printed over 10,000 copies of the catalog when they realized that some post offices wouldn't deliver it. The catalog artwork was changed so the nipples wouldn't show and they continued to print. Laurie Fuchs of Ladyslipper laughs when she recalls that they had different skids of catalogs, some labeled "tits" and some labeled "no tits."[492] Fortunately, the unchanged catalogs could still be handed out at events although a few were still sent through the mail when they ran out of the "safe" ones. Those had "pasties" over the nipples with a sticker that exclaimed "New Releases!"

There were times when it was downright dangerous to be in women's music. More than once Memphis LGBTQ radio DJ Pat Jones remembers slipping out the back door of the station after one of her shows because of a threat of violence. Jamie Anderson recalls protesters at an early LGBTQ pride celebration in Boise, Idaho where she was to perform. One was grilling hot dogs on the bed of a pickup truck. A big sign proclaimed he was "grilling weenies for Christ." A rack in his truck held guns.

Sue Fink remembers an eighties era pride march and rally in Columbus, Ohio. She was in a convertible at the head of the parade of several thousand. As she smiled and did her "best Elizabethan wave" a preacher ran up to her and started screaming that she was "...an aberration and how sick I was...I tried to ignore him and just kind of laughed and he added 'And your hair looks terrible'—that's the one that got me—he knew he got me when he saw that look on my face, then went off to bother someone else."[493] She thought the streets would be crowded with people watching the parade but they were strangely empty. Instead, the crowd was waiting at the capitol steps where the rally would be held. The parade was greeted with a roar. "They had bused in thousands of right-wingers chanting something like 'two-four-six-eight Jesus will make you straight.'"[494] Fortunately, there were many supporters, too, probably as many as the right-wingers, and about five police officers. They drove past the yelling mob. Organizers pointed to the empty stage and told Sue to start entertaining. "I thought, Oh my God, someone's going to kill me. I walked out on stage and said something like 'one-three-five-nine, gay people are mighty fine.'"[495] Instead of the two groups facing off, they faced the stage and the show went on with no one getting hurt.

Some straight feminists had difficulty with lesbians. Deidre McCalla remembers an early NOW conference where the fighting between the two sides took so long that Meg Christian's concert couldn't happen at the scheduled time and place. Instead, she sang on the steps of the convention center.

Canadian performer Heather Bishop had success in both straight and women's music arenas. Sue Fink commented, "I think someone like Heather Bishop is such a good example of how it's perfectly okay; she does children's shows and she does women's/lesbian shows. And she never compromises who she is."[496]

Even though folk musicians sing about many issues, they could be uncomfortable about feminist and lesbian issues. The Folk Alliance, an international organization for folk music, has a huge annual conference. Wanting to connect with other LGBTQ folks, Jamie Anderson organized a support group at an early conference. A small number showed up, some of them straight supporters, while a notable group of lesbian performers avoided it, one confiding that she was afraid she'd lose gigs if she came. The conference organizers were supportive of this group and it continued for several years, gaining in numbers. Most attending were lesbians.

Audiences could have a tough time, also. Many of them took a tremendous risk to be at shows and festivals. To be seen could mean coming out as a lesbian and losing jobs, children, and homes. Some were careful about being photographed. The Michigan Festival had this in its 1979 program: "If you don't wish to be photographed…'Don't Steal My Image' buttons will be available at WWTMC's table under the merchant's tent to serve as negative releases."

In 1979, Canadian women headed to the Michigan Festival had trouble crossing the border at Port Huron. They were stopped by US border officials, questioned about sexual activities, and denied entry. They found another crossing and entered the US. At the second border crossing they had a map on which they'd circled a campground. Instead of telling this second group of border guards that they were attending the Michigan Festival, they told them they were going camping. One of them even shaved her legs to appear "more heterosexual."[497] Because of festival workshops, letters to the government, and other activism, harassment stopped and for future festivals, Canadians weren't usually hassled at the border.

It wasn't just straight people who could cause problems. Gay men weren't always supportive, either. Jamie Anderson recalls shows produced by LGBTQ groups where only the women came. At one show, men helped with set up, then left before the music began. Rock musician Flash Silvermoon recalled a negative experience at a New York City Pride event for a huge crowd in the early seventies. Her band was whisked away to a nearby apartment along with Bette Midler who was also performing. Their only contact with the event was through closed circuit TV. "…the organizer disappeared without telling us when we'd be on. I knew Bette would be on in maybe a half hour. I told the women in my band to follow me. When Bette walks out, we'll walk behind her and jump into the next car. We started to pull away and one of the guys with walkie-talkies said 'Wait, they aren't supposed to go anywhere.'"[498] They arrived at the event where things weren't going well—an unpopular boy band had played, and then organizers had thrown a transgender woman off the stage. One of the organizers wanted to throw Flash and her band offstage as well—"I grabbed the mic and said, 'If you think I'm going to let a skinny little fag push me around you're crazy.'"[499] Her band did their scheduled two songs.

For artists such as Robin Flower, there was another set of issues. She toured with her all-women's band in the late seventies and early eighties, and while she loved playing in women's music venues, she didn't have to convince them that women could really play. Straight venues were sometimes more of a sell. "The men who ran the folk clubs were probably threatened by the women coming up who were different than all the other women they'd ever met before…(there was a) clash of cultures with the women…wanting to be treated as they were in the women's movement."[500] She played as many straight venues as she could "…

because that's where the real work happens. Women's music venues were great, too, but we were preaching to the choir."[501] One time she called a folk venue in North Carolina and was told to call the women's music producer. The folk venue wouldn't even consider her.

She had an especially tough time at the Pickin' Parlor in Johnson City, Tennessee: "The club guy meets us at the door and says...'we'll put you up in a motel but we don't want you to play.' I said here's our contract and we're playing. The way he treated us was incredible. They put us in a dressing room with a lot of people coming in and out. It was a gig from hell and I know it was because we were lesbians."[502]

Robin adds that there are straight venues that have always been welcoming to many kinds of audiences. She's especially fond of the Freight and Salvage in Berkeley, California, because, "They really did the bridging between the two (folk and women's music)."[503]

Musician Nancy Vogl offers this view of women's empowerment and working with men:

"We alienated a lot of men because it was important (laughs). We *had* to. It's not blaming, it's the stage of the movement. When you've always put yourself second and finally you put yourself first, it seems rude but if you don't do that it doesn't make this seismic shift that changes the critical mass."[504]

Women were so angry that some decided to be separatists and shut out men all together, even if it meant missing a concert at a straight venue by a strong women's band like Robin Flower's. It was important to Robin that she have an all-women's band and it didn't matter to her if they were lesbians. At one point, it was her and three straight women. "That kind of stuff never mattered to any one of us. I just wanted a strong impression of women playing together."[505] Folk venues sometimes called them an 'all-girl band' and that made her bristle. "I just wanted to be a band...I had a responsibility that I wanted to show that women can really play, be a tight band and make an impression in the world and I know we did."[506]

Selling Recordings

It became harder to sell recordings of women's music in the eighties. Stores and distributors couldn't carry everything that was released. There were many records and too little shelf space. Sometimes stores and distributors made decisions based on the quality of the recording. If it looked and sounded like a homemade recording, it was rejected. If it was on Olivia, Redwood or from a musician with a strong local following, they carried it. Women's music was sold in big chains like Tower Records, but it received less space in the late eighties when they added CDs and videos to stores already packed with LPs, tapes, T-shirts, and posters. Stores like Tower also had a challenging time deciding where to put women's music. Often it was all thrown into a dusty bin in the back labeled "Folk," whether it was comic Robin Tyler or techno-pop artist Sue Fink.

The people who ran the stores didn't always know women's music. If someone asked for Holly Near, it might be met with, "Who?" Women's and LGBTQ bookstores knew more about the music they sold and while some did well with the recordings, they were a sideline.

The Death of Women's Music?

In the eighties, the refrain started that women's music was dead. Judy Dlugacz told *Bitch* magazine, "I hear 'women's music is dead' comes up to me a lot. I think, You wouldn't say that to someone who is Black or Jewish…but with women and lesbians there's not even a thought process yet that there's something wrong with that constant questioning of what I'm doing and the value of what I'm doing."

Olivia proved that women's music was still alive, with 1988 concerts celebrating their fifteenth anniversary. Shows included Cris Williamson, Tret Fure, Deidre McCalla, Lucie Blue Tremblay, Dianne Davidson, and more. They performed in several cities including a return engagement to Carnegie Hall. It was just a couple years later, though, that things indeed began to change for them. In 1990, they offered their first lesbian cruise, with entertainment from Teresa Trull, Dianne Davidson, Cris Williamson, and Deidre McCalla. Their last recording was released in 1993.

Audience numbers for women's music declined in the late eighties. Deidre McCalla commented to *HOT WIRE* in 1986, "The days of 'it's women's music so I'll automatically go and check it out' are long gone." Some artists continued to tour and record but not as many as previous years. Some performers, such as Sweet Honey in the Rock, had a strong following outside of women's music so they weathered the storm. The next decade would hold many changes for women's music.

CHAPTER SIX

•◦✦◦•

BUILDING A NETWORK FROM THE GROUND UP

Technicians, Media, and More

Performers were the most visible part of women's music. Also vital to the movement was a whole network of sound and light technicians, women in print media, radio DJs, concert producers, distributors, and more. Some of these women learned their jobs while in women's music, then went on to a career in that field. Most worked for little or no money but the rewards were many. An article about producer/booker Tam Martin in *HOT WIRE* (July 1987) reported, "The rewards of working in women's music can't be measured, but when Tam has received letters saying, 'Thank you, you changed my life,' or 'Keep up the good work'; you do make a difference. She says there is no feeling like it."

What follows is a selection of some of the women who worked in the many areas of women's music.[507]

Sound and Light Technicians

At first, the technical aspects of women's music shows were rudimentary. Maxine Feldman remembers early shows where there were no microphones. "They'd say well, you know, you sing loud enough."[508] At one show, she was given two megaphones, one for her voice and one for her guitar. She recalls, "I looked at them and I said, 'What the hell is this?' And they said, 'Well, we don't want to learn the—you know, that's the men's equipment. That's the men's stuff.'"[509] She joked that if they didn't want to use "Mic," they could call it "Michelle."

Sue Fink remembers at least one of her concerts where someone hooked up their home stereo and it didn't have enough power to amplify the music without distortion. Sometimes the lighting was a lamp brought from someone's home. Stage crew member Retts Scauzillo remembers an early Campfest after they'd finished a full light and sound setup on the first day of the event. The festival director asked if they needed all that equipment and Retts advised her, "You come back to me on Saturday and tell me if you think we need it. After the first night, she agreed we needed all that. A lot of people needed convincing."[510] We learned quickly how important good sound and lights were. Women were recruited for sound positions simply because they were available and wanted to learn. Some had related skills—sound engineer Shelly Jennings is a licensed electrician, and lighting designer Cindi Zuby was earning her MFA in Scenography (lighting, theater design, and costuming). Mountain Moving Coffeehouse made it a priority to teach women technical skills as did other women's performance venues and production companies.

Margot McFedries was an art history graduate when she attended an early women's music concert and decided she could do better sound than what she heard. She bought a sound system at Radio Shack and taught herself. Later she worked with a respected San Francisco sound company, furthering her education. She worked sound boards at women's events all over the United States, including the National and Michigan Womyn's Music Festivals, the Women on Wheels Tour, the International Women's Year conference in Houston in 1977, and for touring Broadway musicals. She was the first female sound engineer to be accepted into the stagehands union in San Francisco. Margie Adam recalls, "She was the definition of unflappable—even at 7:45 p.m. with the doors about to open and a buzz in the speakers, she could track it down and make it go away."[511]

Shelly Jennings and Myrna Johnston, 1990 Michigan Festival.
Photo by Toni Armstrong Jr.

In 1975 Myrna Johnston helped a friend with sound for a Jade and Sarsaparilla show. She remembers, "I found it totally exciting, and soon became their clueless sound engineer—seat of the pants school of sound."[512] Later that year she did sound at the Boston Women's Music Festival. Two other women, Marilyn Ries and Carol Bellin, joined her.[513] For five years after that, she freelanced, then joined Hanley Audio. With them, she worked many shows, from the Philadelphia Folk Festival to Boston's Berklee Performance Center where she mixed sound for Smokey Robinson, Gladys Knight, and many others. In the eighties, she worked with Allegra Productions, Boston's women's music production company. Not only did Allegra provide Myrna with work, they also created an atmosphere where other women technicians could learn their skills. That group of women, including Myrna, worked at the first NEWMR in 1981 and that led to positions at many other women's events—the Michigan Womyn's Music Festival, Sisterfire, National Women's Music Festival, and more. Myrna started her own sound company, Myrna Johnston Audio, working in many women's music venues as well as Carnegie Hall and other mainstream venues. Myrna offers, "We set high standards for our productions—the audience and the artists deserve the best."[514] Shelly Jennings and Moira Shea are also a part of her company. Both have been technicians for many years. Shelly is also known for her guitar skills, performing with Ferron and others.

Boden Sandstrom started Woman Sound in 1975 with partner (and musician) Casse Culver. Because she played the French horn, she already had an ear for music. A big music fan, she was especially interested in supporting women and political groups. Based in Washington, DC, she ran sound for many women's music festivals such as Sisterfire, Michigan, West Coast and others. She toured with performers Cris Williamson, Casse Culver, and Lily Tomlin; she also did mainstream events like hotel conferences and university graduation ceremonies. Boden was also the production manager for many events including the LGBTQ national marches on Washington.

Kris Koth learned sound on her own and from "the boys." She owned a little PA and ran sound for cabaret performer Suede, among others. Later, she worked with Boden Sandstrom. As a musician, she had a unique perspective, playing in bands with Lifeline, Toshi Reagon and others. She was part of a group of women who worked several different women's festivals. Kris loved the sisterhood and comraderie between crew members. In later years she retired from all her sound tech jobs except for the Virginia Women's Music Festival where, until 2017, she ran sound on a system she designed.

Kaia Skaggs is a musician and sound technician who's worked in many venues including the National Women's Music Festival and The Ark in Ann Arbor, Michigan. She recalls a story that illustrates the difficulties of women engineers. She worked with a male engineer at a live show who initially told her he didn't think that women engineers were treated differently. The show went well, with Kaia running sound inside and him, in a nearby truck, operating the recording equipment. After the show, he came inside to talk with her. Several people complimented the sound, addressing their comments to him even though he wasn't even in the room during the show. Each time, the male engineer would correct them. Kaia recalls, "The reactions ranged from silent stares of incredulity or disbelief to 'oh, well…' to 'Really? Good job anyway (to him!)', etc…After a parade of these people, when we were finally packing up and getting ready to leave, he turned to me and said, 'I just want you to know that now I get it.' We still work together and he said he's never forgotten how eye-opening it was for him to have his male privilege laid bare like that."[515]

Cindi Zuby did lights at productions in Lincoln, Nebraska in the seventies and eighties. Because she was earning a theater degree, she already had gained some experience. The rest she learned on the job. She recalls, "When there were (contract) riders stating that only women could be on the crew, smaller venues had a difficult time in staffing. I was pretty much it in Lincoln."[516] It was difficult if the show was held at a union venue because she was not a member and was viewed as a scab. There were other challenges, some of them technical, like the time she had to search for a turquoise gel (a cover that adds color to a light), so that Holly Near's red hair wouldn't turn a horrible shade of purple. At a Sweet Honey in the Rock show, a circuit blew and all the lights went dark except for one spotlight. She could only catch four of the performers at a time. They never missed a beat as she lit them as best she could. She fondly remembers the artists at shows where things went right—Cathy Winter and Betsy Rose, Adrienne Torf, and Alive!

Leni Schwendinger is a lighting designer who worked extensively with Margie Adam, as well as at various festivals including National, Michigan, and West Coast. She currently works with an urban design group. Margie recalls, "She is brilliant—willing to work with the constraints of any situation—from desk lamps in church basements to the most sophisticated light boards in major venues."[517]

Karen "K.C." Cohen's friend Lauren Heller told her about the Michigan Festival and encouraged her to go in 1986. Both had taken lighting classes in college and it didn't hurt that K. C. was a huge music fan. On the plane to the festival, K.C. met Linda O'Brien, lighting designer for the festival. Linda told her they needed a stage electrician—someone who ensured that everything on stage is running well. So, when K.C. arrived, that was the job she took. "I had mostly worked with men so it was so empowering to have women running all the lights, sound, stage, security, etc. I thought the festival was a Woodstock for women. I felt like I was tripping the whole time because of the sensory overload."[518] This experience was so phenomenal, she went on to work at the festival for twenty-nine years, as stage engineer and then, crew chief. In 2003, she took over as lighting designer. K.C. has also worked on the stage crew at Southern, West Coast, Rhythmfest, National, and Campfest. When she isn't working at festivals, she's employed as a lighting designer in the San Francisco Bay area.

In 1980 producer Boo Price toured nationally with musician Margie Adam and a tech crew. They raised money for women politicians at each stop. Local venues provided some support. Boo laughs when she recalls asking for monitors at one venue. Monitors are the speakers you see pointed at the performer so they can hear themselves well. Boo didn't see monitors so she asked about them. Organizers pointed to six women standing at the edge of the stage and was informed that there were the monitors and she could tell them where to go.

Teching at events often included long hours for little or no pay. Festivals, with multiple acts in a variety of genres, could be especially grueling. Crews worked long hours, sometimes sunup to midnight, and didn't usually get to go a nice hotel room at the end. Kris Koth joked, "Sometimes you need to worry about where you're sleeping because your tent is floating away."[519]

Because everyone was learning, inexperienced musicians sometimes had difficulty working with a sound crew. They didn't know what to ask for or how to ask for it. Experienced musicians could be unreasonable, too. Kris dealt with a few who were divas. She reasons that because the world outside didn't treat them well, they could turn into terrors within the confines of women's music. Technicians could also be difficult. Robin Flower remembers a women's music gig somewhere in the east where they were happy to see that the sound board they were using was the same as the one Robin's band used at home. They tried to tell the sound woman what they needed but she didn't take it well and refused to work with them. Robin had to find someone else at the event to run sound for them. She was frustrated but realized, "Things happen…you learn how to be as flexible as you can."[520]

Leslie Ann Jones, 1984.
Photo by Irene Young © 1984.

Women learned how to be recording engineers too. Leslie Ann Jones was a musician who started recording when her band broke up. She trained on the job and got some formal schooling. After touring as mainstream rock band Fanny's live sound engineer, she got a job at ABC Records as a recording engineer. For the first six months, they had her making copies of tapes. Her big break happened when another engineer wasn't available and she stepped in to engineer her first album. In 1979, after she'd logged four years' experience, June Millington asked her to engineer Cris Williamson's *Strange Paradise*. She went on to engineer albums for Ferron, Holly Near, Margie Adam, June Millington, and Meg Christian. Leslie has also worked extensively in mainstream music, with Joan Baez, Herbie Hancock, and others.

Karen Kane got her start in the industry in 1970, managing a recording studio in New York. She then moved to Boston to run another studio. In her off time, she got to know the equipment. When she told her boss she wanted to learn recording, he started her as an apprentice. She moved mics and swept the floor. Gradually she was given more to do. The first album she engineered was one by Joanna Cazden in 1976 or 1977. Joanna wanted a woman and even though Karen had little experience, she jumped right in. Then she got involved with Bright Morning Star, a radical folk group that included four men and two women. As her reputation grew, she worked with other folk performers including Fred Small, and Kay Gardner, Betsy Rose, Suede, and other women's music artists. She was the engineer for a demo recorded by a young Tracy Chapman. It wasn't always easy. Karen remembers sitting behind a studio sound board in the seventies when the engineer for the next project glanced around and asked her where the engineer was. Later, when she was looking for work at Boston studios, she was offered two managing jobs and nothing that involved the technical aspect of the work. So, she took out an ad in a trade paper and went freelance. Karen's also a live sound engineer. For twenty-one years she ran sound at the Acoustic Stage at the Michigan Womyn's Music Festival.

Tret Fure began as a recording engineer in the seventies when she was recording her second album. When she asked questions about the recording process, she came up against a wall of attitude from the engineer. Her response was that she didn't like feeling stupid and informed him that she wanted to learn about recording. The studio owner gave her a book, *Modern Recording Techniques*, which was a bible for engineers in that decade. She returned the next day after reading it and began telling Randy, the engineer, what she had learned. He asked her to be the second

Karen Kane, 1987.
Photo by Toni Armstrong Jr.

engineer. For five years, she made her living as an engineer as she looked for another record deal. She feels fortunate because many musicians must take low-paying jobs in restaurants and offices while between labels but she never had to leave the industry. Still, it wasn't easy—"…women couldn't possibly know what they were doing in the studio…every new client I had, I had to prove myself."[521]

Concert Producers[522]

In the 1987 publication, *Women's Music Plus*, a directory of resources in women's music and culture, they listed over a hundred production companies and coffeehouses, most in the US. Some had their own space, such as Bloomers (Pittsburgh, PA) and Herizon (Binghamton, NY) while most rented space in churches, YMCAs, and performance halls. It could be hard to find a suitable space. Budget was always a consideration and some rental spaces balked at giving space to a show featuring an out lesbian or a concert that only women could attend. Musician Jamie Anderson jokes that if it wasn't for Unitarian Churches and Quaker Meeting Houses, she wouldn't have a career.

Starting in 1975, Artemis Productions was one of the earliest women's music production companies and was responsible for the Boston Women's Music Festival. Organizers included Emily Culpepper, Andrea Gillespie, Betsy York, Jean MacRae, and Linda Barufaldi.[523]

The Women's Music Union, in Columbus, Ohio, also began in 1975 and featured many touring and local artists. For a while, they offered a concert every three months.[524] Cincinnati had Mound of Venus, a group of women who produced shows featuring mostly local talent. Also in Cincinnati, Kate and Company brought in touring acts. With Estelle Riley at the helm, they raised money for these shows with women-only dances.

Lin Daniels started producing shows after attending a consciousness-raising group in 1974. Around that time, she discovered Mother Courage, a feminist restaurant in New York City, and was excited to hear Maxine Feldman there. She produced her first concert at Rockland Community College in Suffern, New York. She recalls, "I started a Gay Alliance, and brought Alix Dobkin, Kay Gardner, and Patches Atom (Lavender Jane) to play for about a dozen lesbians. The college paid for a few, very enthusiastic dykes to listen to Lavender Jane that night."[525] Not long after that, she attended the second National Women's Music Festival where she learned more about producing at a Malvina Reynolds workshop. In addition to concerts, she produced the East Coast Lesbian Festival.

Virginia Giordano started in the seventies and grew with the network, producing shows in New York City in several venues including Town Hall and Carnegie Hall. Concerts featured Holly Near, Sweet Honey in the Rock, Ani DiFranco, and more. She was also a distributor.

Starting in 1981 Christine Pattee produced shows in Connecticut, under the moniker Women's Music for Everyone. For a while she did four concerts a year, at least two of them featuring well-known names such as Holly Near or Cris Williamson, and one that presented a local performer. Sometimes they did two shows in a day, one in the afternoon and one in the evening, filling the hall both times. For the first few years, there was enough of an income that she could donate money to a women's group. Christine was also one of the original group that produced NEWMR.

Brynna Fish was an active member of Oven Productions in Cleveland. Inspired by Cris Williamson and Therese Edell concerts in the early eighties, she first became involved with Oven in 1983, as part of the sound crew. She went on to work in many aspects of women's music including stage managing, sound reinforcement, artist booking, and finally, starting her own production company, Bluefish Productions. That was true of many who were active in women's music—they didn't just produce concerts, they also had a hand in other areas. Houston's Pokey Anderson produced shows with Hazelwitch Productions, was a DJ on KPFT, and for a few years, distributed albums before she opened Inklings Bookstore with Annise Parker. In Iowa City, Laurie Haag organized shows at the University of Iowa, was a musician, and later became involved with the

Iowa Women's Music Festival. Linda Wilson works with Willow Productions in Kansas City, is a radio DJ and in more recent years, produced the National Women's Music Festival. Karen Hester founded a bookstore/performance venue (Sisterspirit) in San Jose in 1983, started two radio shows, and worked for Olivia. Terry Grant ran Goldenrod Distribution and produced concerts in Lansing, Michigan. Tam Martin produced a festival in Washington State for a few years, is a booking agent and at one time, worked for Olivia. She once joked, "The only thing I do besides women's music is sleep!"[526]

Boo Price got her start producing when she was a student at Holyoke College and kept learning as she did more productions. Later, as Margie Adam's manager, she found and mentored women across the country to produce concerts even if they'd never done it before.

Michelle Crone began producing concerts in 1986 when she started Elword Productions in Albany, NY.[527] She brought a young Melissa Etheridge to town in the late eighties when her fee was a mere $200. Starting in 1979 at the Michigan Festival, Michelle also had a hand in twenty-five different women's music festivals and was one of the founders of Rhythmfest.

As Women's Studies, LGBTQ Studies, LGBTQ groups, women's groups, and women's centers opened and gained prominence on college campuses in the seventies and eighties, they brought in women's music artists. Funding was often strong so performers were eager to do these gigs to finance much of a tour. Feminist musicians knew they could count on college gigs in March for Women's History Month, and in October for LGBTQ events. African-American musicians could do well in February because it was Black History Month.

Sometimes, university engagements became interesting because college students didn't always have the experience needed to do a show. Also, personnel changed often as students graduated, so they couldn't always train each other. Flash Silvermoon recalls an early college gig where she asked for a piano. The organizers found one but it wasn't in the building. They wheeled an upright piano across campus and up a flight of stairs. They had to take the hinges off the door to get it in the room. When Flash started to play, one of the hammers hit her in the head. She laughs when she says, "What these women lacked in good sense, they had in bravery."[528]

LGBTQ pride celebrations also featured women's music performers. National marches started in 1979. The 1993 march in Washington, DC, drew a million people and was covered by major media including CNN. Performers included Holly Near, Cris Williamson, Margie Adam, the Washington Sisters, Eartha Kitt, and the Lavender Light Choir. Through the years local celebrations across the country also featured women performers although it was sometimes hard to find them among the drag queens and dance divas.

Mainstream venues featured women's music performers too. Freight and Salvage Coffeehouse in Berkeley, California, has brought in many over the years including Meg Christian, Cris Williamson, Linda Tillery, and Teresa Trull. It's one of Robin Flower's favorite venues. The Ark in Ann Arbor, Michigan has featured Ferron, and Cris Williamson. The Palms Playhouse in Winters, California, has hosted Teresa Trull, Barbara Higbie, and others. McCabes, in

Los Angeles, has brought in many women's music performers, from Vicki Randle to Ferron. In San Francisco, the Great American Hall was the place to go to hear Lucie Blue Tremblay, Linda Tillery, Teresa Trull, and others. For several years the Canal Street Tavern in Dayton, Ohio, featured women's music on Sundays, including Ann Reed, and Jamie Anderson.

Regardless of the type of venue or company, productions all had a varied shelf life. Some producers did one concert and that was it. Some producers offered events for years and a few continue today. It all depended on community support, organization, and energy. Burnout was a big problem as the years progressed.

Radio Shows

Concerts could not happen without promotion. While word of mouth was a strong way to get out the word, women's and LGBTQ radio programs were vital too. Also important were public radio stations like KPFA in Berkeley which featured women's music as part of their regular programming. Almost every major city in the US and some smaller cities had women's music programming, usually on a public radio station.

It was in the early seventies, on Washington, DC's women's radio show *Sophie's Parlor*, that Cris Williamson suggested to Ginny Berson and Meg Christian that they create a women's record label. On the radio show, started in 1972 by students at Georgetown University, the women of *Sophie's Parlor* learned the skills necessary, then trained other women. By 1987, over one hundred women had gone through their extensive training program. Their two-hour show featured public affairs programming in the first half and music in the second. The show ran for many years.

Begun in 1974 by a collective of three women, *Amazon Country*, on WXPN in Philadelphia, is the longest running women's music program still on the air in the US. DJ Debra D'Alessandro got involved in the nineties. A long-time fan of women's music and of the program, she started work with them after they announced on the air that they needed another volunteer. Sue Pierce trained her. In the summer of 2003 *Amazon Country* almost went off the air. After management announced its cancellation, a public outcry, including an online petition and a picket line, forced them to reconsider. Debra was touched by the widespread support the show received, not just from lesbians but from straight people too. A sympathetic station receptionist printed every positive email received from fans to present to management. The collaborative effort was successful and the show stayed on the air. WXPN also has a long running LGBTQ show, Q'Zine, that has featured women's music artists.

Started in 1978, *Fresh Fruit*, on KFAI in Minneapolis-St. Paul, is the longest running LGBTQ radio program. Featuring many women's music artists, they also present public affairs programming.

This Way Out is a syndicated LGBTQ radio show that not only interviews and plays the music of women's music artists but presents international news of interest to the community. Begun in 1988, it is available on more than two hundred stations around the world.

Her Infinite Variety is a long-running women's music program on WORT in Madison, Wisconsin, which began in 1976 or 1977 with Maggie Harth and has been hosted by a number of women over the years including Deb Andersen. She started there in 1977. Later, Deb moved to Lincoln, Nebraska and in 1984 began at the *Wimmin's Show* on KZUM, where she's still a DJ.

Yellow Springs, Ohio, offered several women's music shows in the seventies, including the *Lesbian Leisure Hour* and *Women in Music*, both on community radio station WYSO. Enid Lefton hosted a long-running women's music program on KLCC in Eugene, Oregon. In Tucson, AZ, KXCI broadcast *Broad Perspectives* starting in the nineties.

Inspired by a visit to an early National Women's Music Festival, Sue Goldwomon worked with many feminist and lesbian organizations including *Her Infinite Variety* on WORT. Calling herself a lesbian cultural worker, she was also involved in many other groups including singing in both of Madison's women's choirs. For a brief time, she was a music distributor.

Tara Ayres has a long history with radio. Starting with a gay college radio show in New Haven, Connecticut, she moved to Madison in the eighties where she was a programmer at WORT for thirty-one years, from feminist news show *Her Turn* to music program *Her Infinite Variety*. She held a variety of jobs for these shows—DJ, writer, producer, and engineer. Tara is also a musician and a concert producer.

Lori Lambert was a radio DJ and musician in Massachusetts and Florida. She was a huge fan of mainstream women artists before she discovered women's music. "When I realized that Olivia was an all-female operation, I was all in."[529] In the early nineties, she wanted to interview Ani DiFranco so she asked her station engineer for use of their digital recorder. His response? "'For Ani DiFranco? Are you kidding? If it was Annie Lennox, sure.'"[530] Lori rented a recorder and did the interview anyway.

Because she was involved in producing women's music shows through Willow Productions in Kansas City, Linda Wilson was contacted in 1989 by community radio station KKFI and asked about doing a women's radio show. She started *Womansong*. The first LP she played on the air was the *Michigan Womyn's Music Festival Tenth Anniversary* album. Over the years, she's moved to cassettes, then to CDs and finally to songs from the station's database, entered from the CDs she has stashed all over her house. "I have entered over five thousand songs in the computer at KKFI. Even with this number of songs in the computer, music by men far out numbers the amount of songs by women, more than two to one."[531]

Pam Smith started *Amazon Radio* in 1990 on WPKN in Bridgeport, CT. Featuring a wide variety of music, from hip-hop artist Hanifah Walidah to folk singer Laura Berkson, she was on the air until 2015.

Almost every community radio station in the US offered a women's and/ or LGBTQ radio program at one time or other. They ranged from programs that featured only women's music artists to those that offered a wider selection, featuring any woman or LGBTQ musician. Some continue today. In later years, Internet stations started, including *Queer Music Heritage* with DJ and LGBTQ music archivist J.D. Doyle, and *Rainbow World Radio*, offered by founder Len Rogers.

Laney Goodman has enjoyed a radio career spanning twenty-five years on several stations including WXPN's *The Women's Music Hour* in Philadelphia. She currently hosts *Women in Music with Laney Goodman*, a syndicated show broadcast on more than one hundred stations internationally.

Women's music shows draw an eclectic audience. Most of the phone calls Linda Wilson receives while on the air for *Womansong* are from men. "Some are to thank me for turning them onto new music, but a good number of them are asking when the men's music hour is. I tell them to listen to any other radio station for the men's music hour. The majority of the donors during my show are women, but I do have a few men who donate and thank me for helping them understand women by listening to the music that I play."[532]

Musician Jamie Anderson was a community radio station DJ for six years, usually for a general music program where she occasionally played women's music artists. One of her favorite stories revolves around Alix Dobkin's "Some Boys." After playing it, she got a call from a guy and as soon as she heard his voice, braced herself for negative comments. Instead, he wanted to know who sang the song and where he could buy it. The phone rang again and this time it was a woman who read her the riot act because the song "portrayed men in a negative way." Jamie wasn't the only musician working on the other side of the mic. In 1988 Kay Gardner co-founded *Women's Windows* on WERU in Maine. Starting as a fifteen-minute spot within another show, it grew to an hour-long weekly show of its own.

Distributors

As artists began to tour and record, they needed companies to sell records to stores. For Olivia, that meant asking women at their concerts. Soon, they had dozens of women to help them. Terry Grant was one of those women who volunteered. Smitten

Terry Grant and Laurie Fuchs, 1991 AWMAC.
Photo by Toni Armstrong Jr.

with Meg Christian's first album *I Know You Know*, she wrote to Olivia when she heard that Meg was coming to her hometown of Lansing, Michigan. She sold

LPs for them at the concert and when she asked about returning unsold records, was asked to keep selling them. So, in 1975, she started Goldenrod Distribution. She holds a B.A. in psychology and a Masters in criminal justice so original-ly, record distribution was not a part of her life plan and even while running Goldenrod, she had a second business, an accounting firm. Her place in women's music is important to her. She told *HOT WIRE* in November 1985, "I can do this (distribution) because every day I can do work that has some impact on—and contributes to—changing women's lives or increasing awareness." She's also had a skilled staff, including long-time manager Susan Frasier, to manage the day-to-day operations. One of the two largest distributors of women's music, Goldenrod moved out of their warehouse and greatly pared down operations in 2011. Now they distribute only a few titles and sell at Midwest women's music festivals.

Laurie Fuchs attended her first women's music festival, National, in 1976 and the next year put together her first catalog of music by women with Olivia distributor Kathy Tomyris. The eight-page catalog featuring thirty or forty recordings was produced in three days, in time for the Michigan Festival. In 1978 Liz Snow joined Laurie—Kathy was no longer involved—and they became Ladyslipper Music. At first, they only sold directly to customers but it wasn't long before they began selling wholesale to stores. They added staff members and grew. Run as a feminist business, everyone's concerns were taken into consideration. It was a unique business model and while it usually worked there were issues. At one point in the early eighties, the three full-time staff members went into counseling to work things out. They kept learning, growing the business about ten percent each year, selling about a thousand units (LPs, cassettes, and CDs) a day. Over the life of the company, they've sold millions of recordings. In 1995, they bought their own building. More than a hundred people have worked for them over the years. In addition to titles considered women's music, they took on albums by any strong female artist such as reggae performer Judy Mowatt, Celtic/World Beat performer Loreena McKennitt, and spiritual musician Lisa Thiel. Known for their selection of spiritual and international music, they counted many mainstream stores and individuals all over the world as customers. In 2018, they started transitioning into an archival website only and at some point, will stop selling recordings.

WILD (Women's Independent Label Distributors) began in the mid-seventies. It offered distributors networking and training opportunities.

As it was in other areas of women's music, they learned from mainstream distributors but also created something new. Run on feminist principles, distributors weren't usually managed by one person who made all the final decisions. Often, they were run with input from all employees even though they weren't officially collectives. Also, it wasn't unusual for women's music distributors to add radio promotion, concert production, and their own record labels to their list of work.

At one point, there were over a hundred distributors. As women's music grew, it was too much work for some distributors. Before dropping out, they offered their business to another WILD member. So, as members left, the territory for the remaining distributors increased. In 1985, there were nine distributors left, each covering a specific part of the US. In the nineties, that number decreased to two, Goldenrod and Ladyslipper. Even though Ladyslipper was one of the earliest online, Internet sales started to affect it. Big online retailers didn't usually buy from them or Goldenrod. Brick and mortar stores closed, affecting wholesale income for the entire music industry.

Record Labels

Olivia and Redwood were the two best known labels but they weren't the only ones. Icebergg Records started up because they wanted to help Ann Reed get her second album out. Other artists on their label included Casselberry-DuPreé and the Washington Sisters. Many record labels were artist-run and included only their own records—Woody Simmons recorded on Deep River Records, Cris Williamson's later releases appeared on Wolf Moon Records, and Margie Adam recorded for Pleiades Records. Some of these independent recordings were distributed by Olivia in the seventies and eighties.

Kay Gardner's label, Urana/Wise Women Enterprises, included her early recordings as well as Casse Culver's *3 Gypsies*. Kay's later CDs were on the Ladyslipper label, the same company that distributed albums. Ladyslipper didn't start out to be a record label. It was unusual for any distributor, mainstream or indie, to also be a label. However, they saw a need when a label going out of business offered them Marie Rhine's *Tartans and Sagebrush* in 1982. To keep this great album in print, they bought the master, added a new cover and carried it. The same label had an album by feminist acoustic group Rosy's Bar and Grill so they bought that one too. These releases were already completed when they got them. The first album they did from start to finish was Kay Gardner's *A Rainbow Path*. Already successful in women's music, Kay kept putting off doing another album because of the lack of funds so Ladyslipper offered to produce the album. Ladyslipper put together a budget of $20,000 with no idea of where they were going to get the money. Funded with loans from local women in the Durham NC area, they started the project, learning as they forged on. It helped that they already had a trusted relationship with Kay because they'd carried her albums for years. They appreciated that she was organized and believed that a new release of her beautiful instrumental acoustic music would be popular. Based on her research in music, healing, and spirituality, she made each of the eight sections of the album correspond to a chakra, using a myriad of acoustic instruments, from her flutes to others on cello, light percussion and more. Falling somewhere between folk and classical, she also incorporated elements of Irish, Eastern, and medieval music. When they began *A Rainbow Path*, there wasn't a New Age category in the record industry at large. By the time it was released, *A Rainbow Path* was at the forefront of this new genre. Appearing in 1984, it sold 10,000 in the first six months and was number one on the new New Age charts. It was enjoyed by a wide spectrum of people, not just women's music fans. They followed that up with 1989's *Garden of Ecstasy* and others.

Booking Agents and Managers

Some artists handled their own business while others worked with booking agents and managers. A booking agent secured concert engagements for performers. A manager oversaw an artist's career, and duties might include advising them about goals, making sure that projects ran smoothly, and coordinating with booking agents, publicists, and others working for the performer.

In the early years, Boo Price managed Margie Adam. Mary Spottswood called herself a "womanager"—her artist was Casse Culver. In later years Donna Korones managed several acts including Ronnie Gilbert, Barbara Borden, Linda Tillery and the Cultural Heritage Choir, and Margie Adam. Judy Werle started at Olivia Records, then went on to manage Cris Williamson.

After handling promotion and more for Olivia Records, Tam Martin started Beachfront Bookings in 1987. She booked concerts for several artists over the years including Margie Adam, Meg Christian, Tret Fure, Barbara Higbie, Deidre McCalla, Ferron, Holly Near, Teresa Trull, Suzanne Westenhoefer, and Cris Williamson.

Roadwork was an arts agency that booked thirty different acts over the years including Sweet Honey in the Rock, Holly Near, and the Wallflower Order Dance Collective. Starting in 1977 and based in Washington, DC, they made a commitment to be a multiracial and multicultural coalition. When they incorporated as a non-profit organization, three of the four women signing were African-American. Board members included Bernice Johnson Reagon and Evelyn Harris (from Sweet Honey in the Rock), Konda Mason, and Amy Horowitz. Amy had come from Redwood Records, where she'd worked closely with Holly Near. When she heard Bernice Johnson Reagon sing, she knew she had to meet her. Soon after, she was booking a tour for Sweet Honey even though she'd only heard Bernice sing. It freaked her out so much that she rushed to the phone to call Holly collect; however, she never regretted the decision. Roadwork's first major project was the Varied Voices of Black Women tour in the late seventies. From 1977 until 1994 they booked thousands of concerts for a variety of artists. From 1982 until 1988 they also produced Sisterfire, a DC area festival.

Amy remembers a long drive with Holly Near where they discussed a recent concert Holly had done with Bernice Johnson Reagon in Hiroshima. As they drove through the mountains of North Carolina, they couldn't get much radio. No matter—they were deep in discussion about nukes and their effect on our planet. They did some brainstorming about how to put what they had learned into practice. After they came out of the mountains, they turned on the radio and for the first time heard the news about Three Mile Island. Amy recalls, "We had to pull over to the side of the road—that's where Holly's anti-nuke tour was born...that's a story of being awake to magic that just happens."[533] She found many moments of magic with Sweet Honey in the Rock, too, including a huge stadium tour in 1990 with Nelson Mandela not long after he was released from prison. She remembers Bernice telling her, "'You've done it! Sweet Honey was in a church basement and you were the architect and now this has happened. What do you want to do, how will you take this training?' She suggested I get a grad degree and agreed to be on my committee."[534]

Penny Rossenwasser was also a part of Roadwork, where she was one of the organizers for Sisterfire. Starting in 1980 and for the next ten years, she booked national tours for Cris Williamson, Meg Christian, Toshi Reagon, Betsy Rose and Cathy Winter, June Millington, and many more. She was one of a group of women's music and culture booking agents who called themselves The Booker Sisters, including Trudy Wood, Denise Notzen, and Jill Davey. They offered booking workshops at the National Women's Music Festival. Penny was also a long-time worker at the Michigan Festival, working in performer support for thirty years with coordinator Barbara Edwards (B. E.) who was also a booking agent, for jazz band Alive!.

Print Media

From the beginning, women sought out ways to explore women's culture, including periodicals. Early publications included *Musica*, a newsletter edited by Indy Allen that existed in the mid-seventies. It covered the national women's music scene including tour schedules, festival details, and information about artists.

In the late eighties *Women's Music Newsletter* was published in the Seattle area. It contained a calendar and artist profiles of Alix Dobkin, Rhiannon, Dianne Davidson, and others.

Larger and better known was *Paid My Dues*, a journal of women's music published from 1974 until 1980. Founder Dorothy Dean and a group of women printed early editions with stock clip art, fuzzy-looking photos, flimsy covers, and amateur writing. However, they quickly progressed to a more professional presentation with a durable cover. Inside were well-written articles and clear photos. Included were letters to the editor, tour schedules, artist profiles, sheet music, festival coverage, LP reviews, and how-to articles for musicians. They covered a wide variety of musicians from Maxine Feldman to Sirani Avedis.

Toni Armstrong Jr. was one of the staff members of *Paid My Dues*. The demise of this publication left a huge hole and in 1985, Toni filled it with *HOT WIRE: The Journal of Women's Music and Culture*. Publishing thirty issues over ten years, this resource was the bible for women's music. Armstrong's *HOT WIRE* brought coverage of women's music to an even higher level than any of its predecessors. Encompassing a larger focus, it also presented news about film, books, plays, and more—anything cultural that encompassed lesbian and feminist ideals. Feature articles focused on women's music artists Holly Near, June and Jean Millington, the Washington Sisters, Ronnie Gilbert, and more, as well as comics Karen Williams and Suzanne Westenhoefer. Mainstream culture was represented also, with actor Patricia Charbonneau and comic Kathy Najimy. Inside, a reader would expect to find a letter from Armstrong, artist interviews, dialogue about issues in women's music, festivals coverage, letters from readers, news items, historical articles, classified ads, and much more, packed into sixty-plus pages. Later issues included a sound sheet that could be played on a turntable. It was a huge undertaking requiring a large group of volunteers, from proofreaders to photographers. In the last issue, Toni Armstrong Jr. told us that she had put in seventy-hour work-weeks, all volunteer,

Toni Armstrong Jr. and Bonnie Morris, 1992
Photo by Zoe Lewis.

in addition to her regular job. Despite a strong reader base and advertising, the periodical was underfunded from the start. They applied for many grants but only secured one. After ten years, it was time to stop. Toni didn't see this as a sign that women's music was declining, only that she had committed from the start to doing ten years and her time with the periodical was finished. She continues to work in women's music.

Toni was also the publisher for *Women's Music Plus* (initially called *We Shall Go Forth*), an extensive directory of resources in women's music from 1977 until 1995. It was the only directory of its kind. Collecting the info and keeping it current was challenging but Toni recalls, "I still can't believe I got so many women to cooperate in sharing the contact information they had...ordinarily the entertainment business is so cutthroat. But women's music...was much more cooperative in general."[535] Cartoonist Alison Bechdel created the illustration for the 1987 edition. The typist in the illustration was modeled after writer Jorjet Harper and the sound engineer, Karen Kane.

Other feminist and lesbian publications had a part in women's music too. The *Lesbian Tide*, *off our backs*, *Sojourner*, and *New Directions for Women* carried occasional coverage. The *Lesbian Connection* contains news about women's music in almost every issue. Started in 1974 and still publishing, this reader's forum features music and festival reviews as well as ads for festivals. Contributors include many fans as well as lesbians active in women's music, from artist Alix Dobkin to festival producer Lisa Vogel.

Individual writers also became known for their work in women's music including Bonnie J. Morris, Connie Kuhns, Laura Post, Jorjet Harper, and Toni Armstrong Jr. Some wrote for periodicals such as *HOT WIRE*. Artists also wrote for that publication. For a while, Kay Gardner wrote a regular column, *Freestyle*, as did Janna MacAuslan and Kristan Aspen (Musica Femina), *Noteworthy Women*. Morris wrote the book *Eden Built by Eves* as well as articles in various publica-

1987
Women's Music Plus
Resources in Women's Music and Culture

Production Festivals Coffeehouses Performers
Writers Writers' Resources Distributors Directories
Dance Theater Film & Video Bookstores Journals
Publishers & Editors Record Labels Newspapers
Newsletters Photography/Photographers & Visual Arts
Music Resources Addresses & Phone Numbers

Women's Music Plus, 1987.
Private collection, Toni Armstrong Jr. Art by Alison Bechdel.

tions. In addition to writing for *HOT WIRE*, Laura Post is the author of *Backstage Pass* (1997), a collection of artist profiles including Alix Dobkin, June Millington, Rhiannon, and many more.

Photographers

From the beginning, lesbian photographers documented our movement. JEB (Joan E. Biren) was one of those. She learned photography while she was a member of radical feminist collective the Furies and excelled at portrait photography, especially of lesbians. Her work appeared in *off our backs*, *Gay Community News*, on album covers, and in two book collections. She's photographed many in women's music including Margie Adam, Meg Christian, Holly Near, and the Olivia Collective. She's published two books of her photos, *Eye to Eye: Portraits of Lesbians* (1979) and *Making a Way: Lesbians Out Front* (1987).

In the seventies Susan Wilson took photos and wrote articles for Boston women's papers *Equal Times* and *Sojourner*. That led to work for the *Boston Globe* where she became a full-time staff member in 1981.

Toni Armstrong Jr. first picked up a 35mm camera as a teen, learning her skills through the seventies, eighties and beyond. She's worn many hats in women's music, from musician to photographer to publisher of *HOT WIRE*. Her portraits appeared frequently in the journal as well as in books, on album covers, and much more.

A photographer since 1967, Pat Gargaetas is a lesbian activist who took photos at the events she attended, especially early women's music events.

Irene Young began her professional photography career in her twenties, encouraged by her friend Janis Ian. After photographing mainstream musicians, she was asked by Olivia to photograph Teresa Trull. This led to much more work for Olivia, including album covers and publicity shots. Her photos capture the personality and style of artists from Deidre McCalla to Laura Nyro. Her work appears on over six hundred CDs and LPs and in many publications, from *the New York Times* to *Rolling Stone*.

Sign Interpreters

Early on, American Sign Language (ASL) interpretation was important at women's music events, especially festivals, because there was a commitment to accessibility, education about different cultures, and creating community for everyone. Julia Cameron Damon first went to the Michigan Festival in the eighties and she loved connecting with the deaf community there. "For me as a person who became deaf as an adult and has often been told I am not really deaf it was/is the first place I was able to truly relax and enjoy my deaf sisters."[536]

Susan Freundlich was one of the first interpreters, fostering a connection with artists and their deaf audience members. She's worked with many artists in women's music including Holly Near, Linda Tillery, Margie Adam, Robin Flower, and Ronnie Gilbert, as well as those in mainstream music and theater. She was also an executive director for Redwood Records.

Sherry Hicks is well known for her work at women's music festivals, Olivia's fifteenth anniversary show at Carnegie Hall, civil rights marches, and more. She's worked with a wide variety of artists such as Holly Near, Indigo Girls, and Ferron.

Pam Parham was popular at the Michigan Womyn's Music Festival. The first time she saw music interpreted was in the eighties at a Jamie Anderson show in Tucson, Arizona. It was inspiring to her and not long after that, she started her interpreter education.

From the beginning, Sweet Honey in the Rock made a commitment to make their music accessible to the deaf community. Interpreter Shirley Childress Saxton joined them in 1980.

Every large festival had a group of ASL interpreters, some who worked more than one event. While interpreters were there to make the performance accessible to the deaf community, they entertained everyone. One joke was to wait until the musician took a drink of water, then the interpreter would dip her fingers in a glass of water. Comic Elvira Kurt kidded with Pam Parham at the Michigan Festival, claiming that Pam was the rock star who got all

Holly Near and Susan Freundlich, 1981 Crystal Moon Coffeehouse.
Photo by Pat Gargaetas (PGar)

the attention. Elvira's playful, "Damn you Parham!" at the Michigan Festival always brought down the house.

Emcees

A good emcee can enhance a concert, especially at large events with multiple performers. Musicians Sue Fink, the Topp Twins, Jamie Anderson, The Washington Sisters, and Lisa Koch were recruited to introduce acts and keep the energy up while the stage was readied for the next performer. They got creative. Sue Fink made up chants, the Topp Twins wore vintage bathing suits, Jamie Anderson twirled the baton, and The Washington Sisters pretended they were really triplets. Lisa Koch dressed in a habit and emceed as Sister Mary Agnus Labia while carrying a ruler and chastising the audience for their "naughty" behavior. Comics made great emcees too. Kate Clinton told funny stories and Elvira Kurt went through the program to highlight actual workshop titles like "Chicken Chat." Maxine Feldman was well known as an emcee at the Michigan Festival even after she stopped doing musical performances. She sometimes dressed in a tux, and her booming "Welcome women!" was as much a part of the festival as the music. Therese Edell became known as the Voice of Michigan, her smooth alto voice covering the night stage bowl.

Entertainers appreciated a good emcee. Maxine Feldman fondly remembers a time she was getting ready to introduce Toshi Reagon—"I said, 'Toshi, is there anything special you want me to say?' And she said, 'My mom told me that if you have Max for your emcee you're going to be fine.'"[537] (Her mother is Bernice Johnson Reagon, founder of Sweet Honey in the Rock.)

Other Workers

Every women's music event had volunteers who did everything from staffing the ticket table to artist transportation. For many years, the Michigan Festival required the work of over four hundred women.

Denise Notzon was a publicist who learned her craft first at Goldenrod Distribution in the early eighties, then branched out to work for others. Clients included Margie Adam, Kate Clinton, the Michigan Festival, and others.

Sandy Ramsey started in women's music in 1974 as a distributor for Olivia. Two years later she worked full-time with them in a variety of jobs including office manager, road manager, and distribution. In the early eighties, she took the skills she learned in women's music to form a consulting firm, offering business guidance to musicians, distributors, and managers. She also worked at the Michigan Festival.

Boo Price has held a dizzying array of positions in women's music, including distribution, artist management, concert and festival production, and stage production. In the seventies, she was attending law school when she got a call from Ginny Berson at Olivia who told her, "While you're in law school you've got to learn everything about entertainment law because we don't have any women lawyers."[538] She wasn't planning on entertainment law but decided to take Ginny's advice. Armed with her law education and mentoring from one of the few female entertainment attorneys (as it turned out, there were one or two), Boo negotiated a contract between Cris Williamson and Olivia for *Changer and the Changed*. Boo recalls, "It was a totally feminist practice. We met, I think, three days in a row, ten hours a day. (It was) the whole Olivia collective, Cris, Margie (Adam) and me."[539] The contract was different from the standard entertainment agreement. "I wrote the contract so that both parties to the agreement had equal share of the decision-making and the artist retained maximum decision-making in the process."[540] Her list of legal clients reads like a Who's Who of women's music and

Boo Price, 1991.
Photo by Marcy Hochberg.

culture: Margie Adam, Cris Williamson, Linda Tillery, Teresa Trull, Robin Tyler, Carolyn Brandy, the Women's Philharmonic, Olivia Records, Redwood Records, Naiad Press, Judy Chicago's Dinner Party Project, Michigan Womyn's Music Festival, West Coast Music and Cultural Festival, and the New England Women's Music Retreat.

Retts Scauzillo attended her first women's festival in the eighties. Under the tutelage of Boo Price, Alix Dobkin, and others, she learned to be a stage manager. In the eighties and nineties, she attended almost every major

women's festival, usually as part of the stage crew. At the Michigan Festival, her crew dressed in costume according to that day's theme. Sunday was leather day. With multiple acts on one stage, it was important that the stage run on time and one of her jobs was to confirm time lengths with each act. On Sunday, she firmly told comedy duo Dos Fallopia (making their first festival appearance) they had exactly forty minutes. A brief time later one of them approached her and meekly offered that their set was forty-five minutes. Years later she found out the two women fought over who was going to tell Retts. "They thought I was a big bad leather dyke," recalls Retts, laughing.[541] Those festivals gave her such good management skills that she was able to leverage the experience into a management job outside of women's music. Retts also produces concerts in New York State and performs as a drag king.

In 1979 Debbie Fier had just finished a piano tuning apprenticeship in Colorado. She was called to tune a piano for a Holly Near concert in Denver. Nervous about her new tuning skills and not knowing who Holly Near was, she did the job admirably enough that it led to work at many more concerts, including tuning pianos for the Michigan Festival for fifteen years. In that time, they went from two pianos to six—not a small job, especially outdoors where weather can wreak havoc with wood and metal.

Educators were important in women's music also. In 1975, Karlene Faith taught a class at University of California Santa Cruz, *Women in American Music*. It covered a broad spectrum of history, right up to the (then) new women's recording company Olivia. Holly Near, Cris Williamson, and Margie Adam were guest lecturers. One class project included producing a Meg Christian concert. Mary McFaul was one of the students involved. It led to a lifelong career for her in music that included concert production, management, and booking.

Music Industry Conference and the Association of Women's Music and Culture (AWMAC)

With so many involved in this vibrant industry, it became clear that women needed a place to meet, learn skills, and hear new performers. Starting in the early eighties at the National Women's Music Festival, the Music Industry Conference provided that place. Workshops and networking proved a valuable tool for many attending. *HOT WIRE* (November 1985) noted that about fifty concert producers attended the 1985 conference, including two who made their sole living producing shows. The conference was offered for three or four consecutive years.

In 1986 planning began for a new women's organization, AWMAC. The founding steering committee—Deidre McCalla (musician), Sue Fink (musician), Lisa Vogel (festival producer), Leslie Ann Jones (engineer), and Judy Dlugacz (record label owner)—appointed a bylaws committee and organized the first conference for 1987 as part of the National Women's Music Festival. This conference and later ones included artist showcases, workshops, and networking. It was a place for performers to meet concert producers and for everyone to learn skills, from writing songs to feminist business ethics. The next conference in 1988 was also at the festival. In 1990, they separated from National and convened in San Francisco. Durham, N.C. hosted the next one in 1991. AWMAC disbanded in the nineties.

CHAPTER SEVEN

••✦✦••

OUTSIDE THE US

Performers and More in Other Countries

The women's music culture that thrived in the United States was carried by musicians into other countries. Holly Near and Meg Christian represented the US at the first International Women's Music Festival in Copenhagen in 1978. There was also a festival in Israel in 1986 that featured Americans Sue Fink, Beth York, Casselberry-DuPreé, and performers from around the world. The Michigan Festival drew a large number of workers and attendees from countries around the globe, some coming back year after year. Sweet Honey in the Rock toured internationally. Alix Dobkin toured Europe with German band Witch is Which in 1979. Later in her career she toured Australia. Robin Flower and her band played a number of Canadian folk festivals and folk clubs. The music itself was passed around too. Naomi Littlebear Morena's "Like a Mountain" was sung at the Greenham Common peace camp in England. Mosa Baczewska did a concert in St. Louis where she performed her song "Rainbow" and a woman in the audience told her that she'd learned the song from two German women in Greece who were dancing under the full moon.

For American acts, performing across borders often meant appearing as part of a big event so they could tour there later. Canadian folk festivals and clubs were especially open to Americans. There were some issues though. The Berkeley Women's Music Collective had trouble during one trip to Canada because border officials labeled them "undesirables." Sue Fink had a memorable trip to Calgary in the eighties. It was her first time playing in Canada and she didn't realize she needed a work permit. She and bass player Diane Lindsay were detained in Vancouver and missed their connecting flight. Officials finally decided to let them fly to Calgary where they were met by a border guard who informed them with a sigh that she didn't want to be late for a concert that night. Sue recalls, "I said, 'What concert are you going to?' and she said, 'Sue Fink and Diane Lindsay.' I said, 'That's us!' All the papers went in the wastebasket and we were only late fifteen minutes and she drove us there. That's the essence of what we were doing…we were everywhere."[542]

Holly Near toured internationally, learning about different cultures and issues in other countries. When she talked about gay and lesbian community, sometimes the translator would stop because there were no words for those concepts in that particular culture. Sue Fink also had an interesting time with language when she performed at a women's festival in Israel. Scheduled to perform with Israeli musician Korin Allal, Sue struggled to learn the Hebrew in the song "The End Is Near" and jokes that she knew she got it right when she was mumbling it under her breath near Israeli soldiers and they looked alarmed. Some of the words translate to "the bomb is in your hand."

There were also issues with international artists coming to the United States. In the eighties, some musicians had trouble getting visas to tour here. New laws stipulated that artists had to have "eminent stature." Too often, the musicians banned were lesbian. Canadian Lucie Blue Tremblay racked up thousands of dollars in legal fees—so much that Olivia started a legal fund for her.

A vibrant women's music scene existed in other countries also.

Canada

Women's music started here around the same time it did in the US although the network wasn't as prominent because the population is smaller and more spread out. The Kootenays Women's Festival began in 1974 in British Columbia; in 1979 there was a festival in Toronto; and the eighties saw the emergence of the Canadian Women's Music and Cultural Festival in Manitoba. Quebec offered the Festival International de Musiciennes Innovatrices. There were coffeehouses, too, such as Full Circle in Vancouver and Co-op Lesbienne in Montreal. Concert production companies included Sappho Sound in Toronto.

Women's bookstores and radio shows were established too. In 1975, *The Lesbian Show* started in Vancouver on radio station CFRO. It featured music and interviews from Canadian performers Heather Bishop and Ferron, as well as US musicians Meg Christian, Holly Near, Sue Fink, and Cris Williamson. It enjoyed a wide access to women's music artists because the Vancouver Folk Festival booked them. It is still on the air, under a new name, *Gender Queeries*. Another long-time radio show is *Matrix Women's Show*, on CINQ in Montreal. Started in 1980, they still broadcast.

While there were a few women's music spaces in Canada, it was through the folk festivals that many Canadian feminist and lesbian artists gained prominence, some who then toured in the United States. Starting in 1980, the Vancouver Folk Festival booked women's music, much of it from the US—Sweet Honey in the Rock, Cathy Winter and Betsy Rose, Robin Flower, Nancy Vogl, and

Holly Near—as well as Canadians, such as Ferron. The Winnipeg Folk Festival followed suit and in 1982, brought in Ginni Clemmens, Meg Christian, and others, as well as Canadian Heather Bishop. This festival also had a women's tent from 1984 through 1986, with Judy Small, Ronnie Gilbert, and many more. Booker Rosalie Goldstein dismantled it, though, when she decided that women should be dispersed throughout the festival, not consigned to one stage.

There were many Canadian musicians who became known in the women's music network in the US. Lucie Blue Tremblay first played in the states in 1985, at the Michigan Festival.

Manitoba-based singer Heather Bishop had a varied repertoire that included blues covers, folk tunes, lesbian originals, kids' songs, and stories about her life on the prairie. With her rich alto voice and engaging stage presence she became well-known at women's music festivals. She recorded fifteen albums, starting in 1979, selling nearly 200,000. Four are children's albums and most were released on her own label, Mother of Pearl. She toured extensively in the US and Canada as well as overseas. At one point in her career she appeared at between 250 and 300 shows a year. She helped to establish women's music in Canada. Her partner, Joan Miller, would book a tour by calling women's and lesbian groups in various Canadian cities. Many of them had never produced a show before. From the beginning, Heather was an out lesbian. She recalls her first festival appearance, at the Regina Folk Festival in the late seventies: "I knew that if I was going to be a musician, that I had to be out, because I was already out in my life in every way."[543] She received a standing ovation. She included lesbian material in every show. In the beginning of her career, she'd place it about three-quarters of the way through a concert. "I decided that if by that time I had won their hearts and *then* did a song about being a lesbian and they got all freaked out, then at least the problem would be theirs."[544] Being out created some problems for her at folk festivals. "Most of the men did not know what to do with me at all…they would just avoid me like the plague. And a lot of women avoided me too, because they didn't want people thinking that *they* were lesbians."[545] In the mid-eighties that started to change. What makes all of this even more remarkable is that all along, she was also a popular children's entertainer, a regular on *Fred Penner's Place*, a well-known kids' show in Canada. In 2005 she was awarded the prestigious Order of Canada.

Connie Kaldor is also from the prairies, Regina, Saskatchewan. Her professional music career began in 1978 and since then she has played all over Canada and the United States. A pop/folk singer-songwriter, she started recording in 1981, releasing eleven albums. *Moonlight Grocery*, her 1984 recording, was distributed by Redwood. Her original songs encompass many topics, from heartache to the beauty of the prairies to jerks who whistle at women. Like Heather Bishop, she helped pave the way for other feminist performers. She and Heather toured western Canada together in 1981.

Sara Ellen Dunlop co-owned the Music Room in Toronto, one of the first gay and lesbian clubs in the sixties. Also a well-loved singer-songwriter, she released a four-song LP as well as a forty-five in the seventies. She was one of the original members of Mama Quilla, an all-women's rock band that formed in the seventies and broke up in the early eighties. Some members went on to form the Parachute Club. Later, some of Mama Quilla reunited and released one album, *Mama Quilla II*, and played at the Michigan Festival.

Faith Nolan was born in Nova Scotia and later moved to Toronto. This folk-blues singer-song-writer/activist played her political songs at Canadian folk festivals as well as the Michigan Festival and other US venues. She started recording in 1983 and has fifteen albums, one recorded with Mary Watkins. Faith sings passionately about many issues, from Afro-Canadian history to women in prison.

Masa, and Faith Nolan, 1991 East Coast Lesbian Festival.
Photo by Toni Armstrong Jr.

From western Canada, Ferron began her performing career in the seventies. Perhaps the best-known of the Canadians, she released several albums and toured extensively on the women's music circuit as well as the folk scene.

Lillian Allen performs dub poetry, a political form that influenced rap and hip-hop. Much of her work was interwoven with music. She's released several books and recordings. In 1986 and 1988, she won Junos (the Canadian equivalent of the Grammys) for *Revolutionary Tea Party* and *Conditions Critical*. The former was distributed by Redwood. She performed at the Michigan Festival as well as elsewhere in the US.

Lorraine Segato was the driving force behind the socially-progressive band the Parachute Club. She wasn't prominent in the women's music scene but she did appear at the Michigan Festival.

Sherry Shute is known mostly for her guitar work with Heather Bishop. Her self-titled album was released in the eighties.

Australia

Although, like Canada, it was limited by a sparse population, Australia had a vibrant women's music scene that included venues, radio shows, performers, and a distributor. American music in general has always been popular there so it was natural that artists such as Holly Near and Cris Williamson were enthusiastically received. In 1994, a compilation of Australian women's music, *More Than a Pretty Face*, was released. It included "Coming Out Blues" by Vicki Bennett.

Lavender Blues was an Australian lesbian band from the late seventies. Their album, *Wake Up Sister*, was released in 1978. Included was the title cut as well as "Lesbian Nation." Judy Small opened for them at an early show.

Inspired by the rise of folk music in the sixties, folksinger Judy Small got her first guitar at age fourteen. Influenced by Joan Baez and Mary Travers, she started performing locally in Sydney, her hometown. Her first big break performing internationally was at the Vancouver Folk Festival in 1982 where she met Holly Near. That same year, she released her first album, *A Natural Selection*. Touring took her all over the world, including stages in the US. Known mostly in the folk world, she also appeared at women's music venues. One of her best-known songs, the anti-war "Mothers, Daughters, Sons" was also recorded by Holly Near and Ronnie Gilbert. She sang a lot about LGBTQ issues including the humorous "Turn Right, Go Straight" and "Influenced by Queers." When *Queer Music Heritage* asked if she'd ever had problems being out, she replied, "I've sort of blithely gone ahead and assumed it doesn't damage my career and just sung about it anyway. I've always seen my lesbianism as being similar to being right-handed. You know, everything I do I do as a right-handed person, whether or not I'm using my hands."[546] She released twelve albums, at least one of them on Redwood.

New Zealand

The Topp Twins started recording in the eighties and toured internationally, including appearances at the Michigan Festival. Best described as folk/country, these lesbian identical twins are known for whimsical performances. You never knew if Lynda and Jools were going to yodel or wear vintage bathing suits (as they did when they emceed at Michigan one year). They could venture into serious songs, too, with beautiful harmonies only sisters can do. In their home country they have their own TV show and movie. In 2008, they were inducted into the New Zealand Music Hall of Fame.

There were other women performers, and several of them released a compilation recording in 1982, *Out of the Corners*. The first of its kind in that country, it was carried by Ladyslipper and included Jess Hawk Oakenstar, who later moved to the US.

England

At the same time Americans were discovering women's music, a similar movement was happening in the UK. The Women's Liberation Music Archive lists over a hundred musical acts who were active in the seventies and eighties, a broad range, from punk band Abandon Your Tutu, to eclectic folk band the Fabulous Dirt Sisters, to jazz group the Guest Stars. Many offered original music and some recorded the music they heard from Americans. The Stepney Sisters, a feminist rock band, covered "Keep on Truckin' Mama," by the Chicago Women's

Liberation Rock Band. Bad Habits performed Holly Near's "Mountain Song." The Brazen Hussies played songs by Cris Williamson and Alix Dobkin. Humor had a place too—Clapperclaw specialized in satire, including their own "History is No Place for a Lady."

Some of the acts toured, usually in Europe. A few made it across the pond. Punk/art duo Frank Chickens played at the Michigan Festival, as did the folk/pop Lizzy Smith Band. Even if they didn't tour in America, some of these performers were an influence. Ruth Barrett considers British folk singer Frankie Armstrong a mentor and Willie Tyson covered Peggy Seeger's engineer song. (Peggy is American but lived in England for many years.)

The best-known English act in the US was Ova. Rosemary Schonfeld and Jana Runnalls did three tours of the States including an appearance at the Michigan Festival in 1980, and later at NEWMR. They toured Europe, had a strong following in Germany, and released three albums on the Stroppy Cow label starting

Ova, 1986 Michigan Festival.
Photo by Toni Armstrong Jr.

in 1979. This eclectic duo played several instruments and presented mostly political songs, sometimes in an improvisational style.

Although it wasn't as cohesive as in the US, there was a network of places to play, including folk and rock clubs, women's centers, conferences, and festivals. Some gigs were women-only. Feminist magazine *Spare Rib* covered the scene. Women's Revolution Per Minute (WRPM) distributed the albums, including those by American musicians. Recordings were found at record shops and women's bookstores.

Ireland

Maria Walsh and Carole Nelson are Zrazy, a pop/jazz duo that offers songs with piano, sax, vocals, flute, bodhran (traditional Irish drum), and more. They toured extensively in Europe and the US including the Michigan Festival. Their song, "679-4700," advertised the number for the abortion helpline in England. At the time, it was illegal to publicize the number in Ireland. Another controversial song, "Cool to be Queer," resulted in some audience members walking out;

however, women's music audiences and others loved them. Also known for less political numbers such as "I'm in Love with Mother Nature," they released six albums, starting in 1993.

Germany

In addition to featuring touring British bands, Germany had the Flying Lesbians, a rock band popular in the mid-seventies. They released one album with songs that included "The Battered Wife" and "I'm a Lesbian How About You?" Witch is Which came along in the late seventies with a repertoire including "Marlene," a love song to a woman, and "Suzanne," about body image. Alix Dobkin toured with them. Out lesbian singer-songwriter Carolina Brauckman started recording in 1982. American women's music was also popular in the country. Women's music distributor Troubadisc carried the most requested, including Alix Dobkin and Cris Williamson. In 1985 the first Lesbenwochen Festival occurred in Berlin. This weeklong lesbian festival featured American Debbie Fier and British duo Ova. The opening night performance was attended by three thousand. Women's music was covered by *Troubadora*, a short-lived magazine first published in 1978.

Netherlands

In the seventies there were occasional women's events with music—some that were protests for abortion rights or LGBTQ pride. The first Dutch women's festival happened in 1976 and lasted yearly until the eighties. One of the more notable musical acts was the all-lesbian rock band Wicked Lady. Formed in the UK, they moved to Holland because they felt more freedom there. Repertoire included a cover of Jimi Hendrix's "Hey Joe" that guitarist Sue Exley played partly with her teeth. They released three singles including "Girls Love Girls"— when they performed it live they'd stop in the middle and kiss each other. Up until then, they played a lot of Dutch military bases but soon after that song, lost those gigs. They played even more clubs after that, becoming very popular. The band broke up in 1981. Sue went on to be part of a country duo, Gypsy, which was popular in Spain.

Israel

It isn't known if there was a women's music scene in Israel although it hosted a women's festival in 1986, perhaps the only year it occurred. Well-known feminist singer-songwriter Korin Allal performed at that festival. One of her songs, "Alticra li Motec," translates to "Don't Call Me Honey." Popular from the late seventies, she still performs. She came out as a lesbian in 2001.

CHAPTER EIGHT

•••✦•••

IT'S JUST FOLK MUSIC, RIGHT?

Jazz, Rock, and a Whole Lot More

Because many of the early musicians were solo performers, women's music developed a reputation for being pop/folk singer-songwriters. However, women's music was built on the shoulders of women such as gutsy blues singers Ma Rainey and Bessie Smith as well as locally-known all-women rock and country bands popular in lesbian bars such as the Roc-A-Jets (Baltimore), Rail Runners (Kansas City), and the Indavana Blues Band (Phoenix). These artists proved that women could play and enjoy all kinds of music and while there wasn't usually a direct connection to the artists who came after them, they did serve to inspire. Teresa Trull even recorded Ma Rainey's "Prove it on Me Blues" on her first Olivia album.

Toni Armstrong Jr., publisher of *HOT WIRE*, took aim at anyone who thought women's music was only white women with guitars. "We have always been an incredibly diverse network in terms of musical style—a review of festival stage lineups over the years is most educational."[547] And what is folk music? Toni maintains that, "People involved in the genuine 'folk music circuit' do not consider most of what we do to be 'folk music.'"[548] For some, anything with an acoustic guitar is folk music but really, music with a guitar could encompass jazz to classical. For example, Judith Casselberry played guitar for Casselberry-DuPreé, and while some of what they did could be described as folk, they played a variety—reggae, soul, African, and country. Nedra Johnson calls herself a singer-songwriter who is "...more on an R&B tip than what one might expect of a 'girl with a guitar.'"[549] Yet, when she performs solo gigs, she sings and plays a guitar and it's not music that would get her booked at the average folk festival. However, it made her popular at women's music festivals.

While solo singer-songwriters could travel alone or with one support person, it wasn't the same for bands. For many genres—salsa, jazz fusion, rock, R&B—a band was necessary. "Plane fares, hotel rooms, salaries, and equipment all cost money," bandleader Ellen Seeling comments. "For example, to bring the seven-piece version of DEUCE to Michigan can cost anywhere from $2500 to $3500."[550] And that was in the eighties. As a member of the Berkeley Women's Music Collective, Nancy Vogl saw that bands were treated differently: "We had a group of four women, as opposed to one woman that you could create kind of a fantasy for—as a result, talking with all the bands (and we talked to all the bands, of course) it was a particular dynamic that we saw repeated throughout the country. For example—a solo performer would get paid the same or more than a band of four with a sound person. This sets up an odd dynamic of value."[551]

Robin Flower had similar feelings. "I felt that bands were not supported… bands were the ultimate in collectivity and that was never quite understood."[552]

As women's music released albums that embraced a variety of genres, attitudes changed. In 1985, *HOT WIRE* published a list of twenty-six women's bands, from rock power trio Holy War, to jazz quintet Alive! Some released recordings on their own labels. Olivia took notice too. In the eighties president Judy Dlugacz told *Bitch*, "Olivia has done jazz, fusion, R&B, rock and roll, (and) we're doing a blues rock album now—one of the reasons why I started another label, Second Wave, was to get away from that image of soft acoustic music, because that's not all we do."

Rock

Carol MacDonald was early on the scene, first in mainstream music with sixties band Goldie and the Gingerbreads, then on to the all-women's jazz/Latin/rock ensemble Isis, which she co-founded with drummer Ginger Bianco in the seventies. In the eighties, she performed with her band Witch at women's festivals. Carol enjoyed the festivals although her 1984 Michigan Festival performance created some controversy because her act included leather-clad women which some thought presented Nazi-like images. Others strongly disagreed and loved her set. She says, "It had nothing to do with Nazis. It was theater, not political."[553] Carol enjoyed presenting a tough image—something that was popular in mainstream music but not always understood in women's music.

Two early acts, the Chicago and New Haven Women's Liberation Rock Bands, made one album in the seventies and while they did some touring, they didn't receive much attention. At the time, there wasn't a women's music network for them. Even after the network took hold, music with drums and bass was misunderstood. Pianist Mary Watkins recalls playing with Linda Tillery and Teresa Trull: "There was some resistance because each of these artists performed with a full band. Many women saw women's music as a style of folk music for voice accompanied by guitar or piano…To these women, adding drums and bass was a violation of women's music."[554]

Flash Silvermoon noticed a difference depending on the event. Women seemed to be fine with rock at a dance or in a bar, but not at a festival or in a concert hall. Rocker Carol MacDonald echoes that: "Bars don't play Meg Christian."[555] Guitarist Sherry Shute told *HOT WIRE* (March 1988), "I felt from the feminist camp early on they didn't want to *know* about rock music at all—it was just dismissed without giving a listen as being male-identified. And I would say, 'Look, this stuff is written by me and my women friends.'" Toshi Reagon wondered why some thought rock was male—she told *HOT WIRE* (July 1985), "It's unfortunate that most of hard rock is produced by men…" and although much of classical music has also been written by men…"when women play that, are they accused of playing men's music?"

Melissa Etheridge was always a rocker. She told *HOT WIRE* in 1990, "I didn't play the kind of music that was being played in the women's music scene. I played like the way I do, very upfront rock and roll—I guess that didn't set well with some of the real hard political groups." She goes on to say that she did have support, it just wasn't across the board. She was grateful for the few women's music gigs she did get, including three appearances at Robin Tyler's West Coast festival and once at Southern. Melissa never played the two large Midwest festivals—National or Michigan—and although she sent a demo tape to Olivia, they didn't sign her. While she had a huge lesbian following, most of her support came from heavy touring in straight lounges, bars, and restaurants before she was discovered by a mainstream label in 1986.

Even when rock performers played solo, they were met with resistance. Ellen McIlwaine played an early National Women's Music Festival. With her guitar amp cranked, she blasted through a set of rock and blues, causing some women to leave with their hands over their ears while others cheered her on. June Millington came from the rock world and when she started to play with Cris Williamson, audience members asked her to turn it down which was perplexing to her since her guitar wasn't loud. It was, however, an electric guitar. She performed on her own, too, recording and touring through the eighties and later. Tret Fure came to women's music with an electric guitar—"One of the things I was able to do in the early eighties was to show women that they can play electric guitar…"[556] Other glimmers of rock at early festivals included a young Lea DeLaria at a National open mic. After explaining that "Chuck" was a woman, her guitarist thrashed through chords as Lea strutted about the room singing "Chuck, let's fuck."

One of the first rock bands to make an impact in women's music was BeBe K'Roche. This four-piece San Francisco Bay area band released their self-titled LP on the Olivia label in 1976. With keyboard, bass, drums, electric guitar, and vocals, they brought a smooth combination of rock mixed with jazz and Latin sounds. Most songs were written or co-written by keyboard player Virginia Rubino. One of their most popular songs, "Kahlua Mama," was a sensual and danceable love song to a woman. They performed at the first Michigan Festival, at the National Festival, and did some touring, mostly on the west coast.

The Fabulous Dyketones formed in the seventies and played oldies rock, often with new lyrics. Known best in clubs and at dances, they also made appearances at women's music festivals, including National and the Pacific Northwest Women's Music Festival.

Flash Silvermoon played at the Michigan Festival in 1979 and 1982 with two different bands. They were well-received but there were some issues with sound reinforcement. Bands were often more difficult to amplify, especially in the early years.

Kentucky-based Yer Girlfriend had more of a folk/rock bent. Often political, they released three albums in the eighties and nineties.

Gretchen Phillips came out of the punk scene, then went on to two bands, Two Nice Girls and Girls in the Nose, joining several women musicians including Kay Turner, Kathy Korniloff, Meg Hentges, and Laurie Freelove. Always refreshingly out, her bands were known for outspoken songs such as "I Spent My Last Ten Dollars on Birth Control and Beer" and "Honorary Heterosexual Lesbian." They recorded several albums, the first in 1989, and toured, sometimes at women's venues. Gretchen first attended the Michigan Festival in 1982. She credits some of the bands she heard there as inspiration for her work. For many years, she was a common fixture on their stages as an emcee, as well as with her bands. She continues to record and perform.

Rising out of the alt-rock scene, eclectic performer Ember Swift plays a variety styles from jazz to punk. Since the nineties, this Canadian has released twelve albums and played at the Michigan and National festivals.

Later, festivals featured more rock, often bands that were better known on the straight rock circuit although many had a big lesbian following—Lez Zeppelin, Tribe 8, Wicked Jezabel, the Butchies, and others. Although many of these bands identified as feminist and/or lesbian, they didn't always connect with women's music audiences. Tribe 8's guitarist Leslie Mah remarked to *HOT WIRE* (Jan 1994), "My feelings are that we're not exactly embraced by the existing lesbian musical culture. I think that in the history of women in rock, most of the women involved have been bisexual or dykes, but not necessarily out." It would seem likely that the feminist issues in the nineties-era Riot Grrrl movement would influence women's music or vice versa, but that wasn't true. Each had their own scene although one of the early riot grrrls, Kathleen Hanna, did perform at Michigan with her band Le Tigre.

Jazz

When Rhiannon began going to women's music events, she wondered why there wasn't any jazz. She set out to rectify that, co-founding Alive! in 1975. Originally a trio, they soon expanded to five pieces—Rhiannon (vocals), Barbara Borden (drums/percussion), Carolyn Brandy (congas/percussion), Susanne

DiVincenzo (bass/cello) and Janet Small (piano). They released four albums and toured extensively, playing in jazz clubs, women's music festivals, jazz festivals, and more. Touching on a variety of styles from bebop to Latin jazz, they're known for original songs "Spirit Healer," "Call It Jazz" and others. They also covered Ida Cox's "Wild Women Don't Get the Blues" and June Millington's "Heaven is in Your Mind." They did their last gig in 1985 although they've reunited a few times for special performances including one at the last Michigan Festival. The *LA Times* called them, "... one of the most enterprising and entertaining small bands on today's jazz scene."[557]

After the breakup, members branched off to various musical projects. Rhiannon joined several a cappella ensembles. She released six albums on her own label and was popular at the Michigan Festival as a solo performer where her improv solo work was well-loved by audiences. Suzanne found work in pit bands and is the principal cellist with Jersey Shore Pops Orchestra. Carolyn has collaborated with many artists and founded Born to Drum, a music camp for women. Barbara continues to play and teach. Sadly, pianist Janet Small passed away in 2010. Tammy Hall takes her place for reunion shows.

Sax/flute/clarinet player Jean Fineberg first attended the Michigan Womyn's Music Festival in the seventies and while she enjoyed it, felt a little out of place: "There's no doubt that the women's music scene was primarily vocal folk music, played on guitars. I think the first year I went to the Michigan Festival was 1979, backing up Sirani Avedis, then known as Sally Piano. I don't think I saw another horn player there for several years. And that's probably because women weren't accepted and encouraged to play that kind of music and to play those instruments."[558]

In 1980, Jean formed DEUCE with Ellen Seeling on trumpet and flugelhorn. The rest of the players varied and sometimes included Julie Homi on piano and Nydia "Liberty" Mata on Latin percussion. Jean recalls, "We always tried to pick the best players, regardless of gender, race, age, or anything. So consequently, we had a very mixed band. Of

DEUCE — Jean Fineberg and Ellen Seeling, 1991 Michigan Festival.
Photo by Toni Armstrong Jr.

the seven pieces, we would usually be about half women and half men."[559] At first, they played their original jazz fusion around New York City, where they were based, then branched out to tour, mostly at jazz venues but also several times at the Michigan Festival, as well as appearances at National, WIMINfest, NEW-MR, the Southern Women's Music Festival, and the West Coast Women's Music Festival. Their lineup for women's festivals was always women-only. The audiences there enjoyed them, however, Jean remembers some confusion: "I think some women in the community didn't get where we were coming from because we didn't have lyrics. Jazz fusion is a very high energy, electric naughty aggressive jazz, which didn't fit in with most of the women's music of the time. Even the jazz community looked askance at fusion as not being pure jazz. We always had a good audience reaction, probably just because the music was good and the players were good..."[560]

They released two albums—*DEUCE* in 1986 and in 1996, *Windjammer*. Today Jean and Ellen both perform in the Montclair Women's Big Band, recording with them in 2006.

Pianist and composer Mary Watkins was well-versed in many styles including jazz. She was known as an accompanist as well as a solo performer. In the beginning, she came up against some of the same issues as rock musicians: "There were...those who did not like or understand jazz and considered it a male thing. When I performed with bass and drums and sometimes added a horn, I was well-received for the most part but it was a bit of a mixed bag. Jazz musicians traditionally have smaller audiences than rock groups and folk artists so I tended to have more receptive audiences when playing clubs or special Mary Watkins concerts in concert halls—this is not to say that audiences at the (women's) festivals were not receptive. Most of my performing was solo piano and I played ninety-eight percent original music. However, it was very eclectic. And for that, I was usually enthusiastically received."[561]

In addition to her solo albums, Mary worked with many in women's music. She's also known for compositions including a jazz score for the play *Lady Lester Sings the Blues* and a jazz adaptation of Tchaikovsky's "Nutcracker."

Active in the late seventies, Baba Yaga (named for a powerful Russian witch) was a short-lived jazz band with one album, *On the Edge*, distributed by Olivia. Members Barb Galloway (guitar), Jan Cornall (congas), Susan Colson (bass), Bonnie Kovaleff (trumpet), Kiera O'Hara (piano) and Patti Vincent (sax) played in an eclectic improvisational style. They toured primarily on the west coast. Robin Flower was a member for a while.

Boston area band Bougainvillea included Susan Shanbaum and Debbie Lemke who were also members of the Berkeley Women's Music Collective. Beginning in 1978, this all-women jazz/Latin band gigged around Boston. In 1982, they won a contest and were invited to play at the Women's Jazz Festival in Kansas City.

Formed in 1980, Maiden Voyage was an all-women seventeen-piece jazz orchestra led by sax/flute player Anne Patterson. They appeared at numerous jazz festivals and other mainstream venues as well as the West Coast Women's Music Festival.

Active in the eighties and nineties, the Blazing Redheads played high energy Latin jazz in the San Francisco Bay area and did numerous tours that included women's festivals—Michigan, National, and Robin Tyler's events. This seven-piece band released two albums, *Blazing Redheads* and *Crazed Women*.

Mrs. Fun is a Milwaukee-based band that includes elements of avant-garde jazz and neo-cabaret with keyboards, drums, and vocals. Gigs included the National Women's Music Festival. They released seven albums and shared the stage with many, including Janis Ian and the Indigo Girls.

Jasmine started in the late seventies as a jazz duo in St. Louis. Carol Schmidt (piano, vocals) and Michelle Isam (clarinet, sax, vocals) offered upbeat sets incorporating jazz, pop, and blues. Later, they were joined by vocalist Lydia Ruffin and released 1987's *Wild Strings* on Icebergg Records. Rich in vocal harmonies, their collection of songs included originals plus covers. Their dramatic version of "Leader of the Pack" was especially popular, with a breathless Michelle dramatically dropping to the floor at the end. They released a second album, toured and appeared at women's music festivals until 1989.

Together in the early eighties, Sojourner was an eight-piece all-women's band from Chicago and Detroit who played styles from the Black musical experience—jazz, blues, and more. They performed around the Midwest, including a 1981 appearance at the Women's Jazz Festival in Kansas City.

Based in the San Francisco Bay area, Swingshift was an eighties-era jazz band that included Bonnie Lockhart on piano, also known for her work with the Berkeley Women's Music Collective. The band included others on flute, sax, drums, and more. Swingshift performed locally and did some touring.

Also based in the bay area was Wild Mango, a jazz/world beat band. Formed in 1994, they played at the Michigan Feestival as well as many jazz festivals. The original lineup included Jackeline Rago, who also played with Latin women's group Altazor. Guitarist Erika Luckett is a singer-songwriter, too, and later did solo sets at women's music festivals. Bassist Jan Martinelli performed on many women's music albums, as did drummer/percussionist Michaelle Goerlitz. Wild Mango released four albums.

Azucar y Crema was an all-women band that specialized in salsa and Latin jazz. Popular at Latin venues, in the nineties they also played at the National Festival and a women's festival in Las Vegas.

Lea DeLaria is known for her role in the TV series *Orange is the New Black* but long before that she was a comic and jazz singer who played the women's music circuit, Provincetown clubs, and mainstream venues, from the Newport Jazz Festival to Carnegie Hall. She has made several albums including early nineties favorite *Bulldyke in a China Shop*.

Mimi Fox is a jazz guitarist who performed solo and with others in many venues including women's music festivals. Known mostly in mainstream jazz circles, she's released eleven recordings and has performed on many more including women's music performers June Millington, Elaine Townsend, and Robin Flower. Mimi's also played with an impressive array of mainstream musicians, from Diana Krall to Stevie Wonder.

After graduating from the Berklee College of Music, pianist Kellie Greene moved to Los Angeles and performed with many artists including Frank Sinatra. In 1976, she became the first woman musical director for a network TV show, *The Harrison and Tyler Show*. She and Robin Tyler kept in touch and in later years, Robin hired her to play at her festivals.

Classical/Opera

Kay Gardner was the first to demand that women's music include classical music, incorporating it into her performances, co-founding the New England Women's Symphony in 1979, and encouraging venues to book classical artists. It wasn't always easy. She told *HOT WIRE* (March 1986), "It's a constant fight as a so-called classical performer to get the attention of the festival producers and audiences...it should be on the main stage right along with the pop acts." Kay composed a staggering number of pieces over her career—over fifty chamber works, choral pieces, orchestral works, operas, solo instrumentals, and vocal pieces. Two of her orchestral compositions were performed at the National Festival, *Ouroboros* and *A Rainbow Path*. The latter was performed twice, the second time in 2012, with a twenty-one piece orchestra directed by Deborah Freedman. Musicians included Mary Watkins.

Kay was so moved by the 9/11 attacks that she composed "Lament for Thousands" in two weeks and offered it to the Bangor Symphony Orchestra, the same group she had sued for sex discrimination twenty years prior. She had applied to be a conductor and was turned down, and sued when she discovered that a survey had been passed around the orchestra, asking if they would welcome a woman conductor. By 2000, she was asked to guest-conduct a special ensemble of women from the orchestra who performed pieces by female composers. After Kay's passing in 2002, the orchestra performed "Lament for Thousands" for its opening season concert.

Improvisational pianist/guitarist/singer/composer Beth York was greatly inspired by Kay. Her five-movement chamber piece, "Transformations," debuted in Atlanta in 1981. She performed it at the National Festival in 1984 and 1985. Beth has also appeared at other festivals, including Campfest and Michigan, and additional venues in the late eighties, sometimes with Kay. Her recording, *Transformations*, was produced and recorded by Ladyslipper in 1985. Currently, she's a professor of Music Therapy at a southern college.

Mary Watkins composes classical pieces that have been performed by the Women's Philharmonic Orchestra, the Berkeley Symphony Chamber Orchestra, and others. In 2016, she was commissioned to perform an orchestral piece for the National Women's Music Festival. Her repertoire also includes film scores and opera.

Flute player Kristan Aspen was involved with women's music almost from the beginning, as an original member of The Fabulous Dyketones. She also toured and recorded with Izquierda. She hired guitarist Janna MacAuslan, sight unseen, to run sound on Izquierda's final tour. After a whirlwind romance, Kristan convinced Janna to move to Portland, Oregon. In 1981 Musica Femina was born. Presenting original work as well as pieces by other women composers, performances by Kristan and Janna were as much a lesson in women's classical music history as they were performance. Concerts included stories and a photo of each composer. Each performance was not a responsibility taken lightly. Research could take months. Concerts began with a lighting of candles and an invitation to the muses. Janna told *HOT WIRE* (July 1985), "We are not trying to fit in with the model of what a classical concert should look or sound like; we're trying instead to create an intimate, warm, together feeling with the audience." They launched their first national tour in 1984. Appealing to traditional women's music venues, they were also popular on college campuses. Kristan recalls: "We met classical musicians everywhere we went. They were encouraged that there were women in classical music. It was very exciting. Often the students would come and talk with us after our performance. We inspired a lot of people to see possibilities they hadn't seen before. Previously they only knew men as important people in music."[562]

Musica Femina—Janna MacAuslan and Kristan Aspen, eighties. *Photo by Tee A. Corrine. Tee A. Corinne Papers, Coll 263, Special Collections and University Archives, University of Oregon Libraries, Eugene, Oregon.*

They released four recordings and toured until 1996. Kristan comments, "We toured long enough to feel like progress had been made on the campuses where we played. Toward the end, there were scholars who were doing their own concerts of women composers. In the beginning, we were the only ones…We worked our way out of a job."[563]

The Bay Area Women's Philharmonic began in 1981. Presenting works by female composers, it offered varying styles of classical work, always with a high level of musicianship. The philharmonic didn't draw the usual classical fans. The *San Francisco Gate* noted, "They were not habitual concertgoers, by and large, and what they lacked in experience they made up for in enthusiasm and passionate attentiveness. No one ever went to a Women's Philharmonic concert out of a sense of obligation or routine."[564] They presented concerts for twenty-three years, until 2004. Some thought that like Musica Femina, it had worked its way out of a job. However, the *San Francisco Gate* wrote, "Just last month, the San Francisco Symphony announced its 2004-05 season, with a schedule featuring only music by male composers, led by male conductors. Other major orchestras haven't done any better on that front."[565]

The New England Women's Symphony began earlier, in December 1978, and existed until November of the next year. Founders included Kay Gardner, Leslie D. Judd, Gail Perry, and Nancy Barrett-Thomas. Their repertoire included only women composers, from Baroque to the 1970s. They released one album on the Galaxia label.

Therese Edell started composing chamber and choral works in 1987 when her advancing multiple sclerosis prevented her from her work as a singer-songwriter. With a modified computer, she created several commissioned pieces including "38:3 Sections, 8 Years" for classical duo Musica Femina. She also composed "This Longest Night" and "Goddess and Guru," for MUSE, Cincinnati's women's chorus.

Barb Glenn and Susan Nivert, the Derivative Duo, presented opera parodies. Dressed in gowns and high-top tennies, they warbled through "Eine Kleine Visit from Mama" (melody borrowed from Mozart, with original lyrics about de-dyking the house) and "Honolulu Chorus" (a sendup of "Hallelujah Chorus"). They released two albums in the nineties and played women's music venues including the National Women's Music Festival.

Over the years, other acts were featured at women's festivals. Well-known classical guitarist Sharon Isbin played at the Michigan Festival. A few times, a duo or small ensemble played on their acoustic stage. Kay Gardner started an orchestra at the National Festival. Later it was organized by Leslie Judd. In 1978, the festival orchestra performed with renowned conductor Antonia Brico, and in 1979 with another conductor. The festival's classical series featured a variety of performers from 1982 to 1992, so many performers wanting to do this series that it was rare to book anyone twice although flute/cello duo Skaggs and Powell were featured several different years. Leslie Judd recalls, "This was an amazing mix of educators, authors, and performers all wanting a space to share, compare, and learn about women composers."[566] The Ohio Lesbian Festival featured string quartet Quartetto di Lesbos in 1999 and 2000.

Others

Women's venues presented many other genres of music. From the late nineties, the all-women klezmer band Isle of Klezbos has offered a selection of folk dance, reworked standards, and more. Their energetic sets at the Michigan Festival usually resulted in a rambunctious Hora line that filled the night stage bowl. They've toured internationally and released two albums.

Suede is a cabaret performer known for smooth jazz standards and pop on keyboard, trumpet, and guitar. Since the eighties she's been popular in Provincetown, at women's festivals, and on Olivia cruises. Suede started releasing albums in 1988, with four in total plus one with a cappella group, the Flirtations.

Other kinds of music were heard at festivals—an eighties West Coast Festival featured a koto player (a Japanese stringed instrument), Michigan featured a flamenco guitar player and a pipa player (Chinese stringed instrument). Even disco was represented in women's music. Olivia released an album, *Hocus Pocus*, by disco artist Alicia Bridges in 1984. President Judy Dlugacz thought that since disco had a huge gay following that this would be a good direction for the label. Although it reached as high as the fifties on dance charts, Olivia lost money on the album.

Olivia released a 1977 LP featuring poets Pat Parker and Judy Grahn. However, spoken word artists weren't popular at women's music venues until the nineties, when they were featured at festivals—Alix Olson, Stacyann Chin, Sister Spit, C. C. Carter, Storme Webber, Slanty Eyed Mama, and Andrea Gibson all offered a feminist perspective in their work, sometimes accompanied by music.[567] Theater and dance were also presented at festivals, mostly at Michigan and National.[568]

CHAPTER NINE

•• ⚬✐⚬ ••

INSTRUMENTALISTS

Making Other Performers Sound Great

As women's music grew, solo musicians and bandleaders hired women to perform with them. Sometimes it was another solo performer and sometimes a side player who worked for hire on albums and for shows.

In the early days of women's music, it wasn't unusual to see Kay Gardner sitting in with someone at a festival, or Cris Williamson jumping onstage to sing with a friend. In later years, the Chix Lix set at the Michigan Festival was a favorite, with musicians who'd done their own set earlier in the festival contributing a song with the festival band. The National Festival has an all-performer jam, with performers from earlier sets each getting up to do a song, the others joining them. There's a great energy in this kind of spontaneity that audiences and musicians love.

That same kind of synergy was evident on recordings. Cris Williamson's *Changer and the Changed* was packed with women who had (or would soon have) their own solo careers or own bands: Woody Simmons (banjo), Margie Adam (vocal and piano), June Millington (guitar), and Meg Christian (vocal and guitar). We saw that on others' albums as well, Robin Flower on Casse Culver's *3 Gypsies*, Nancy Vogl on Trish Nugent's *Foxglove Woman*, Naomi Littlebear Morena on Maxine Feldman's first forty-five, and Carolyn Brandy (Alive!) on Gayle Marie's *Night Rainbow*.

In later years, artists also got together for duo albums. Cris Williamson and Tret Fure made many recordings together. Barbara Higbie and Teresa Trull teamed up for two albums. In the nineties, Kay Gardner and Nurudafina Pili Abena joined to record *OneSpirit*. Teresa Trull and Cris Williamson's *Country Blessed* came out in 1990. Cris Williamson and Holly Near released an album together in 2003. Holly Near also did a recording in 2011 with folk duo Emma's Revolution, *We Came to Sing*. Barbara Higbie, Linda Tillery, and Laurie Lewis formed Hills to Hollers. Their several performances together included the Michigan Festival and the release of an album in 2011.

Side Players

One of the main principles of women's music was its goal to support women and that included who you hired for recording and for live performances. Some of these selected women were already professionals and some were hired because they had potential. For these players, women's music offered them an opportunity not present in mainstream music. Seventies-era jazz/rock band Isis had many musicians over the years including Ellen Seeling on trumpet and Nydia Liberty Mata on drums. The Fabulous Dyketones name was owned by bandleader Char Priolo. She hired a host of musicians over the years including bass player Lisa Koch (Dos Fallopia and Venus Envy), and guitarist Lisa Rogers (Therapy Sisters).

It continues to be extremely difficult for women instrumentalists in mainstream music. Ellen Seeling knows this well. "I can't tell you how many women musicians I know from way back who were really great players and had the background and the education and the skills. Then they got into their thirties and forties and they start feeling like they've just been beaten up for so many years that they're going to try something else."[569]

Jean Fineberg had to push through many barriers to learn her instruments: "My first saxophone teacher, who was shorter than I was, tried to discourage me from playing the tenor and told me he thought I should play the alto because my hands were so small. Meanwhile, I think they were bigger than his! Many famous saxophonists would come to New York and I would take a lesson with them. One, who is dead now, chased me around his hotel room until I left with no lesson. When I was young and vulnerable, another one had me lie on the floor and he put his hand on my stomach under the pretense of trying to teach me how to breathe and told me that playing was like having an orgasm."[570]

Jean's own father told her she was too old to play professionally, even though she'd played most of her life. In her early professional life, she played in bands with men. She had to play twice as well as them to keep those jobs. Trumpet player Ellen Seeling likes to tell about the time a woman stopped her and complimented her singing at a recent concert. Ellen isn't a vocalist. The woman was so used to seeing women only as singers, she didn't even remember Ellen's instrument. Pianist Julie Homi performed in the New York jazz scene and found similar barriers. "I'd played with some really good women musicians, and we wouldn't get certain work because we were women. But the good side was that the women were very supportive of one another. We had to have a really strong network, and we did provide each other with work whenever we could."[571]

Women's music offered these musicians more and, sometimes, better opportunities to play. Ellen Seeling comments, "I really don't think we would have been able to make a living the way we did without the psychological support allowing us to say, 'I can play, I am worth getting paid, and what I have to say is worthwhile listening to,' without women's music."[572] Jean Fineberg agrees. "The women's music scene provided an opportunity for instrumentalists as well as vocalists to have the experience that you absolutely need to become a professional player, to be a leader of a group, to play a prominent role in an ensemble, to get the solos, to accompany all kinds of vocalists, and to play in many different genres."[573] Women's music gave them opportunities even their male colleagues didn't have, like playing for almost ten thousand at the Michigan Womyn's Music Festival. It was great for the audiences too. For some fans, it was the first time they'd seen a woman ripping through an electric guitar solo or anchoring a great groove on a set of drums.

What follows are a few of the women known for their performances on women's music recordings and in shows and concerts. It's certainly not an exhaustive list, merely a selection of some of the better-known players.

Bass Guitar

In 1973 Barbara Cobb heard the New Haven Women's Liberation Rock Band at a New York City club. The next day, she bought a bass guitar and started to play. She's worked with Alix Dobkin and many bands including Isis and the Harp Band.

Diane Lindsay first recorded with Margie Adam on her debut album, *Songwriter*, and in 1977, with Meg Christian for her second album, *Face the Music*. She went on to work with a host of others—Teresa Trull, Linda Tillery, and Cris Williamson. Also a pianist and songwriter, her "Sweet Darlin' Woman" was covered by Meg Christian and was an often-requested song at Meg's shows. Her own album, *Open Up*, was released in 1984.

Meg Christian and Diane Lindsay, 1981 Crystal Moon Coffeehouse.
Photo by Pat Gargaetas (PGar).

Jan Martinelli calls Diane Lindsay a talented player and a great inspiration. Jan first encountered women's music in the late seventies when she played with Mary Watkins and Linda Tillery. She worked with many others including Holly Near, Woody Simmons, Gayle Marie, Robin Flower, Wild Mango, and the Blazing Redheads. Performances included the Michigan Festival in 1978 and later years, as well as other festivals and concerts over the years. She loved her experience in women's music. "I feel lucky to have met such incredible women—it was very inspiring."[574]

There are others—Joy Julks performed with Teresa Trull, Mary Watkins, and Linda Tillery. Carrie Barton was a popular player with several artists including Cris Williamson and Tret Fure. Toni Armstrong Jr. played on several projects starting in the seventies including Mosa's *Turning Tide* and in Alix Dobkin's Lavender Jane reunion shows. Susan Abod performed with the Chicago Women's Liberation Rock Band and toured with Willie Tyson. Laurie Lewis had her own band but also played upright bass on Woody Simmons's *Oregon Mountains* and Robin Flower's *Green Sneakers*. She performed shows with Robin too.

Piano

Holly Near introduced us to a whole host of talented pianists, starting with Jeff Langley in the seventies. Later, she worked with J.T. Thomas, John Bucchino, Julie Homi, and Adrienne Torf. Julie Homi studied classical and jazz before she started performing in the seventies with many in women's music, from Holly to Linda Tillery to Teresa Trull. She also had her own band that performed at the Michigan Festival in 1989. Adrienne Torf studied piano from a very early age and had a short stint with an all-women disco band. In 1979, she began working with Holly Near. She worked with many in women's music including Ferron, Linda Tillery, and Kay Gardner. She was also a popular solo performer at festivals and was in the band for the Meg/Cris Carnegie Hall album and performance. Her solo recordings were released in 1986 and 2003. She also appeared on Ferron's *Shadows on a Dime*, Kay Gardner's *Garden of Ecstasy*, and Cris Williamson's *Portrait*. In the eighties, she began a collaboration with poet June Jordan that included an opera and an album.

In addition to her own projects, Mary Watkins played on many women's music releases including those by Meg Christian, Holly Near, Linda Tillery, and Cris Williamson.

Colleen Stewart appeared on several women's music recordings including Linda Tillery's first Olivia album. She also worked with Mary Watkins, June Millington, and Vicki Randle. Performances included women's music festivals.

Julie Wolf was a regular at the Michigan Festival in later years, playing with many different performers. She toured and recorded with Ani DiFranco, and performed with Zoe Lewis, Lisa Koch, the Indigo Girls, and Carly Simon. She released a jazz album and scored music for films.

Drums/Percussion

In addition to her work with Latin and world beat bands, Michaelle Goerlitz played live and in the studio with many performers in women's music—Cris Williamson, Tret Fure, Altazor, Margie Adam, Ferron, and Holly Near.

Nurudafina Pili Abena first performed at the Michigan Festival in 1978, accompanying jazz singer Rashidashah. Known mostly for her work with Kay Gardner, she also performed her African traditional/Afro-Cuban/Caribbean drumming with her own band.

Carolyn Brandy was a co-founder of jazz band Alive!. She also recorded with Holly Near, Margie Adam, and Robin Flower, as well as with her own bands, Sistah Boom and the Carolyn Brandy band. She's an expert in Cuban folkloric drumming.

One of Nydia Liberty Mata's major influences was Cuban music. She recorded and toured with Laura Nyro in the seventies and eighties. Nydia also performed with jazz/rock band Isis, dub poet Lillian Allen, eclectic group the Harp Band, and jazz band DEUCE. For many years she was seen at the Michigan Festival, often accompanying other artists.

Guitar

Nina Gerber got her professional start playing with folk artist Kate Wolf. Proficient in many styles, from bluegrass to rock, she recorded and performed with many including Ferron, Cris Williamson, and Dianne Davidson and made three recordings of her own. Sherry Shute is best known for her electric guitar work with Heather Bishop. Shelly Jennings has worked with Ferron, appearing on several of her recordings, as well as Sirani Avedis's *Tattoos*, and Lucie Blue Tremblay's *I'm Ready*. Shelly also plays bass. Jerene Jackson played electric guitar on Linda Tillery's first album and Teresa Trull's early albums. She was also a member of BeBe K'Roche. Later, she formed and led her own band.

Horns/Woodwinds

Jean Fineberg (saxophone, flute) and Ellen Seeling (trumpet, flugelhorn) played with a variety of artists—Isis, June Millington, Teresa Trull, Linda Tillery, Margie Adam, David Bowie, and Chic. In the seventies, they toured and recorded with Laura Nyro. Percussionist Nydia Liberty Mata, already in Nyro's band, recommended them. Ellen remembers, "Laura called us at Indiana University, where I was finishing up school and Jeanie was auditing classes. I picked up the phone, and this voice said, 'This is Laura Nyro.' I didn't believe her, and I wanted to say, 'And this is Miles Davis,' but I went ahead and listened. She asked us to pick up her *Smile* album, learn some tunes, and she would fly us to Philadelphia for a concert with the band. If she liked us, we would do the rest of the tour."[575]

When they walked onstage in Philly, they were gobsmacked to find well-known players they admired. The show went well, so they toured with Nyro and had an amazing time. She was different than other musicians they'd worked with. Instead of charts (sheet music), they were given directions like "play pine trees." "Nobody had ever asked us to play pine trees before," Jean recalls. "Laura would just express feelings and we would just do whatever our interpretation was."[576] Nyro only played at two women's music festivals (Michigan and Sisterfire) so she wasn't a part of the women's music scene; however, she shared some similarities with the singer-songwriters of women's music, including an emotional depth that connected with audiences. Jean and Ellen played with other mainstream acts, including disco band Chic, although they found the experience wasn't as positive. They also performed on Sister Sledge's "We Are Family" and they still receive royalties when that music appears on TV and in movies.

Vocals

When women's music artists were looking for a great vocalist, they often called Vicki Randle. She appeared on countless recordings and at concerts with Linda Tillery, Meg Christian, Cris Williamson, and Ferron, as well as a host of mainstream artists. She released her own album, *Sleep City*, in 2006. Vicki's a multi-instrumentalist, too, and plays guitar, mandolin, drums/percussion, and bass.

Multi-Instrumentalists

Robin Flower must not ever sleep because in addition to having her own band, and in later years member of a duo with Libby McLaren, she's played mandolin, fiddle, and guitar with jazz band Baba Yaga, rock band BeBe K'Roche, and on many albums with Barbara Higbie, Holly Near and others.

Barbara Higbie, first known for her work on the Windham Hill label, later joined Teresa Trull for two duo albums and several tours. Proficient on piano and fiddle, she's played with women's music artists Holly Near, Ferron, and Vicki Randle, as well as mainstream artists Bonnie Raitt, the Kronos Quartet, and Pete Seeger. She's released five solo albums.

Kara Barnard played with so many artists at one National Festival that Jamie Anderson joked she was the house band. Skillful on guitar, mandolin, banjo, autoharp, dulcimer, and musical saw, she's worked with Ferron, Tret Fure, Wishing Chair, and Jamie Anderson at festivals and in the studio. Kara has three solo albums.

CHAPTER TEN

•◦◦✦◦◦•

THE GODDESS NEEDS MUSIC

Spiritualty and Religion in Women's Music

Musician and choral director Melanie DeMore told *HOT WIRE* (Jan 1993), "Music can...change the way you feel about yourself, and make you feel connected to a community." That was certainly true for those who found spiritual community with women's music.

When the second wave of feminism burst forth, spirituality wasn't welcomed. Musician/ Dianic Priestess Ruth Barrett theorizes that was because feminism was "...very influenced by Marxism and the idea that 'religion is the opium of the people' and many feminists were

Ruth Barrett, nineties.
Private collection, Ruth Barrett. Photo by Kim McElroy.

thinking that this was just another distraction from political work."[577] However, the seventies saw the emergence of the Goddess Spirituality Movement, a departure from male-dominated religions. Influenced by the work of Z Budapest and her book *The Feminist Book of Light and Shadows* (later reissued as *The Holy Book of Women's Mysteries*) and later, Starhawk's *The Spiral Dance*, women began to explore women-centered spirituality as a form of feminist activism. The movement needed music. In 1975, Kay Gardner's *Mooncircles* answered the call. Through the years she made music appropriate for rituals and other spiritual pursuits. Eclipse Neilson remembers a time with her in the late seventies: "She shared her knowledge of ancient musical scales and instructed us in simple rituals. As she sang in her haunting voice, tears welled up in my eyes more than once, although I did not know why. I felt as if we had traveled back in time to a place where all that had ever been—still existed. As we honored the land and the spirit guardians of the place, I could feel the ancestors emerging from the forest to join us. I felt like I had come home."[578]

In the eighties and nineties, Ruth Barrett and Cyntia Smith added music that was drawn from traditional folk sources as well as original compositions inspired by goddess mythology and female-centered spirituality. One of Barrett's most important songs is "Every Woman Born," which she wrote for a 1980 Take Back the Night March. In it, she sings of the goddess of the hunt, Diana. Ruth explains, "Pictured with bow and arrow, she can offer protection and defend herself, women, and the creatures of the earth. She can take care of herself and that obviously connects with the idea of women taking back the night."[579] Despite the strong female imagery in her music, Ruth wasn't always embraced by women's music. In fact, it was hard to know where she fit in—she was too spiritual for folk music, and too straight for women's music (in later years, she came out as lesbian). That started to change when she met Kay Gardner at the tenth Michigan Womyn's Music Festival. Excited to share an interest in the Goddess and the healing power of music, they became friends. Ruth's Dianic Goddess community in Los Angeles sponsored workshops given by Kay. Kay was the original director of the Candlelight Concert, a spirituality-themed closing concert for the Michigan festivals—a celebration of women's music, dance, and spoken word that included many spiritual traditions and was entirely lit by candles and hand-held torches. Many found it powerful. Kay offered Ruth the position of director in 1993, which Ruth held until the festival ended in 2015.

Ruth continued to teach and facilitate rituals, co-founded Temple of Diana, and authored *Women's Rites, Women's Mysteries: Intuitive Ritual Creation*. Her later solo recordings contain chants and spiritual songs, some in collaboration with others—*Invocation to Free Women* (1987), *Parthenogenesis* (1991), *The Year is a Dancing Woman, Volumes One and Two* (2003), *Garden of Mysteries* (2008), and *Songs of the Otherworld* (2010).

Goddess rituals became popular at women's music festivals, from opening ceremonies to croning rituals. Leaders in the movement sometimes facilitated workshops. At their first festival in the eighties, goddess worship was a surprise to Southerners Wanda and Brenda Henson. Wanda told *HOT WIRE* (Jan 1993),

"...it's difficult to assure the women here (in the South) that women's spirituality has nothing to do with devil worship. This was about the Goddess, of course, and reclaiming a pre-Christian religion that celebrates women." Wanda grew up in a Pentecostal family. Attending her first festival transformed her. For Brenda, who grew up Unitarian, it was an easier transition. After that festival, the two of them started the Gulf Coast Women's Festival in Mississippi.

Christians weren't as visible at women's music events although some came from that tradition. Melanie DeMore joined a convent in the seventies. Duties included teaching music at an all-female Catholic high school. The sisters were also involved in the community, working in a variety of settings. In 1993 she told *HOT WIRE*, "I found out more about the role of women in religious and spiritual life than I did as a lay person. Women have been running things for themselves in the church for hundreds of years. They taught me what it meant to be a feminist from a spiritual point of view. They ran their own lives." Although she was only with the order for five years, she carried these beliefs into her later work as a choral director and popular solo performer at women's festivals. "It's important for me to sing the truth, to sing for God/Goddess or whatever. I always write 'sing for God' at the top of my set lists."[580]

Over the years, a few workshops by and for Christians appeared at women's music festivals but in general, they maintained a low profile.

An LGBTQ Christian music network began in the eighties. Musicians appeared at Metropolitan Community Churches (MCCs) and other affirming churches. Many of the artists were men. A notable exception was Marsha Stevens. One of her best-known songs, "For Those Tears I Died," was written before she came out and recorded by many in mainstream music including Pat Boone. Christian music of this kind was rarely featured at women's music events; however, some artists from women's music performed at MCC churches as well as for Unitarian and other liberal congregations. Sometime in the eighties, Casse Culver talked about being a Christian during her set at a West Coast Women's Music Festival. Sweet Honey in the Rock includes spirituals in their concerts and it's a part of their mission statement. One of their recordings, *Feel Something Drawing Me On*, is all gospel. Melanie DeMore includes spirituals at her concerts also. She recorded "Balm in Gilead" on her 2012 release *In the Mother House*.

Judy Fjell plays in a variety of religious settings, most often for Unitarian Universalist churches, as has Kiya Heartwood. Carole Etzler Eagleheart has performed her woman-centered music there, too, as well as in other venues. She is also a certified teacher of the Seneca Wolf Clan Teaching Lodge. Songs include "She Calls to Us" and "Chant for Mother Earth."

In later years, the Michigan Festival had a sweat lodge for native, Indigenous, and First Nations Women. It was a spiritual experience—a place to honor ancestors and to remember traditions. Native blessings were included in festival opening ceremonies and at the closing Candlelight Concert. The festival also had the One World Inspirational Choir. Led by Aleah Long, it sang spiritual music from several traditions.

One of the reasons Meg Christian left women's music was to follow a spiritual path. In 1986 she released *The Fire of My Love for You: Songs for Gurumayi Chidvilasananda*. Meg sometimes traveled and appeared with the charismatic guru.

In the nineties, Redwood Records organized the New Spirituals Project. These popular Thanksgiving weekend concerts featured commissioned music from a variety of musicians including Bernice Johnson Reagon, Ysaye Barnwell, Mary Watkins, and Jackeline Rago.

Jewish women have been a strong part of women's music. Author Bonnie J. Morris wrote: "Women's music festivals offer a setting of natural beauty and spiritual energy—an ideal time and place for Jewish women to find one another and network under green trees, whether we choose to address our complex oppression—as Jews, as women, and/or as lesbians—or to celebrate our lives through energetic song and dance."[581]

Maxine Feldman, Alix Dobkin, and Laura Berkson celebrated their Jewish culture in their performances. Berkson released her first album in 1989 and performed at folk and women's music venues. She holds a degree in Jewish Communal Service and works as a cantor. Her "Marie," about two high school girls who attend their prom together, was made popular by Ronnie Gilbert. Linda Hirschhorn released her first album, *Skies Ablaze*, in 1984. It was distributed by Redwood and included the beautiful "Circle Chant" that has been sung all over the world in spiritual gatherings. She also performed at women's music festivals and released nine more albums, some solo and some with the Jewish women's a cappella group Vocolot.

Cabaret artist Lynn Lavner told *HOT WIRE* she was, "...a cultural Jew (the food, the music, the humor), an ideological Jew (show me the underdog and I'll show you my cause), an intellectual Jew (having raised brooding to an art), an analytical Jew (arguing either side of any argument with equal passion), and most of all I am stubborn."[582] In 1987, she performed at the tenth International Conference of Gay and Lesbian Jews. Also that year, she played at the thirteenth General Conference of the Universal Fellowship of MCCs and Dignity (LGBTQ Catholics). She joked with *HOT WIRE* (Nov 1987) that, "I'm just filling the vacuum left by Jim and Tammy Faye."

Pianist Dovida Ishatova performed with her mother, Henia Goodman, a Holocaust survivor. No stranger to women's music, Dovida had performed with Kay Gardner, Ginni Clemmens, and the New England Women's Symphony. For several years she tuned the pianos at the Michigan Festival. While performing a short set at the 1979 West Coast Women's Music Festival, she recited a moving poem she'd written to her mother. At its conclusion women leapt to their feet with applause and tears. In 1980, the mother-daughter duo performed together for the first time at a conference, on a double bill with June Millington. They also appeared at women's music festivals. Her mother was so moved by the support at these shows that she would smile and comment, "I think that I am now going to try women."

Comic/producer Robin Tyler was also vocal about her Jewish culture. Lynn Lavner had enormous respect for her because of the support she offered other Jewish lesbians. When J.D. Doyle (*Queer Music Heritage*) asked Lavner in 2003 about the connection between out-LGBTQ performers and their Jewish culture, she had this to say: "Robin was born in Winnipeg. Winnipeg was one of the great Canadian sites for Jewish immigration...(their) values included family and learning and a love for culture. They flocked there, the way that the Russian and European Jewish immigrants flocked to Ellis Island, where my people came from. So, I suppose that being have-nots at the beginning, we were raised with a great consciousness of right and wrong, and a sense of justice."

Wanda and Brenda Henson offered a Seder at an early Gulf Coast Festival. Wanda recalls, "...Jewish women brought all this wonderful information in. It was liberating just to hear it."[583] Gatherings for Jewish women were often included at women's music festivals.

CHAPTER ELEVEN

••◦✂◦••

WOMEN'S MUSIC ISN'T FUNNY?
Comedic Musicians and Stand-up Comics

The myth that feminists weren't funny was disproven many times in women's music. Almost every well-known musician incorporated at least one funny song or some amusing stage patter into their work. Meg Christian's "Ode to a Gym Teacher" was a lighthearted look at a crush that always got laughs. Margie Adam did "Sleazy," a sexy song that didn't take itself too seriously. Heather Bishop sang an emotional ballad in French that was drolly translated to English by someone else. Partway through the song the audience realized it was about dust balls. Cathy Winter had a humorous song with words taken directly from a nuclear accident evacuation plan. She didn't have to change the words to get laughs. A capella trio Yagottawanna performed "It Must be in the Water," a song from a straight couple whose kids are all gay. Folksinger Ginni Clemmens gave us "Fat White Dyke and Over Forty" with tongue planted firmly in cheek. Mosa Baczewska offered "Heavy Metal." Decked out in leather and dark aviator shades, she introduced the song by telling audiences she was inspired by a button labeled "heavy metal" on her electric keyboard. Then she played a song about actual heavy metals—iron, lead, and uranium. For a performance at the National Women's Music Festival in the nineties, her interpreter Ruth Rowan also wore dark shades and played the part of a bad-ass heavy metal artist.

Leah Zicari did several funny songs including one to Martina Navratilova where, of course, love should be the score. Audiences also enjoyed "Torque Me Baby," a blues tune about riding a motorcycle. A skilled fingerstyle guitar player, Leah proved that funny songs didn't have to be accompanied in a simple way.

With songs such as "Role Playing Tango," "I'd Rather Be Cute," and "Shelly, You've Gone Nelly on Me," it was clear that Lynn Lavner liked making us laugh.

This Week in Texas called her "America's Most Famous 'Left-Handed, Vertically-Challenged, Jewish, Lesbian, Activist, Politically Incorrect' Comic."[584]

In recent years, singer-songwriter Cheryl Wheeler made appearances at the National and Michigan festivals. Her deadpan delivery of stories between songs was as funny as any stand-up comic. Songs were sometimes off-kilter, also, including "My Cat's Birthday"—about a grand affair that included cats in pirate attire who were blissed out on catnip—and "Handy House"—a list of rules in gross detail for what one cannot do in a portable toilet.

Singer-songwriter Lisa Koch released her first solo album *Colorblind Blues* in 1991. She's no stranger to comedy with songs like "Beaver Cleaver Fever," "You Make My Pants Pound," and "I'm a Middle-Aged Woman." She was also a member of Venus Envy, whose *I'll Be a Homo for Christmas* came out in the early nineties, selling thousands. Songs included "The Twelve Gays of Christmas," and "Rhonda the Lesbo Reindeer." Later Koch formed comedy duo Dos Fallopia with Peggy Platt.

Dos Fallopia — Lisa Koch and Peggy Platt, 1995 National Festival.
Photo by Toni Armstrong Jr.

Their *My Breasts are Out of Control* cassette was released in 1992. It contained songs by their alter egos, faux grunge band the Surly Bitches, and country act the Spudds, a skewed version of The Judds. Also included was a sendup of women's music performed by two women, Compost Morning Dew and Dolphin-Free Tuna Woman. Both Peggy and Lisa were well-known in their hometown of Seattle for an annual sketch comedy/music holiday extravaganza "Ham for the Holidays." Lisa's solo work is popular at festivals and on Olivia Cruises.

Jamie Anderson is also known for funny songs including "Wynona Why Not," "Menopause Mambo," and "I Miss the Dog (More Than I Miss You)."

Lea DeLaria wears several hats along with comedy. She is a jazz/pop singer who also does stand-up.

Monica Grant did both stand-up comedy and music too. This California-based artist released three albums (1989-1996) and appeared at festivals. Her act included a funny parody of Ferron's "If It's Snowing in Brooklyn," with a dead-on imitation of her voice, as well as serious songs such as "Lover's Lullaby." She also did theater, including a two-woman show *Goddess on a Payroll*.

Anne Seale was a cabaret performer with humorous songs "Lesbian Cemetery" and "Sex for Breakfast." She performed at Campfest and is also an author.

Dianne Davidson didn't do funny songs but her stories between songs could be hilarious. At the 1996 National Women's Music Festival she told us, "I grew up in West Tennessee where we write songs pretty straight ahead. (For instance) 'You hurt me and I hate you.' Then I started hanging out with Cris Williamson who writes songs no one can understand.(laughs)"[585] Everyone knew that she and Cris are friends.

Teresa Trull and Barbara Higbie made humor a part of their shows. Teresa told *HOT WIRE* (July 1985) "...when people are laughing it inhibits those bad feelings that can happen...People are more open." Like Davidson, Trull was also funny with her between-song patter. At several shows she remarked to the audience, "I don't have relationships, I take hostages."

While they didn't perform music, lesbian stand-up comics made use of the women's music network. Audiences responded so well that comics could use the same venues and media.[586]

Canadian Robin Tyler has led quite a life and sometimes draws on it for her comedy routines. One of her favorite stories was about her joyful discovery of lesbianism— she ran through her school's hallways shouting, "I'm a lesbian!" She jokes that administrators didn't bat an eye because it was a theater school and they thought she said "thespian." In another story she relates how she went to her first drag show at the young age of twenty-one, only to be arrested along with forty-four queens and charged with female impersonation. Her comedy career began in 1968 as part of the duo Harrison and Tyler. Later she became a solo performer—touring, and releasing an album in 1979, *Always a Bridesmaid, Never a Groom*, distributed by Olivia. TV performances included a 1980 appearance on *Funny Women*, a show hosted by Phyllis Diller. Robin went on to produce women's music festivals and much more.

Kate Clinton was a high school English teacher for several years before she made her way to comedy in 1981. Her political humor is well-known in venues all over the world. She's appeared on the *Rachel Maddow Show*, *The L Word* and hosted *In the Life*, an LGBTQ newsmagazine on PBS. She's the author of three books and has made several CDs and DVDs.

Suzanne Westenhoefer has been a professional comic since 1990. She's performed her irreverent comedy about relationships and more in venues all over the world. Suzanne was the first openly lesbian comic with an HBO special, in 1994.

Karen Williams romps through a variety of topics, from racism to getting older. She's popular in many venues including Olivia cruises and is a well-known emcee at women's festivals. Karen is also a motivational speaker and educator.

Starting in the nineties, Marga Gomez was a regular at women's music festivals as well as clubs, theaters and on TV. Robin Williams called her the lesbian Lenny Bruce.

CHAPTER TWELVE

•◦✄◦•

BEYOND THE EIGHTIES

Changes, Decline, and Hope

The women's music network experienced profound changes after the eighties. Audience size decreased. More gray hair appeared in the crowds and the question became how to draw younger women. While some artists such as Lisa Koch and Nedra Johnson were starting their careers in women's music, others, including Lynn Lavner and Maxine Feldman, ended theirs. A few festivals ended and at least six new ones began. Olivia celebrated their twentieth anniversary and released their last album. As feminists made progress and lesbians gained rights and visibility the question became whether the work was done.

Holly Near was talking about the end of *HOT WIRE* but she could have been speaking for the women's music network when she said: "The big word in 'movement' is MOVE. The big word in 'activism' is ACT. It's not good for ourselves or for the world to stay in one place out of habit or guilt or fear of change."[587]

New Festivals

Rhythmfest was a southern festival begun in 1990 and organized by women who'd worked at other events. They drew twelve hundred in their first year and in later years, topped three thousand. In 1994, organizers included Michelle Crone, Barbara Savage, Mandy Carter, Kathleen Mahoney, and Billie Herman. The first festival was in Georgia; later they moved to North Carolina. In additional to women's music favorites like Holly Near, they also booked performers not often featured at other women's music festivals, like rock band Tribe 8. Melissa Etheridge made two surprise appearances. One year, she worked in the office, even answering the phone for unaware women wanting to know if the rumor of her performance was true. Difficulties in finding a suitable site forced the festival to end in 1996.

Booking agent Tam Martin produced the Pacific Northwest Women's Jamboree for five years, 1990 to 1994, at Western Washington University in Bellingham. For one of the few festivals held indoors, she worked hard to insure a balance of performers including comedy, Northwest performers, and nationally touring musicians. Entertainers included Kate Clinton, Washington Sisters, Dos Fallopia, Seattle Women's Ensemble, Righteous Mothers, Dianne Davidson, and Jamie Anderson.

The Virginia Women's Music Festival began in 1990. They own their wooded property with a lake that is situated between Charlottesville and Richmond. Over the years they've featured a wide variety of musicians, from rock cover band Wicked Jezabel, to singer-songwriter SONiA.

From 1990 until 1995 the Lone Star Women's Festival took place in the fall, outdoors on rented land close to Austin. Entertainers included Texas artists (fifty percent of the performers) as well as nationally touring musicians: Venus Envy, Leah Zicari, Odetta, the Therapy Sisters, Sue Fink, Dianne Davidson, Nancy Scott, Girls in the Nose, Jamie Anderson, and many more. Activities also included skinny-dipping and rafting in the Guadalupe River that bordered the festival. Three hundred to twelve hundred women attended each year.

Houston had its own festival, Houston Women's Music Festival, 1995-2009 and again in 2011. This one-day festival featured local and nationally known artists: Deidre McCalla, Zrazy, Catie Curtis, SONiA, Elaine Townsend, Ferron, Melissa Ferrick, Ellis, Ruthie Foster, Wishing Chair, and Tret Fure.

Organized by Athena Productions, Midwest Womyn's Autumnfest was held in Dekalb, Illinois starting in 1995 and running through the early 2000s. It featured many in women's music, from Ferron to Nedra Johnson.

Madison, Wisconsin, was the home of 2003's and 2004's Tomboy Girl Fest, organized by Jane Weldon and Tret

Nedra Johnson, Lucie Blue Tremblay and Sue Fink, 1991 Michigan Festival. *Photo by Toni Armstrong Jr.*

Fure. Held indoors at a convention center, it included Ubaka Hill, Ember Swift, Lucie Blue Tremblay, Deidre McCalla, and others. Jane went on to produce the National Women's Music Festival 2005 through 2011.

The Northampton (Massachusetts) Lesbian Festival ran for at least four years in the nineties. Produced by WOW Productions, it featured music, comedy, a crafts area, and workshops.

In the 1990s, Heart of the South and Heart of the West happened in New Orleans and Las Vegas. Produced by Maile Klein and Marina Hodgini, performers included Azucar Y Crema, Lisa Koch, and Suede.

New Performers[588]

New performers were a diverse lot, from hip-hop to punk. Whether or not they performed in many women's music venues, they benefitted from women's music. Nedra Johnson told *HOT WIRE* in 1994, "I have much respect for Alix Dobkin and all the women who have been performing as out lesbians for the past twenty-plus years of women's music; I acknowledge that I could not do what I do without that foundation."

Nedra Johnson's mother played guitar, and her dad was a jazz musician. Growing up, she learned several instruments including tuba and bass guitar. At the age of twenty-three she did her first professional gig, at the Michigan Festival in Toshi Reagon's band. She also performed with Helen Hooke (Deadly Nightshade). Helen discovered that Nedra's dad had played on one of the Deadly Nightshade's albums. Today, when Nedra isn't playing bass with someone else, she's doing her own R&B-infused girl-with-a-guitar act. She released two albums—1993's *Testify* and 2005's *Nedra*. A popular performer at the Michigan Festival, she also played at the 1993 March on Washington and other venues.

Ubaka Hill, 1993 National Festival.
Photo by Toni Armstrong Jr.

Inspirational performer/drummer Ubaka Hill started playing in the seventies when she met drummer Edwina Lee Tyler at Washington Square Park in New York City. It was the first time she'd seen a woman play a djembe. She furthered her musical skills at a women's space in Brooklyn where she jammed with other drummers. In the eighties, she co-founded and played with several ensembles before moving to solo work. In the next decade, she became known in women's music for performances that incorporated poetry, song, and percussion. This charismatic performer played at the 1993 National LGBT March, at the National

Festival, the Michigan Festival, and more. At the 1995 Michigan Festival she started and led Drumsong Orchestra, a participatory drumming experience that was very popular until the event's last year in 2015. She's also led drumming groups at Campfest, and Sisterspace. Ubaka has three recordings, two of them on the Ladyslipper label. Songs include "Dance the Spiral Dance," "The Womyn United" and "If the Drum Is a Woman." She lives in upstate New York.

A cappella group DykeAppella hail from Madison, Wisconsin. They only played in venues that were wheelchair accessible and their group included an ASL interpreter. Member Tara Ayres recalls, "It was great for us as musicians to have an interpreter as part of the group, since we had to discuss the lyrics and meaning of each song in depth, so we had a shared understanding of everything we sang."[589] Active from 1991 until 2001, this five-woman group performed at several festivals, Mountain Moving Coffeehouse, and more. Their only recording, *At the Gates of Heaven*, was released in 1998. Songs included "Lesbian Picnic" (a sendup of "Teddy Bear Picnic"), "Wake Me Up Gently" (Deidre McCalla), and "Amazon" (Maxine Feldman).

Multi-instrumentalist Zoe Lewis calls herself a "world beat vaudeville extravaganza." Incorporating jazz to folk, she's done her show in a variety of venues, from the Virginia Women's Music Festival to the Kerrville Folk Festival to Olivia tours. Originally from Britain, she now resides in the US. Zoe's toured internationally since the late eighties and released eight recordings.

Susan Herrick released four albums in the nineties and performed at several women's music festivals including the Ohio Lesbian Festival. Centered in folk and pop, this singer-songwriter focused on themes of healing and spirituality.

Singer-songwriter Catie Curtis started performing at the Michigan and National festivals in the nineties. An award-winning songwriter, she's released fourteen albums and toured extensively, including concerts for Olivia Travel and two appearances at the White House. Early songs include "Radical," released in 1995, where she coyly sings to a lover that a display of affection isn't done to make a statement.

Hip-hop duo Goddess and She is known mostly outside of women's music but have been popular at women's festivals including National, Michigan, and the Ohio Lesbian Festival. Many lesbians discovered them through TV show *The L Word*.

There was a lot of speculation in women's music circles about singer-songwriter Cheryl Wheeler because of her androgynous look and her relationship songs that avoided pronouns. Known on the folk circuit, this personable musician started dropping hints in the nineties, in a matter-of-fact way, about a break-up with a woman. Known for her talented songwriting, she's released many albums starting in the eighties, and performed at National and Michigan. Holly Near has covered her biting commentary on gun control, "If It Were Up to Me."

Punk band The Butchies made appearances at the Michigan Festival. The Durham, N.C.-based band released four albums from 1998 to 2005. In their repertoire was Cris Williamson's "Shooting Star." One year at the festival they performed it with Williamson.

Atlanta area singer-songwriter Doria Roberts released *Radio Doria*, in 2000. Performance credits include Lilith Fair and the Michigan Womyn's Music Festival. For several years she was the producer for the Queerstock compilations that featured many in LGBTQ music including Catie Curtis, Angela Motter, Holly Near, and Toshi Reagon. Also from Atlanta is gender queer pop/blues singer-songwriter Bucky Motter who released two albums in the nineties (as "Angela Motter"), *Outta Control* and *Pleasure and Pain*. Bucky has shared the stage with a wide variety of musicians, from Doria Roberts to Jamie Anderson, and played at Rhythmfest every year it was in existence.[590]

Pam Hall's sensuous performances were popular in the early nineties at women's festivals Campfest, East Coast Lesbian Festival, and the Gulf Coast festival. *Honey on My Lips* was recorded with June Millington and released in 1992.

The duo Emma's Revolution is known in peace and justice circles as well as for their performances with Holly Near. Beginning in 2004 Pat Humphries and Sandy O released four albums together, plus one with Holly Near, *We Came to Sing*.

Bitch and Animal first burst on the scene in the late nineties. This violin-bass-percussion-ukulele duo were popular for songs "Pussy Manifesto" and "Drag King Bar." Frequent performers at the Michigan Festival, they toured in the US and Europe with Ani DiFranco as well as on their own. They released three albums. Bitch went on to solo work and released several albums including one on noted indie label Kill Rock Stars. Animal released one recording. In the 2000s Bitch worked with Ferron on two recordings and a movie. She also continued solo work at the Michigan Festival and other venues.

Alt rock/singer-songwriter Ani DiFranco didn't regularly appear in women's music venues but she credits women's music with support in her early years. Ladyslipper and Goldenrod were her first distributors. She appeared at the Michigan Festival and at Rhythmfest.

Charming singer-songwriter Ellis released her first recording in 1996 and ten albums followed. A favorite at the Michigan Festival, she's also played at the National and Virginia festivals. Her fan base includes many lesbians as well as straight folk followers.

Singer-songwriter Melissa Ferrick made her first recording in the nineties. She was popular at the Michigan Festival, especially for the sexy "Drive," and toured extensively.

Born in Venezuela, Irene Farrera is a singer/songwriter/guitarist/quarto player who offered songs in a variety of Latin styles. She lived in the US for a time and toured there in the nineties. Appearances included the Michigan Festival. She released four albums, one of them on the Redwood label.

SONiA started as part of alt rock/folk band Disappear Fear in the nineties. Now she tours solo, appearing in over twenty countries, including women's music festivals. She covers a wide range of peace and social justice issues.

Originally from Zimbabwe, guitarist/singer/songwriter Jess Hawk Oakenstar lived in New Zealand where she worked with other musicians including the Topp

Twins. She moved to the US in 1990. Until 1996, she toured the US, Australia, and New Zealand, playing in folk and women's music venues. Jess released two albums and is now based in Phoenix, Arizona.

Pianist/singer/songwriter Lynn Thomas released her first album, *Courage*, in 1992, and performed at many festivals. She penned "Together Proud and Strong" for the 1993 LGBT March on Washington. It was recorded in several cities with a chorus that included many in women's music as well as a few men and performed at the march.

Folk duo Justina and Joyce released two albums on their own label in the nineties. Their ethereal harmonies were heard at women's music festivals including Campfest, Gulf Coast, and the Northampton Lesbian Festival, as well as pride events and the International Gay Games.

Americana duo Wishing Chair (Kiya Heartwood and Miriam Davidson) started recording in the mid-nineties. Playing guitars, accordion, banjo and more, they released eight albums of mostly original work. They were popular at women's music festivals as well as folk venues. Kiya went on to solo gigs. Miriam is now the director of several choirs including Anna Crusis in Philadelphia.

Singer/songwriter/guitarist Pamela Means started releasing albums in the nineties. On her website she states, "...I've been called both 'a white Tracy Chapman' and a 'black Ani DiFranco.' But, really, I'm just me." Her unique style and great guitar chops made her a favorite at women's music festivals including Michigan. She's toured internationally and released eight albums.

Established Performers

For some performers, the nineties and later marked the end of their performing career. In 1998, after years of touring that included forty-one states and eight foreign countries, Lynn Lavner retired. Maxine Feldman, who had health and financial issues, stopped musical performances in the eighties, and emceeing (and other work) in the nineties. Naomi Littlebear Morena stopped playing music after injuring her hand in a 1999 auto accident. She hopes to return to music. Others transitioned into different work. Robin Flower had been teaching music since the seventies and transitioned to doing it full time in 1995. She still performs with Libby McLaren and they've been together over twenty-five years. Bernice Johnson Reagon retired from Sweet Honey in the Rock in 2004. She now does public speaking in a program that includes songs. June Millington, along with Ann Hackler, started the Institute for Musical Arts (IMA) in 1986. They offer music and music business workshops and camps for women and girls. She released two albums in the nineties as well as *Play Like a Girl* in 2011, and published a memoir, *Land of a Thousand Bridges*, in 2015. In 2018 she joined sister Jean and friend Brie Howard for an album by new band Fanny Walked the Earth. Not long after the release of the album Jean Millington had a stroke. As of 2019, she is recovering. Heather Bishop expanded her work to include public speaking and devoted more time to painting. In 2011, she published a book featuring her art, *My Face is a Map of My Time Here*. She's also a hypnotherapist. Ginni Clemmens moved to Maui and released another album in 2001, *Underneath Hawaiian Skies*.

Sue Fink released *True Life Adventure* in 1990. She quit touring later in that decade because she wanted to have a family, spend time with her partner, and put energy into other work. In 1993 she started the Angel City Chorale. Today, she writes music, teaches voice, and conducts the 160-voice choir. They've performed all over the world and in 2018 the Chorale was a semi-finalist on the reality TV show *America's Got Talent*.

Kay Gardner continued to compose and perform. In 1990, she conducted a live performance of "A Rainbow Path" at the National Women's Music Festival and in 1993, at the festival, premiered her hour-long classical piece "Ouroboros" with a choir and a forty-piece orchestra. Her orchestral work, "Rainforest," was performed by four orchestras in the early nineties.

In 1992, Linda Tillery formed the Cultural Heritage Choir. With music rooted in the Deep South and reflecting West African and Caribbean traditions, they perform at many venues internationally and release albums including the most recent *A Retrospective* (2012). Linda continues to perform her own show. In 2015 she appeared with Mary Watkins at the National Women's Music Festival's fortieth anniversary and in 2017 at the Ohio Lesbian Festival.

In 1993 Gwen Avery recorded a live performance at June Millington and Ann Hackler's IMA (Institute for Musical Arts). In the liner notes, June mentions a recent tough period for Gwen: "She has emerged from personal struggles stronger than ever…" Gwen adds, "To all the wonderful people who loved me through the rugged years, thank you for your time, love and patience."[591] She released

Alix Dobkin, 1992 Michigan Festival.
Photo by Toni Armstrong Jr.

2001's *Sugar Mama*, featuring her well-known title song, as well as standards such as "Georgia on My Mind." Producer Linda Tillery first heard her in the seventies. For the liner notes Linda wrote, "She would just pour out The Blues, and I'm not talking about an imitation. I can remember feeling the hair on the back of my neck stand on end…" While the album was well-received, four years later Gwen went through another difficult period. She told *Queer Music Heritage* in 2011, "I became homeless…which has now been the most trying time of my life..." Fortunately, she got back on her feet and in later years resumed performing until her passing in 2014.

Jamie Anderson continues to tour and has released eleven albums. She was one of the producers, along with Sue Fink and Dakota, of *A Family of Friends*, a 1993 compilation of women's music. In addition to solo shows, she started performing in 2014 with Dianne Davidson and Deidre McCalla, as "We Aren't Dead Yet."

Alix Dobkin released two albums in the nineties and in addition to other gigs, did four 1994 Lavender Jane reunion concerts with Kay Gardner and Toni Armstrong Jr. Her memoir, *My Red Blood*, was published in 2009. She's currently a co-director for Old Lesbians Organizing for Change. She still performs but since 2011 is doing fewer concerts.

Lucie Blue Tremblay continues to tour. She represented Canada at the 1992 World's Fair. She appeared at the fortieth anniversary of the National festival in 2015 and at an anniversary celebration for Olivia in 2018. In 2017 she released *Counting My Blessings*.

The Washington Sisters performed on the night stage at Michigan in 1993, a special appearance because their mother was in the audience. Their last gig together was in March of 1996. They went on to other careers, Sharon in academia and Sandra with the US Park Service.

Holly Near published her memoir in 1990 and in 1993, took her one-woman show *Fire in the Rain* to several venues, including one off-Broadway. She continued to record, releasing solo albums and some with Ronnie Gilbert and Cris Williamson. Today she maintains a busy touring schedule performing in a variety of venues, from folk concerts to the fortieth anniversary of the Michigan Festival. Still very much involved in social activism, she has raised awareness for Planned Parenthood, border issues, School of the Americas and much more.

After a several years sabbatical, Margie Adam returned for more shows in the nineties. *Another Place* was released in 1993 and in 1995, *Soon and Again*. She also toured with pianists Liz Story and Barbara Higbie, as the Three of Hearts. Margie released three more recordings in the 2000s (including a greatest hits album), then retired from music after performing at the Million Strong March for Women's Lives in Washington, DC in 1995. Now she works as an integrative counselor in the San Francisco Bay area.

The Fabulous Dyketones released their only recording, *Live in P-town*, in 1988 and their last performance was in 2004; however, there were several reunions in the nineties, perhaps without co-founder Char Priolo. One of the original members, Kristan Aspen, recalls at least one reunion performance organized to help fight an anti-gay measure in Oregon. She jokes that they can't fit into the costumes anymore.

After thirty years of performing, Australian Judy Small retired from music. She is now a federal judge.

Teresa Trull and Barbara Higbie released their second album, *Playtime*, in 1997. Teresa now lives in New Zealand, working as a horse trainer and doing the occasional gig. Barbara released five solo albums since *Playtime* including

2014's *Scenes from Life*. Recent performances include the Michigan Festival and on Olivia tours.

Jean Fineberg and Ellen Seeling (DEUCE) continue to play music in various projects, including the Montclair Women's Big Band. They also teach and love being role models for their female students.

Vicki Randle continued working with women's music artists as well as mainstream acts including Elton John, Bonnie Raitt, Herbie Hancock, Taj Mahal, and many others. She was the lead singer and percussionist for the Tonight Show Band for eighteen years. Vicki has recorded soundtracks for dozens of movies and performed worldwide, from London's prestigious Albert Hall to the White House.

Dianne Davidson retired from music after a serious car accident. Jamie Anderson pulled her out of retirement in 2014. She now lives in Nashville where she's involved in various music projects. A new album is planned.

Deidre McCalla continues to perform and maintains a busy music teaching practice. She's one of the artists on *Glass Half Full*, a 2006 compilation produced by Irene Young that raised money for breast cancer research. Her 2018 performances included an Olivia anniversary celebration and one with "We Aren't Dead Yet" at the National Women's Music Festival. She lives in Atlanta.

In 1998, Therese Edell was awarded the Jane Schlissman Award for Outstanding Contributions to Women's Music at the National Women's Music Festival. That same year she released another recording, *From Women's Faces Plus*, that contained cuts from her earlier album as well as songs that were previously unreleased. She also continued to compose music. Miffed at rumors that she would soon or had already passed away, she wrote this letter to *Lesbian Connection* (July/August 2000): "Dear Lesbos — Last Saturday night before her concert, my old friend Kate Clinton came up to me and chatted for about ten minutes, catching me up on her life and hearing about mine. Then for the first time ever, I got to sit in a box seat—very fun! Imagine my surprise when during the evening many of the audience members (who had obviously sung 'Happy Birthday' to me at Michigan) sang the song to me once again! Then Zrazy, the duo from Ireland, dedicated the last song of their set to me! And finally, Kate Clinton began her set by telling everyone that she had just spoken with me out in the lobby. What is this? Are all these people afraid I'm at death's door or something? I may be quadriplegic these days, but I'm certainly not feeling that I'm going to be checking out anytime soon!"

Ferron released four albums in the early nineties and continued to tour. In 1991, her *Shadows on a Dime* was listed in *Ms* as one of the landmark albums of the prior twenty years. In recent years her arthritis became so bad that she couldn't play the guitar. She cut back on touring. Ferron performed at Michigan's fortieth anniversary in 2015 in a round robin on the day stage, admitting that she hadn't touched a guitar for a year. When Melissa Ferrick canceled her night stage performance, Ferron and band filled in for her. The audience jumped to its feet at the end of her triumphant set. After that, she booked more dates, including a headlining spot at the 2017 Vancouver Folk Festival, an event she first played at in the seventies.

Cris Williamson's *Changer and the Changed* was also on that list from *Ms*. Cris continues to record and perform, including a 1993 tour to Russia with Tret Fure. Tret and Cris toured and recorded together for many years. In the nineties, they began making albums with both names on the cover, *Postcards from Paradise* (1993), *Between the Covers* (1996), and *Radio Quiet* (1998). Tret is especially fond of *Between the Covers*, calling it their best. "We were at our peak musically. We were happy and sharing music equally. I love *Radio Quiet* but I've had people tell me that they could hear the impending trouble/breakup in that CD. *Between the Covers* had a lot of love in it."[592] They were together for nineteen years. Tret remembers, "…the more our relationship became public, people sort of fell to us as role models and comes a point, I think, in anyone's professional life, that if you become too identified with someone else you lose your own identity…Because it was always 'Cris and Tret' and I was feeling like 'and Tret' more than I was feeling like 'Tret.'"[593]

Tret decided to end the relationship, calling it one of the hardest decisions she's ever made. There was backlash. For the first two or three years it was difficult for her to get booked for shows. While some fans were supportive, others were angry and refused to attend concerts. Not only did their audiences love their music together but they were relationship role models. Tret recalls, "(We were) the poster children for co-dependency and it was just wrong…we never should have put ourselves out there so much like that because it just made it very difficult to move on."[594] It was a good thing while it lasted. "We had a great relationship musically and personally…"[595] Tret released eight solo albums after that and continues to tour. While she has fans in the folk world, women make up the bulk of her following. "I'm still considered a women's music artist and I have no problem with that, they've been there for me."[596]

Cris poured out her grief in 2001's *Ashes*. Produced by Teresa Trull, it featured her friend Bonnie Raitt on the heartbreaking "Cry Cry Cry." She released several more albums on her own label, some including previously recorded songs, and one with Holly Near. Cris is the biggest selling women's music artist. She maintains a busy touring and teaching schedule. In recent years she toured with a show where she sang every song from *Changer and the Changed*. Side players included Vicki Randle, Teresa Trull, and others. Excited audiences sang along and offered standing ovations. Cris is grateful to the music and to her fans, "I love my job. Music saves lives. It saves mine too. For an hour on stage or two I'm doing what I do best. And that's about as good as a person could hope for."[597]

Community Drumming

From the beginning women gathered and played drums at women's music festivals. Drumming was especially popular in the nineties and later when Ubaka Hill started and led Drumsong Orchestra at the Michigan Festival. Wahru

Cleveland co-founded something similar at the National Festival—the Drum Chorus—and led drumming at the Ohio Lesbian Festival. Women playing drums together created spiritual connection and community. Attendee Sue Fitzgerald recalls, "Drumming put me back in touch with the five-year-old girl that loved rhythm but was told drumming was for boys."[598] Some women attended the festivals primarily to drum—at workshops, around campfires, and on stage. At the Michigan Festival, Drumsong Orchestra performed on the Sunday Acoustic Stage and at National, the Festival Drum Chorus performed on the last day.

Drummer Debbie Fier remembers great jams at Michigan—"When rains would come, drummers would gather backstage and have mind-blowing jams with the best of the best drummers—Edwina Lee Tyler, Carolyn Brandy, Annette Aguilar, Nydia Mata, and more!"[599] Edwina was a mentor to many drummers. Fier exclaims, "Edwina was the first female djembe player that many of us witnessed…she inspired a whole new generation of wimmin drummers."[600]

Professional women's drumming groups have been popular onstage at festivals, also, from taiko drummers Sawagi Taiko to groups celebrating the diversity of the African diasporic culture, such as ASE Drumming Circle.

Drumming is a powerful force. Michigan Festival worker Tess Wiseheart recalls a festival with so much rain that she joked even the raccoons were dining at a restaurant in town. It was an effort to get anything done because the rain kept on and on. Spirits were low as workers prepared for opening night: "We were so wet and so miserable that none of us could stand in our own power. How the hell were we going to pull off the night stage opening? And then, it happened. The drums began. I MEAN the Drums. Carolyn and Edwina and Annette… the drummers. Suddenly, our shoulders were back and we were being big in our power. The drums were loud, and rhythmic, and diverse. It was a symphony of percussion played by the womyn who knew how to do it. And they kept it up and kept it up, and they chased the rain away. The sun broke through the clouds for the first time in days, and we were going to have a festival!"[601]

Mainstream Music and Women's Music

Women's music and culture continued to draw mainstream notice. *The Arsenio Show* featured Lea DeLaria and Kate Clinton. A 1994 Geraldo Riviera show about lesbian visibility included Olivia president Judy Dlugacz. Until 2014 Vicki Randle was a regular in the *Tonight Show* band. NPR's "Morning Edition" and "All Things Considered" used Margie Adam's *Naked Keys* between stories throughout the eighties and nineties. While these exposures aren't more important than what happened within the women's music network, they do illustrate how women's music became more visible and, perhaps, introduced even more people to the music and its artists. For some, hearing BETTY on *The L Word* was their first exposure to women's music.

Some fans first found women's community through mainstream artists, and later, women's music. Many lesbians discovered Canadian k.d. lang after her first album release in the eighties. She never appeared at women's music festivals or on a women's music label but her androgynous look and powerful voice made her popular with lesbian fans. There was much speculation about her sexuality until she came out in the pages of *The Advocate* in 1992. For a few years, interviews focused on her sexuality and while she publically supported LGBTQ rights in the nineties and later, she was adamant that she be remembered for her voice. She once told Barbara Walters that when she sang a love song, she was thinking of a woman. For other lesbians following mainstream music, their first love was Melissa Etheridge. Julie King attended her first Etheridge show in 1991 when she was a freshman in college. "I remembered being shell-shocked, looking around at all the women. Women were everywhere! They were kissing fervently in the bathroom line or bravely taking over the men's bathroom (since there were no men in sight). I immediately found what I didn't know I had been looking for."[602] She became a huge fan, attending every Etheridge show she could, married a man for a few years but realized she was a lesbian and found the Michigan Women's Music Festival, attending every year from 2007 to 2015. Connie Daily also started her journey to women's music through mainstream artists, including Etheridge and k.d. lang.[603] A few years after becoming their fans, she was encouraged by a friend to attend the Michigan Festival. After wandering into the Goldenrod booth (where recordings were sold), "Someone offered to help me and I told her I had no idea what I was looking for. She sat me down with a pair of headphones and put on Cris Williamson. 'Waterfall' played. The tears flowed. It was an epiphany."[604]

Lilith Fair, a series of concerts in the late nineties and 2010, featured female solo singer-songwriters and woman-fronted bands—founder Sarah McLachlan as well as the Dixie Chicks, Queen Latifah, and many more. While it was promoted as the first of its kind, women's music fans knew that wasn't true. Sue Fink comments, "It was never the same as women's music where the women built the stage and the sound system, ran it all themselves and did the promo themselves—it wasn't just the performers—the women's community built all that...from the ground up..."[605]

More Changes

Olivia celebrated its twentieth anniversary in 1993 with a concert attended by two thousand in Berkeley and twelve hundred the next night in San Francisco. The all-star celebrations included former and current Olivia performers. Also in 1993, they released their last album, Cris Williamson and Tret Fure's *Postcards from Paradise*. Over forty albums were released by Olivia overall with *Changer and the Changed* their biggest seller.

Three years prior they had offered their first cruise. Six hundred women sailed with them and they were planning more trips. In the early nineties, the company had twelve employees with an annual budget close to four million. They are now a vacation company for women, and Olivia artists are often featured on their trips.

In 2018 Olivia was honored by the Americana Music Association. Judy Dlugacz and Cris Williamson accepted the award. Cris noted, "We've sold out Carnegie Hall three times. This is the first time we've been acknowledged by the industry."[606]

In the early nineties Redwood continued to release Holly Near's recordings and also developed a following for their Latin and World music recordings. They commissioned work for live performances, too, including the New Spirituals concerts. Financial difficulties forced them to close in 1996. Although they had achieved success with releases from a variety of artists—Judy Small, Inti-Illimani, Lillian Allen, and Altazor, among others—Holly Near's albums sold the most, by far. It wasn't enough to keep them solvent. Their final release, by Latin Jazz group Ritmo y Candela, was nominated for a Grammy. Holly's recording career did not end with Redwood. She continues to release albums.

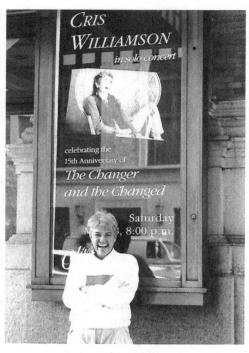

Cris Williamson, Carnegie Hall, 1991.
Photo by Toni Armstrong Jr.

HOT WIRE ceased publication in 1994 amid an outpouring of thanks. In their last issue, September 1994, producer/writer Dr. Ruth J. Simkin wrote "...I will be saddened not to receive it any longer but will always be grateful for what I got from it, how I was fed, how my ideas were challenged, how my beliefs were validated, my culture honored..."[607]

Many women's bookstores closed in the 1990s and 2000s partly because online entities increased in popularity. No longer could we depend on these brick and mortar stores as places to buy women's music or where we could check the bulletin board for concert flyers. In 2016 there were thirteen women's bookstores remaining in the United States and Canada, down from over a hundred in the eighties and early nineties.

In the 1993 LGBTQ march in Washington, stages included many well-known performers in women's music—the Washington Sisters, Lynn Lavner, Pam Hall, and Cris Williamson. Also that year was Stonewall 25, a milestone anniversary of the Stonewall riots. Held at Carnegie Hall, the celebration concert included Kay Gardner, Nurudafina Pili Abena, and Alix Dobkin. Local pride celebrations continued in communities across North America, sometimes with lesbian musicians.

Performance spaces closed, including long-time Chicago coffeehouse Mountain Moving. It held its last show on December 10, 2005 with Deidre McCalla.

Producer Lin Daniels wondered about the viability of the network, especially for venues: "I'm not sure that women's music can continue the way it has been. It's getting harder and harder for women to make a living doing women's music because there are fewer producers out there...It seems to me that...lesbians... don't feel the need as much to go to a lesbian music concert. They can turn on HBO and see Melissa or k.d. lang...That's not enough for me."[608]

In 2002 the documentary *Radical Harmonies* was released. The first film devoted solely about women's music, it included concert footage and interviews with many in women's music, from musician Gwen Avery to producer Lin Daniels. The eighty-eight minute film was produced by Dee Mosbacher, Boden Sandstrom, Margie Adam, and June Millington. It played to eager audiences all over the country, including at the Michigan Festival.

Additional visibility was offered to women's music artists through awards. The OutMusic Awards began in 1990, honoring LGBTQ artists, sometimes with a live awards show. *HOT WIRE* also had an annual Readers' Choice Survey with categories ranging from Emcee to All-Time Favorite Performer. While not a formal awards show, it did offer bragging rights to musicians.

With declining audiences and a steadily graying crowd, festivals made the effort to draw younger women. Michigan seemed to be the most successful. Its day stage and late night slots became a haven for acts that largely attracted the twenty-something crowd—Le Tigre, MEN, Medusa, MazzMuse, Von Iva, and Krudas Cubensi. Anyone was welcome to attend, of course, and it wasn't unusual to see sixty-year-old women crowd-surfing.

Perhaps younger women saw the festivals as the sole domain of gray-haired women. Young women created their own events—riot grrl band performances in the nineties and later, gender queer events. Older women were also attending fewer festivals and buying less women's music. Robin Tyler reasoned that the decline for all women was because the mainstream saw an opportunity with us, and used the Chitlin' Circuit for comparison. Through the sixties, the Chitlin' Circuit provided safe venues, record labels, and media for African-American entertainers. Robin recalls, "It's like what happened with Lena Horne and Ella Fitzgerald. My first agent in the seventies used to be their agent. He brought them out of Harlem and even though they couldn't enter the front of clubs he started to expose them to white audiences. The same thing happened in women's music—the minute the Indigo Girls and Melissa Etheridge (entered) or there was a crossover, then it became very commercial."[609]

Robin mourns the decline of women's music festivals. "The festivals, which were the only place where women could gather, started to lose women. Nothing will replace festivals...If you go to Dinah Shore (golf tournament and lesbian events) it's not the same. It's not built by women."[610] Also, the women's music network was built through word of mouth—there was no social media, no YouTube and no cell phones. Now, artists can put something up on YouTube and gain popularity, as Sue Fink did recently with a video of the choir she directs: "(We got) 65,000 hits on a YouTube video—you can do that now. Imagine what we could've done if we had the resources we have now."[611] Videos of her choir's first appearance on 2018's *America's Got Talent* have garnered millions of views.

One of the issues that came to the forefront in the nineties, especially at the Michigan Festival, was the inclusion of transgender women. The festival's women-born-women (WBW) intention was that those attending had to have been born biological females. While producer Lisa Vogel and others maintained that this was not transphobic, others disagreed. In 1991 Nancy Burkholder bought a ticket to the festival but was asked to leave after it was discovered she was transgender. The festival later apologized. People on both sides of the issue were angry. Camp Trans was established in 1994 (some sources say 1993) by a group of activists, some who were transgender and some who identified in other ways. Situated across the road from the festival, they handed out literature and staged demonstrations outside and inside the festival. Debate raged on and escalated in publications and in festival workshops although some attempt at peaceful dialogue was accomplished on both sides. Lisa Vogel told the front gate to sell tickets to people from Camp Trans, as long as they understood the intention of the festival. Included in the first group that came from across the road was Vogel's girlfriend of twenty years. Women who attended the festival had mixed views, according to Vogel, "...the womyn who really wanted the fest to be womyn-born-womyn space [without trans womyn] would say everybody wanted that, or most people want that. And womyn who wanted trans womyn welcomed and sought after would say the majority wanted that too.[612] Some activists advocated boycotting artists who appeared at the festival. Performers scheduled at other events across the country had their bookings canceled, causing many to lose money. In 2015 Lea DeLaria canceled a scheduled performance at the Michigan Festival because of negative criticism. Camp Trans closed in 2012.

Other women's festivals didn't experience protests on the same level but were occasionally painted with the same broad brush, with some women choosing not to attend because of perceived anti-trans bias. That was the reason the promo for the Ohio Lesbian Festival stated, "All womyn welcome, always."

Several festivals ceased in the nineties and beyond, including the Pacific Northwest Music and Cultural Jamboree, and Campfest. Some festivals continued through the decade—the Virginia Women's Music Festival (also known as CampOut), the Ohio Lesbian Festival, and Sisterspace Weekend. The National Women's Music Festival celebrated its twentieth anniversary in 1994 and its fortieth anniversary in 2015. (The festival didn't occur in 1981, hence the discrepancy with numbers.) At the latter, co-founder Kristen Lems performed, along with many others who were there at the early festivals—Holly Near, Mary Watkins, Linda Tillery, June Millington, and Alix Dobkin—plus those who came later—Big Bad Gina, Nedra Johnson, Lucie Blue Tremblay, Melanie DeMore, and Jamie Anderson. This festival has been an inspiration to many over the years, including fan Anne Griffiths: "I started attending National with my mom when I was eight years old, and I firmly believe I am the confident, successful woman

I am today because of these women who created that world for me. It never occurred to me to ask, 'Can a woman run security for a concert?' Or drum or direct a show, because I saw it right in front of me. I owe them so much."[613]

Michigan also celebrated its fortieth anniversary in 2015. Performers included BETTY, Jill Sobule, Toshi Reagon, Ferron, Alive! and many others. Sadly, it was their last festival. While many women grieved the loss of this long-time festival, the final one was celebratory and included a grand fireworks display after the last night stage. Producer Lisa Vogel told us, "The spirit of this community will live on forever, the friends and family we have found on the Land are eternal."[614] She maintains that there were several reasons for the festival ending. One was the enormous amount of energy needed to produce it. She started the festival at the age of nineteen and through her twenties and thirties, had the energy to produce an event of this size. That changed in her forties. "I had attempted for the last fifteen years to reorganize the festival so I didn't have to work equal to two full-time jobs in a year…in my fifties it was really fucking hard…There were many things that influenced the attendance of the festival and certainly the trans debate was one of them…Forty years of a run of doing anything is a long, long time."[615] She was approaching sixty years of age when she decided to end the festival. Festival land was sold to a group of women who plan to open it to rental by various women-positive groups.[616]

Teresa Trull is grateful for the opportunities women's music gave her and others. "Women's music made it possible for women to do what they're doing now—it also meant that women's music will no longer be around. It was a self-fulfilling prophecy. If you achieve your goals, then there shouldn't be anything such as women's music. It should be the point. The whole idea is that women should have the same opportunities."[617]

Cris Williamson is proud of what they did. "Many storms have battered us, but still we cling with our roots—which tend to be pretty strong. And we're rooted in good things—good ethic and well-meaning business."[618]

It was those good things that were held dear, it was much more than mere entertainment. Over and over again women in the network heard how women's music made a remarkable difference in thousands of lives. Cris remembers, "Afterwards the stories that people tell me are amazing….Not, 'You have a real nice voice.' Oh no. We get stuff like, 'I just want you to know, I wouldn't have lived without you.'"[619]

Fan Robin Slicer attended her first women's music performance in utero, when her mother attended a Holly Near/Cris Williamson concert in 1976. "I grew up with women's music. It shaped me…In the tradition, I took my daughter to her first Holly Near concert in utero as well and I hope she will grow up strong for a lifelong exposure as well."[620]

Elisabeth Brook first heard women's music in the seventies and is a lifelong fan. "(It) had the effect of making me more powerful as a woman and giving me a community of women who understood what it means to be feminist and lesbian. It helped me to be more articulate about my wants and needs. Women's music changed the face of my world…"[621]

Marianne Barlow's mother discovered women's music when she came out in 1980. "She used to sing Cris Williamson's 'Lullaby' to me as a kid. I'm now a lesbian singer-songwriter."[622]

Musician Nancy Vogl hopes that younger women stay connected with the work that older women have done in women's music and feminism: "There is such little connection between this generation of young women and the early feminists. It's as if those ideas that were easy and accessible got absorbed by the dominant culture but no one remembers where they came from and older dykes are invisible."[623]

DJ/musician Lori Lambert believes that honoring our foremothers will aid in connection: "There is a long string of pioneers who've paved the way through blood and tears toward full expression of self. As people who witnessed the evolution of these freedoms, we understand how we got here…it is our duty to fight, explain, and express creatively what we see and how we feel. I feel fortunate as an individual to have had even a small hand in the shaping of such a lively, expressive art."[624]

It was wonderful for so many. Sandra Washington adds, "The community we built was an amazing thing…I'm glad I had the experience."[625]

Robin Tyler feels the same, "There's nothing like that era, I'm really happy to be part of it."[626]

Women Who Are Gone

We have lost many in women's music. In 2002 Kay Gardner visited a hospital not long after returning home from the Michigan Festival. Complaining of extreme fatigue and other symptoms, she was sent home where she had heart failure and passed away. She was probably misdiagnosed, as are many women with heart issues. Ginni Clemmens died in 2003 after a car accident on Maui, where she was living. Maxine Feldman had long-term lung and heart issues and was lost to the music world in 2007. Engineer and musician Kris Koth showed up for work at the Virginia Women's Music Festival in 2018. She hadn't felt well for a while but was afraid to see a doctor because she had no health insurance. Two festival workers—a nurse and a paramedic—determined that she should go to the hospital. Diagnosed with liver and kidney failure, she made her transition a few days later. Others who have passed include Bonnie Kovaleff Blackfoot (musician, 1997), Brenda Henson (Gulf Coast Music Festival producer, 2008), Carol MacDonald (musician, 2007), Erika Luckett (musician, 2018), Flash Silvermoon (musician, 2018), Gwen Avery (musician, 2015), Janet Small (musician, Alive!, 2010), Jerene O'Brien Jackson (musician, BeBe K'Roche, 2003), Joy Rosenblatt (Mountain Moving Coffeehouse and *HOT WIRE* staff member, 2004), Karlene Faith (educator, 2017), Kim Kimber (producer, NEWMR, Women's Music Archives, 2018), Marcia Diehl (musician, New Harmony Sisterhood Band, 2015), Marilyn Ries (recording engineer, 2017), Pamela Robin Brandt (musician, The Deadly Nightshade, 2015), Pat Parker (poet, early Olivia LP and Varied

Voices of Black Women tour, 1989), Peggy Mitchell (musician, BeBe K'Roche, 2009), Peggy Platt (comic, Dos Fallopia, 2018), River Lightwomoon (musician, coffeehouse producer, 2019), Ronnie Gilbert (musician, 2015), Rosetta Reitz (label owner, Rosetta Records, 2008), Ruth Rowan (sign interpreter, 2015), Shirley Childress Johnson (sign interpreter, Sweet Honey in the Rock, 2017), Sylvia Meservey (*Face the Music* radio DJ, 2007), Tess Wiseheart (Michigan Festival staff, 2018), Therese Edell (musician, 2011), and Virginia Giordano (record distributor and concert producer, 2015).

These women were honored in many ways. Ginni Clemmens's friends held a memorial on her favorite beach. An empty boat filled with leis was sent out to sea while everyone sang. Ronnie Gilbert's life was celebrated with a concert at Freight and Salvage Coffeehouse in Berkeley, with many in women's music performing—Linda Hirschhorn, Holly Near, Barbara Higbie, Linda Tillery, and more. The show sold out quickly and was streamed live on the web for those who couldn't attend. For others we've lost, there were concerts, rituals, loving obituaries, and more.

Did Women's Music Accomplish What It Set Out To Do?

Women's music set out to empower feminists and lesbians. Its impact cannot be disputed. Musicians agree that women's music helped them. Amy Ray says, "It opened up a lot of doors and it made the people in the record industry also understand that there was a recognizable demographic."[627] Melissa Etheridge told *HOT WIRE* (Jan 1990), "Even though I was not a part of women's music…I definitely would have to say that it being there—and those women doing what they were doing—helped me to do what I'm doing today. I saw that there were women making music that they really wanted to make and doing it as themselves." Robin Flower agrees that it helped women musicians: "It made women musicians more visible in this world. Lesbians, too. Women instrumentalists aren't a big deal anymore and that's really good."[628] Deidre McCalla has seen profound changes: "I do think we changed the world…We set out to change how women were perceived as artists and women's participation in the industry. Even though the overall music industry is male dominated, definitely there are more women in positions of power. When I watch bands on TV it's not uncommon to see a woman bass player or drummer…what this generation sees as normal was a revolution and it's a revolution that we built."[629]

Still, there's work to be done. Robin Flower has a show about the history of music that she presents at schools and, "…little girls will say 'I didn't know girls could play guitar.'"[630] Producer Lin Daniels wonders about visibility— "It's not enough for me to turn on television and see Ellen DeGeneres and Melissa Etheridge and a few others who have made it to the mainstream. That's wonderful, I applaud them. I think their success, in part, is a product of what we'd done in the seventies and eighties. I just don't think it's enough."[631]

Women's music had a personal benefit, not only for the audience but for those involved. Deidre McCalla comments, "What has been moving in my life as a performer are the many connections that I make with people during shows and although I don't recall them individually, the power of that connection remains after the notes have died and that's really the meaning that I have in this. My son said to me yesterday, 'I don't understand why you're going to do this show when there's no profit' and I said, it depends on how you define profit."[632]

Women's music was also one of the driving forces behind the women's movement, helping to raise funds and create awareness for the first rape crisis centers, the women's health movement, and women's bookstores. Nancy Vogl says, "Women's music provided so much of the funding...we would go from town to town doing a benefit for the battered women's shelter, for a women's study group in some other town..."[633] She recalls the announcements at each show—potlucks, protests, and other events going on for women that served to bring them together and empower them for the work they needed to do.

Ginny Berson is conflicted about what was achieved. Her vision was to overthrow patriarchy and capitalism. "We didn't succeed in creating a separate economic institution that hired hundreds and hundreds of women, gave them great benefits, treated them well, and enabled them to learn new skills....(but) I don't feel like we failed. We recorded and produced some wonderful music that truly touched women, helped women change their lives and brought women together and built community and supported women in their own changes, their own work and their own spiritual growth."[634]

Kristan Aspen wonders if we women knew what we'd planned to do: "Women's music in general didn't set out to accomplish something. It was the expression of the culture we were creating. It was the glue that held us together. It was the air we breathed. It was our sustenance. We didn't do that for the outside world. We did it for ourselves. It was our creativity. It was sharing with each other. What the world got was to see that women could perform on a level that was high quality, exciting and fun."[635]

Cris Williamson told the *Boston Globe* in 1988 "There I am hacking with my machete, making my way through the jungle...and I look behind me and Tracy's (Chapman) striding down the path. Part of me is a bit jealous of that success and in my rational mind I say 'Cris...this is why you did it.'" We made it safe for women in music and for their audiences. Janis Ian told *HOT WIRE* (May 1994): "I was talking with Lea DeLaria on a street corner in P-town, my partner and I were watching some little baby butches running up to each other and asking for dates, and we're going 'Good lord!' I mean, none of them were worried about things like violence or shame. Lea said, 'Don't you understand? That's what we've given them.'"

Over forty years ago Maxine Feldman was one of the musicians who told us we were Amazons and that we could do *anything*. We accomplished so much, creating a network that empowered us in a myriad of ways. An army of lovers brought us magical nights in college coffeehouses, Carnegie Hall, and the woods of Michigan. They played for us what was in their hearts and ours. We could not fail.

Acknowledgments

I wrote this book with the help of many people. In no particular order, I'd like to thank them.

Thanks to my first readers—Margie Adam, Ruth Barrett, Karen Colton, Alix Dobkin, Pippa Holloway, and Kaia Skaggs. You helped me with errant commas, you corrected statements, and you let me know when I repeated myself. None of you knew how I should spell "a cappella" but that's okay.

Thanks to Margie Adam, my head cheerleader. She read the first draft *twice*, then spent hours on the phone offering editing advice and encouragement. We killed the battery in three different phones. When the battery on her laptop died, we knew we were done.

I wrote much of this book while housesitting or staying with friends and family. Thanks to everyone in North Carolina who gave me a comfortable bed and unlimited Wi-Fi. Thanks also to my mom, Joy Anderson, and her husband, Mike Soustek, for letting me take over their guest room in Arizona for a couple of months. Mom brought me sugary iced coffee at the exact time in the afternoon when my eyelids started to droop, and Mike made dinner every night. I no longer fit into most of my jeans. I don't care.

The encouragement and support I received from fans and friends was phenomenal. Many of you asked about buying the book before I'd even finished the first draft. Lots of you helped me raise money to pay for a portion of the expenses. Some of you listened to me go on and on about the project. Bless you all.

I often joked with J. D. Doyle that I used his *Queer Music Heritage* site so much, I should've made him co-writer. His unwavering support for this book and for LGBTQ music in general is appreciated so much by me and many other people around the globe.

HOT WIRE was also invaluable. Thanks to Toni Armstrong Jr. and her dedicated band of merry volunteers for a great publication that's just as important today as it was when it was published. Thanks also to Toni for so many wonderful photos. Thanks to the other photographers, too, who never get enough credit for what they do. Your images really make this book come alive.

My appreciation to everyone I interviewed, from grateful fans to musicians I've long admired. Many of you went above and beyond the call of duty, giving me contact info, photos, words of support, and advice. Thank you for the stories and for trusting me.

Writer and women's historian Bonnie Morris has been a great support. I thank her for her work, including the groundbreaking *Eden Built by Eves*. When I got a confusing letter from a university press, she translated the academic speak and told me "They're afraid men won't buy the book." Whatever issue I was facing, chances are good she'd been there first and had sage advice to offer.

Thank you to everyone who made women's music what it is and was. The beautiful music and your incredible support made me the strong woman I am today. I wouldn't have considered being a professional musician or writer without you.

Bella Books, thanks for taking a chance on this enormous project. It's such a relief to work with women who not only understand women's music but realize its importance.

When Bella asked if Katherine V. Forrest, the editor for my first book, would be a good choice for this book, I rocketed out of my chair with a big "Hell yeah." Thanks, Katherine, for all your work and for finally setting me straight on how to spell "a cappella."

Last but not least, love to my long-suffering wife, Pat Laberge, who celebrated with me when I got that coveted photo or found that obscure resource, and who nodded sagely as I processed and vented, often about women she'd never heard of, bless her Canadian heart. Honey, you can talk about your motorcycle all you want. I owe you at least that much.

Appendix A

Women's Music Producers and Venues Featuring Touring Musicians

From *Women's Music Plus* 1987, published by Toni Armstrong Jr., and the author's files.

This does not include festivals, university groups or pride organizations.

A Woman's Coffeehouse, Minneapolis, MN
Allegra Productions, Cambridge, MA
Amber Moon Productions, Lexington, KY
Amethyst Productions, Chicago, IL
Artemis House, Oklahoma City, OK
Artemis Sisters, Morgantown, WV
Athena Arts, Houston, TX
Ava Productions, St. Paul, MN
Bloodroot, Bridgeport, CT
Bloomer's, Pittsburgh, PA
Blue Room House Concerts, Bloomington, IN
Branching Out Productions, Indianapolis, IN
Calico's Coffeehouse, Columbus, OH
Canal Street Tavern, Dayton, OH
Catch Fire! Productions, Halifax, Nova Scotia, Canada
Circle Productions, East Lansing, MI
Coffeehouse Extempore, Minneapolis, MN
Cowrys Productions, Bloomington, IN
Crystal Vision/Flash, La Mesa, CA
Dark Star Productions, Greenwood, VA
Desperate Measures, Bogota, NJ
Electric Woman Productions, Little Rock, AR
Elword Productions, Albany, NY
Everywoman's Coffeehouse, Manchester, NH
Fallen Woman Productions, Madison, WI
Fifield Presents, Los Angeles, CA
Finer Points Productions, Bloomington, IN
First Friday Productions, Roanoke, VA
Folklore Productions, Santa Monica, CA
Free Spirit, Tempe, AZ
Freight and Salvage Coffeehouse, Berkeley, CA
Full Moon Rising, Cambridge, MA

Gatherstretch Productions, Oklahoma City, OK
Granny May Productions, Atlanta, GA
Heatherwood Productions, Hollywood, CA
Hera Productions, Babylon, NY
Herland, Oklahoma City, OK
Hexeba's Productions, Rushland, PA
Highlands Inn, Bethlehem, NH
Homegrown Productions, Ann Arbor, MI
Horizon, Binghamton, NY
Hurricane Productions, Milwaukee, WI
IMA, Goshen, MA
Indy Indie, Indianapolis, IN
Jazzberry's, Rochester, NY
Joyful Productions, Chicago, IL
KKS Productions, Cazenovia, NY
Lavender Triangle Productions, Toledo, OH
Leaping Lizard Productions, Madison, WI
Leonarda Productions, New York, NY
Lincoln Legion, Lincoln, NE
LIP, Utica, NY
Little Feather Productions, Dallas, TX
Lois Marchino, El Paso, TX
Magnolia Productions, Birmingham, AL
Mainstage Productions, Tallahassee, FL
Mateel Women's Music, Redway, CA
Maven Productions, Boulder, CO
Midwest Music, Milwaukee, WI
Modern Times / Amaranth, Cambridge, MA
Moonrise Productions, Flint, MI
Mound of Venus Productions, Covington, KY
Mountain Moving Coffeehouse, Chicago, IL
Muse Productions, Louisville, KY
Muses, Baltimore, MD
New Women Now, Rock Spring, WY
Oh Sure! Productions, Iowa City, IA
Orchid Productions, Atlanta, GA
Oven Productions, Cleveland Heights, OH
Palms Playhouse, Davis, CA
Pleiades Productions, Ft Worth, TX

PMS Productions, Tempe, AZ
Renegade Productions, Kansas City, MO
Rising Productions, Rochester, NY
Roadwork, Washington, DC.
Sisterspirit Productions, San Jose, CA
Snake Sisters Café, Rochester, NY
Sojourner's Coffeehouse, Woodstock, NY
Spiderweb Productions, Trumansburg, NY
Stanford Women's Productions, Stanford, CA
Star Trip Productions, Denver, CO
Strong Again Productions, East Moline, IL
Studio Red Top, Boston, MA
Summer Sound, Denver, CO
Summercor Productions, Mt. Marion, NY
Sun Walk Productions, St. Paul, MN
The Ark, Ann Arbor, MI
Uncommon Partners, Seattle, WA
Unicorn Productions, Portsmouth, VA
Victory Music Productions, Sumner, WA
We-3 Productions, Spokane, WA
Wild Pony Productions, Dowell, IL
Willow Productions, Kansas City, MO
WIMIN, Albuquerque, NM
Wired Women Productions, St. Louis, MO
Womanspace, Philadelphia, PA
Women for Women, Edwardsville, IL
Women in Productions, San Francisco, CA
Women on Stage, New York, NY
Women Producers Alliance, Tallahassee, FL
Women's Building, Albany, NY
Women's Caucus, Rochester, NY
Women's Music Productions, Summitville, NJ
Women's Music Productions, Nashville, TN
Women's Music Union, Columbus, OH
Women's Revolutions Per Minute, Birmingham, England
Womyn on Wheels, Tucson, AZ
Womyn Producing Womyn, Archer, FL
Womynly Way Productions, Toronto, ON, Canada

Appendix B

Performers with a National or Regional Presence

From *Women's Music Plus* 1987, *HOT WIRE* 1984 – 1994, both published by Toni Armstrong Jr., and the author's files.

Abyss
Adrienne Torf
Alice DiMicele
Alive!
Alix Dobkin
Altazor
Ann Reed
Azucar y Crema
Baba Yaga
Barbara Ester
Barbara Higbie
Bay Area Women's Philharmonic
BeBe K'Roche
Berkeley Women's Music Collective
Bernice Reagon
Beth York
Betsy Lippitt
Betsy Rose
Betty MacDonald
Big Bad Gina
Bitch and Animal
Bonnie Hayes
Bougainvilla
Bucky Motter (aka Angela Motter)
Butchies
Carol MacDonald and Witch
Carole Etzler
Carole McCauley-Spearin
Casselberry-DuPreé
Cathy Fink
Chicago Women's Liberation Rock Band
Connie Kaldor
Cris Williamson

Cyd Slotoroff
Deb (DJ) Adler
Debbie Fier
Deidre McCalla
Derivative Duo
DEUCE
Diane Lindsay
Dianne Davidson
Doria Roberts
Dos Fallopia
DykeAppella
Edwina Lee Tyler
Elaine Townsend
Ellis
Ember Swift
Emma's Revolution
Erica Wheeler
Fallopian Tubes
Ferron
Flash Silvermoon
Gal (Janice Perry)
Gayle Marie
Gerri Gribi
Gina Breedlove
Ginni Clemmens
Girls in the Nose
Goddess and She
Gomez and Palacios
Gwen Avery
Haresuite
Hanifah Walidah
Hawkins and Delear
Heather Bishop
Holly Near
Hot Flashes
Hunter Davis
Irene Farrera
Isle of Klezbos
Izquierda

Jackie Robbins
Jamie Anderson
Jan Barlow
Jane Finnigan Quintet
Jane Voss
Jasmine
Jennifer Justice
Judi Friedman
Judy Castelli
Judy Fjell
Judy Reagon
Judy Sloan
Judy Small
Julie Homi
June Millington
Justina and Joyce
Kara Barnard
Karen Beth
Karen MacKay
Karen Ripley
Kate Clinton
Kay Gardner
Kay Weaver
Kitty Barber
Kristin Lems
Labrys
Laura Love
Laura Wetzler
Lea DeLaria
Leah Zicari
Leah Warnick
Leslea Newman
Leslie Judd
Leslie and the Lys
Lifeline
Lillian Allen
Linda Allen
Linda Moakes
Linda Shear

Linda Sheets
Linda Tillery
Lisa Koch
Lori Noelle
Lucie Blue Tremblay
Lynn Lavner
Lynn Thomas
Madeline Davis
Maggie Savell
Make It Mime
Marathon
Marcia Deihl
Marcia Taylor
Margie Adam
Marie Rhines
Margie Adam
Mary Gemini
Mary Waitrovich
Mary Watkins
Maxine Feldman
Meg Christian
Melissa Ferrick
Melanie Demore
Mimi Fox
Mischief Mime
Morgan and Phelan
Mosa
Motherlode
Mrs. Fun
Musica Femina
Nan Brooks
Nancy Day
Nancy Tucker
Naomi Littlebear Morena (Martinez)
Nedra Johnson
New Haven Women's Liberation Rock Band
Nervous But Excited
Nicholas, Glover and Ray
Pam Hall

Pam Sisson
Pamela Means
Party Line Dance Band
Pat Parker
Paula Walowitz
Phranc
Reel World String Band
Rhiannon
Rhythm Method
Righteous Mothers
Robin Flower
Ruth Barrett
Ruth Pelham
Sam Weis
Sidney Spinster
Silvia Kohan
Software
Sojourner
SONiA and Disappear Fear
Sue Fink
Suede
Summer Osborne
Susan Herrick
Susan Savell
Sweet Honey in the Rock
Swingshift
Sylvia Kohan
Teresa Trull
Terry Garthwaite
The Fabulous Dyketones
Therese Edell
Tory Trujillo
Toshi Reagon
Tracy Riley
Tret Fure
Tribe 8
Trish Williams
Two Nice Girls
Ubaka Hill

Venus Envy
Vicki Randle
Wahru Cleveland
Wallflower Dance Brigade
Washington Sisters
Wicked Jezabel
Wild Mango
Willie Tyson
Wishing Chair
Yagottawanna
Yer Girlfriend
Zoe Lewis

Notes

Introduction

1. Cris Williamson, interview with author, March 10, 2008.
2. Sue Goldwomon, interview with Abbie Hill, University of Wisconsin in Madison, June 14, 2010, accessed June 20, 2014, https://minds. wisconsin.edu/handle/1793/57124.
3. Toni Armstrong Jr. and others, "The Mainstreaming of Women's Music and Culture," *HOT WIRE*, May 1994.
4. Nancy Vogl, interview with author, May 27, 2013.
5. Sue Fink, interview with author, August 23, 2014.
6. Judy Jennings, interview with author, August 19, 2016.
7. M. J. Stephenson, interview with author, April 19, 2016.
8. Anne Haine, interview with author, April 19, 2016.

Chapter One

9. Maxine Feldman, interview by J. D. Doyle for *Queer Music Heritage*, April 2002, http://www.queermusicheritage.com/apr2002.html.
10. "Highlights," accessed June 9, 2016, www.now.org/about/history/ highlights.
11. *Gay Community News*, (April 19, 1980).
12. Ibid.
13. Robin Tyler, interview with author, March 19, 2012.
14. *The Advocate*, (April 11, 1973).
15. Ibid.
16. Cullen, Hackman and McNeilly, *Vaudeville Old and New*, (Psychology Press, 2004).
17. Robin Tyler, interview with author, March 19, 2012.
18. Cullen, Hackman and McNeilly, *Vaudeville Old and New*, (Psychology Press, 2004).
19. Ibid.
20. The festival used "Womyn" instead of "Women." Some in women's music preferred alternative spellings.
21. Karen Corti and Toni L. Armstrong, "A Sometimes Serious Person: An Interview with Maxine Feldman," *Paid My Dues*, (Autumn 1977).
22. Martha Meeks, interview with author, January 7, 2015. The spelling of "women" is varied among women's music fans. "Womyn" is the one preferred by Martha.
23. Patricia Brody and Jas Obrecht, "Meg Christian: Feminist Guitarist and Co-founder of Olivia Records," *Guitar Player*, (July 1978).

24.   Meg Christian, interview with Silvana Moscato, Vito Russo's *Our Time*, episode 3, (1983), https://www.youtube.com/watch?v=GYr9F2Fsuis.

25.   Cris Williamson, interview with Kathy Belge, *About.com Lesbian Life*, (October 4, 2005).

26.   Ginny Berson, interview with author, November 14, 2014.

27.   Ibid.

28.   Judy Dlugacz, "If It Weren't for the Music: 15 Years of Olivia Records," *HOT WIRE*, (July 1988).

29.   Ginny Berson, interview with author, November 14, 2014.

30.   Ibid.

31.   Ibid.

32.   Ibid.

33.   Ibid.

34.   *Meg/Cris at Carnegie Hall* LP liner notes, Second Wave Records, a subsidiary of Olivia Records (1983).

35.   Julie Peddicord, interview with author, April 19, 2016.

36.   Julie Sherwood, interview with author, January 30, 2015.

37.   Judy Dlugacz, "If It Weren't for the Music: 15 Years of Olivia Records (part 2)," *HOT WIRE*, (January 1989).

38.   Since it would be difficult, if not impossible, for five women to live on the income earned by one touring performer, it's possible that there were other sources of income, perhaps a trust fund or loans/gifts from private individuals. A reliable source could not be found to confirm this.

39.   Cris Williamson, interview with Kathy Belge, *About.com Lesbian Life*, (October 4, 2005).

40.   Ibid.

41.   Michelle Marquand, interview with author, April 19, 2016.

42.   Barbara Goldman, interview with author, April 19, 2016.

43.   Ginger Starling, interview with author, April 19, 2016.

44.   Karen Escovitz, interview with author, April 19, 2016.

45.   Julie Nicolay, interview with author, April 19, 2016.

46.   It is difficult to get exact sales figures although the consensus among those in women's music is that Cris Williamson has sold more albums than anyone else. SoundScan, a computerized method of computing album sales, did not begin until the nineties. *Changer and the Changed* was cited repeatedly in resources as an album that had tremendous impact.

47.   Toni Armstrong Jr., "The Best of Both Worlds: Teresa Trull," *HOT WIRE*, (May 1989).

48. Cris Williamson with Cindy Anderson, "Music and Life," *HOT WIRE*, (July 1987).

49. Holly Near, Fire in the Rain... *Singer in the Storm*, (New York: William Morrow, 1990).

50. Holly Near, interview with author, January 2012.

51. Ibid.

52. Ibid.

53. Also booked was Beth Elliot, a transgender woman. She didn't perform after the audience voted to ask her to leave, according to an unpublished account by Jeanne Cordova, one of the producers of the event. The vote was 763 for Beth to leave and 742 for her to stay. No mention is made of her in later years at any other events.

54. Margie Adam, interview with author, March 2011.

55. Ibid.

56. Ibid.

57. Ibid.

58. Ibid.

59. Boo Price, interview with author, November 10, 2014.

60. Ibid.

61. Margie Adam, interview with author, March 2011.

62. Ibid.

63. Linda Shear, interview with Tracy Baim, *ChicagoGayHistory.com*, October 27, 2007, http://*chicagogayhistory.com*/biography.html?id=779

64. Ibid.

65. Naomi Weisstein, "The Chicago Women's Liberation Rock Band," *New Politics*, Summer 2014.

66. Ibid.

67. Alix Dobkin, *My Red Blood*, (New York: Alyson Books, 2009).

68. Alix Dobkin, interview with author, March 18, 2016.

69. Mary Forst, interview with author, July 18, 2011.

70. Pat Gargaetas, interview with author, April 19, 2016.

71. Elana Dykewomon, interview with author, April 19, 2016.

72. Alix Dobkin, interview with author, July 18, 2011.

73. Casse Culver, interview conducted for *Radical Harmonies*, date unknown, Sophia Smith Collection, Smith College, Northampton, Mass, Dee Mosbacher and Woman Vision Papers.

74. Ibid.

75. Ibid.

76. Boo Price, interview with author, November 10, 2014.

77.   Willie could not be reached for an interview. There are few resources about her.

78.   Nancy Vogl, interview with author, July 24, 2012.

79.   Ibid.

80.   Standard record distribution agreements allow for one organization to sell another label's product for a cut of the income. It is assumed that this is the kind of arrangement Olivia offered.

81.   Nancy Vogl, interview with author, July 24, 2012.

82.   Ibid.

83.   Linda Tillery, in an interview with Michele Gautreaux, "Sweet Linda Divine," *HOT WIRE*, (March 1985).

84.   *Radical Harmonies*, directed by Dee Mosbacher, (2002: Woman Vision), DVD.

85.   Linda Tillery, in an interview with Michele Gautreaux, "Sweet Linda Divine," *HOT WIRE*, (March 1985).

86.   Ibid.

87.   *Radical Harmonies*, directed by Dee Mosbacher, (2002; Woman Vision, 2002), DVD.

88.   *Sojourner*, November 1983.

89.   Linda Tillery, in an interview with Michele Gautreaux, "Sweet Linda Divine," *HOT WIRE*, (March 1985).

90.   Ibid.

91.   Lin Daniels, interview conducted for *Radical Harmonies*, date unknown, Sophia Smith Collection, Smith College, Northampton, Mass. Dee Mosbacher and Woman Vision Papers.

92.   Robin Flower, interview with author, December 1, 2011.

93.   Sherry Cmiel, interview with author, January 2010.

94.   Jean Fineberg, interview conducted for *Radical Harmonies*, date unknown, Sophia Smith Collection, Smith College, Northampton, Mass. Dee Mosbacher and Woman Vision Papers.

95.   Jean Millington, interview with author, February 25, 2008.

96.   June Millington, interview with author, February 23, 2008.

97.   Jean Millington, interview with author, February 25, 2008.

98.   June Millington, interview with author, February 23, 2008.

99.   Jean Millington, interview with author, February 25, 2008.

100.   Alice de Buhr, interview with author, February 19, 2008.

101.   "The Full Colorful History," accessed June 9, 2014, http://thedeadlynightshade.net/History.html

102.   Ibid.

103.   Ibid.

104.   Loretta Lynn and George Vecsey, *Coal Miner's Daughter*, (Warner, 1976).

105. Sue Fink, interview with author, August 23, 2014.

Chapter Two
106. Margie Adam, interview with author, January 2011.
107. Karlene Faith, interview with author, January 2011.
108. Some sources say it was Santa Cruz, CA.
109. Teresa Trull, interview with author, April 10, 2016.
110. Mary Forst, interview with author, July 18, 2011.
111. Boo Price, interview with author, November 10, 2014.
112. Mary Forst, interview with author, July 18, 2011.
113. Margie Adam, interview with author, January 2011.
114. Ginny Berson, interview with author, November 14, 2014.
115. Kristin Lems, Jo-Ed Videotape Collection, National Festival 1984, Schlesinger Library, Radcliffe Institute, Harvard University.
116. Ibid.
117. Margie Adam, interview with author, January 2011.
118. Casse Culver, interview conducted for *Radical Harmonies*, date unknown, Sophia Smith Collection, Smith College, Northampton, Mass. Dee Mosbacher and Woman Vision Papers.
119. Jon Jorstad," Lack of University Support Blamed for Festival Problems," *Daily Illini*, (June 17, 1975).
120. Lisa Rogers, interview with author, October 12, 2013.
121. Lisa Vogel, interview with author, February 23, 2012. Lisa thinks there may have been others who traveled with them but she couldn't remember for certain.
122. Mary Kindig (Digger), interview with author, March 14, 2014.
123. Lisa Vogel, interview with author, February 23, 2012.
124. Mary Kindig (Digger), interview with author, March 14, 2014
125. Ibid.
126. Ibid.
127. Ibid.
128. Deidre McCalla, interview with author, June 2, 2014.
129. Mary Kindig (Digger), interview with author, March 14, 2014
130. Lisa Vogel, "My First Festival," last modified October 16, 2014, http://www.michfestmatters.com/my-first-festival-by-lisa-vogel/.
131. Lisa Vogel, interview with author, February 23, 2012.
132. Mary Kindig (Digger), interview with author, March 14, 2014.
133. Ibid.
134. Lisa Vogel, "My First Festival," last modified October 16, 2014, http://www.michfestmatters.com/my-first-festival-by-lisa-vogel/
135. Ibid.

136.   Ibid.

137.   Tess Wiseheart, interview with author, March 4, 2013.

138.   Lisa Vogel, "My First Festival," last modified October 16, 2014, http://
        www.michfestmatters.com/my-first-festival-by-lisa-vogel/

139.   Martha Meeks, interview with author, January 7, 2015.

140.   Suji, interview by author, January 2011. You'll see several spellings of
        "women" throughout the book. "Wimmin" is what Suji chooses.

141.   Jane Kreinberg, interview with author, March 30, 2012.

142.   Mary Byrne, interview with author, November 17, 2014.

143.   Martha Meeks, interview with author, January 7, 2015.

144.   Kristie Vogel, "Michigan," last modified January 21, 2016, http://www.
        michfestmatters.com/michigan-by-kristie-vogel/

145.   *Gay San Diego*, December 2010.

146.   July 27, 1985.

147.   Kristan Aspen, interview with author, March 19, 2016.

148.   The *Lesbian Tide* reported in March/April 1976 that final expenses were
        $20,000, about $85,000 in today's money.

149.   There was dialogue in the early years of women's music about Holly and
        her sexuality. After the *Lesbian Tide* put her on their cover in 1976, they
        received letters of complaint. Their response was that she was a great
        advocate for lesbians and that was good enough for them.

150.   Ginny Berson, interview with author, November 14, 2014.

151.   Boo Price, interview with author, November 10, 2014.

152.   Ibid.

153.   Karlene Faith, *Inside/Outside*, (Self-published, 1976). It's assumed that
        "Third World Women" referred to women of color.

154.   Ibid.

155.   Holly Near, interview with author, January 19, 2012.

156.   Pat Gargaetas, interview with author, April 19, 2016.

157.   Mary Watkins, interview with author, January 22, 2016.

158.   Barbara Cobb, interview with author, January 24, 2016.

159.   Attempts to get more information about this tour were unsuccessful
        because memories have faded, some of the women involved have passed
        away, and Roadwork's paperwork was lost when the archive where it was
        stored closed. However, brief mention was made in resources about the
        excitement of these concerts.

Chapter Three

160.   Patricia Brody and Jas Obrecht, "Meg Christian: Feminist Guitarist and
        Co-founder of Olivia Records," *Guitar Player*, (July 1978).

161.   Ginny Berson, interview with author, November 14, 2014.

162. Judy Dlugacz, "If It Weren't for the Music: 15 Years of Olivia Records," *HOT WIRE*, (January 1989).

163. Ginny Berson, interview with author, November 14, 2014.

164. Ibid.

165. Ibid.

166. Ibid.

167. Ibid.

168. Judy Dlugacz, "If It Weren't for the Music: 15 Years of Olivia Records," *HOT WIRE*, (January 1989).

169. Ginny Berson, interview with author, November 14, 2014.

170. Ibid.

171. Some sources say Meg left in 1984.

172. Judy Dlugacz, "If It Weren't for the Music: 15 Years of Olivia Records," part two, *HOT WIRE*, (January 1989).

173. Another source says she was twenty-eight.

174. February 10, 1976.

175. Judy Dlugacz, "If It Weren't for the Music: 15 Years of Olivia Records," *HOT WIRE*, (July 1988).

176. Patricia Brody and Jas Obrecht, "Meg Christian: Feminist Guitarist and Co-founder of Olivia Records," *Guitar Player*, (July 1978).

177. Steve Morse, "An Intimate Evening with Singer Holly Near," *Boston Globe*, October 22, 1990.

178. Autumn 1977.

179. Robin Flower, interview with author, December 1, 2011.

180. Ibid.

181. Ibid.

182. Maxine Israel, interview with author, April 19, 2016.

183. Ibid.

184. Sheri Snyder, interview with author, April 19, 2016.

185. Maxine Feldman, interview with J. D. Doyle, *Queer Music Heritage*, (April 2002), http://www.queermusicheritage.com/apr2002.html.

186. Boo Price, interview with J. D. Doyle, *Queer Music Heritage*, (November 2004), http://www.queermusicheritage.com/nov2004s.html.

187. Boo Price, interview with author, November 10, 2014.

188. Ibid.

189. Ibid.

190. Alix Dobkin, interview with author, July 21, 2011.

191. Lin Daniels, interview conducted for *Radical Harmonies*, date unknown, Sophia Smith Collection, Smith College, Northampton, Mass. Dee Mosbacher and Woman Vision Papers.

192.   Judy Dlugacz, "If It Weren't for the Music: 15 Years of Olivia Records," *HOT WIRE*, (July 1988).

193.   *Radical Harmonies*, directed by Dee Mosbacher, (2002: Woman Vision), DVD.

194.   *Sojourner*, September 1983.

195.   Dianne Davidson, interview with author, July 2, 2014.

196.   Ibid.

197.   Alix Dobkin, interview with author, July 21, 2011.

198.   Boo Price, interview with author, November 10, 2014.

199.   "Transsexual" was the word they used. "Transgender" wasn't in wide use in that period. "Transgender" will be used in later sections of the book. It is a term used to mean anyone who identifies as a different gender than the one to which they were assigned at birth.

200.   Interview with Ginny Berson, November 14, 2014.

201.   Judy Dlugacz, "If It Weren't for the Music: 15 Years of Olivia Records," *HOT WIRE*, (July 1988).

202.   Ginny Berson, interview with author, November, 14, 2014.

203.   Ibid.

204.   Ibid.

205.   Sandy Stone, "Sandy's FAQ: Don't Die Wondering …," accessed June 10, 2014, http://sandystone.com/faq.shtml, which links to https://en.wikipedia.org/wiki/Sandy_Stone_(artist). Normally, an open-source website would not be cited but since Sandy has the link on her website, it was considered reliable. Attempts to reach Sandy directly were unsuccessful.

206.   Alix Dobkin, interview with author, July 21, 2011.

207.   Judy Dlugacz, "If It Weren't for the Music: 15 Years of Olivia Records," *HOT WIRE*, (July 1988).

208.   Annie is also known for writing "Face the Music," the title cut of Meg Christian's second album.

209.   Mimi Fox, interview with author, March 19, 2016.

210.   Alix Dobkin, interview with J. D. Doyle, *Queer Music Heritage*, November 2004, http://www.queermusicheritage.com/nov2004.html.

211.   Ibid.

212.   Teresa Trull, interviewed by Toni Armstrong Jr., *HOT WIRE*, May 1989.

213.   Ibid.

214.   Kate Brandt and T. L. Armstrong, "Teresa Trull: A Step Away," *HOT WIRE*, March 1988.

215.   Toni L. Armstrong, "Interview with Teresa Trull and Barbara Higbie," *HOT WIRE*, July 1985.

216. Teresa Trull, interviewed by author, April 10, 2016.

217. Ibid.

218. Toni L. Armstrong, "Interview with Teresa Trull and Barbara Higbie," *HOT WIRE*, (July 1985).

219. Ekua Omosupe, "The Soul Knows: Mary Watkins," *HOT WIRE*, (January 1993).

220. Jan Martinelli, interview with author, February 18, 2016.

221. Cate Gable, "Still Alive!" *HOT WIRE*, (May 1993).

222. Ibid.

223. Aidin Vaziri, "Gwen Avery, Passionate Singer-Songwriter and Feminist, Dies," *San Francisco Gate*, (February 8, 2014).

224. Ibid.

225. Gwen Avery, interview with J. D. Doyle, *Queer Music Heritage*, November 2011, http://www.queermusicheritage.com/nov2011.html

226. Ibid.

227. Shia Kapos, "Ginni Clemmens, 66," *Chicago Tribune*, March 9, 2003.

228. Tret Fure, interview with J. D. Doyle, *Queer Music Heritage*, January 2007, http://www.queermusicheritage.com/jan2007.html.

229. Tret Fure, interview with author, January 9, 2015.

230. Ibid.

231. Tret Fure, interview with J. D. Doyle, *Queer Music Heritage*, January 2007, http://www.queermusicheritage.com/jan2007.html.

232. Tret Fure, interview with author, January 9, 2015.

233. Cathy Lee Davis, "Reel World String Band," *HOT WIRE*, (March 1985).

234. Kristan Aspen, interview with author, November 17, 2011.

235. Char Priolo, interview by Brian McNaught, *Stonewall Portraits: Profiles in Pride*, Provincetown Community TV, June 17, 2011, https://vimeo.com/25253747.

236. Naomi Littlebear Morena (Martinez), interview with author, September 16, 2011.

237. Kristan Aspen, interview with author, November 17, 2011.

238. Ibid.

239. Naomi Littlebear Morena (Martinez), interview with author, September 16, 2011.

240. Robin Flower, interview with author, December 1, 2011.

241. Ibid.

242. Andrea Warner, CBC radio, https://www.cbcmusic.ca/posts/18805/ferron-unsung-canadian-treasure-candid-interview, accessed May 5, 2018.

243. Karen Escovitz, interview with author, April 19, 2016.

244. Meg Christian, 1984 Southeastern Gay and Lesbian Conference, Jo-Ed

Videotape collection, Schlesinger Library, Radcliffe Institute, Harvard University.

245. Sue Fink, interview with author, August 23, 2014.
246. Ibid.
247. Ibid.
248. Ibid.
249. Toni Armstrong Jr., "True Life Adventures in Women's Music: Sue Fink," *HOT WIRE*, (May 1991).
250. Sue Fink, interview with author, August 23, 2014.
251. Ibid.
252. Ibid.
253. Ibid.
254. John Howard, *Carryin' on in the Lesbian and Gay South*, (NYU Press, 1997).

Chapter Four
255. A distinction is made here between recordings by women—sometimes only a female vocalist with a male band—and music from within women's music, including recordings produced, engineered, and (mostly) performed by women, many with a lesbian and/or feminist message.
256. Staff writer, "Feminist Founded Female Jazz Label," *LA Times*, November 24, 2008.
257. Sandra Washington, interview with author, October 6, 2014.
258. Toni L. Armstrong, "Deidre McCalla," *HOT WIRE*, July 1988.
259. Deidre McCalla, interview with author, May 31, 2014.
260. Toni L. Armstrong, "Moving into the Mainstream: Deidre McCalla's *Don't Doubt It*," March 1986.
261. Toni L. Armstrong, "Deidre McCalla," *HOT WIRE*, July 1988.
262. Toni L. Armstrong, "Moving into the Mainstream: Deidre McCalla's *Don't Doubt It*," March 1986.
263. Dianne Davidson, interview with author, June 4, 2014.
264. Ibid.
265. Ibid.
266. Ibid.
267. Ibid.
268. Toni L. Armstrong, "Lucie Blue Tremblay," *HOT WIRE*, Nov 1986.
269. Olivia bio from the eighties.
270. *Women's Music Newsletter*, ad from Olivia about Hunter Davis's *Torn*, September 1988.

271.   Jennifer Trowbridge, "Feel the Beat: Four Percussionists," *HOT WIRE*, May 1989.

272.   BETTY website, accessed June 30, 2017.

273.   Stephen Holden, "Sharp Satire from a Trio Named Betty," *New York Times*, July 15, 1990.

274.   Laura Post, *Backstage Pass*, (New Victoria Publishers, 1997).

275.   Ibid.

276.   Toni L. Armstrong, "Casselberry-DuPreé, The Making of Their First Studio Album," *HOT WIRE*, July 1986.

277.   Lynn Lavner, interview with J. D. Doyle, *Queer Music Heritage*, March 2003, http://www.queermusicheritage.com/mar2003s.html.

278.   Ibid.

279.   Ibid.

280.   Ibid.

281.   Ibid.

282.   Ibid.

283.   Ibid.

284.   *Radical Harmonies*, directed by Dee Mosbacher, (2002: Woman Vision), DVD.

285.   Laura Love, "The Road I Took to Me," *HOT WIRE*, May 1993.

286.   Ruth Barrett, interview with author, August 18, 2011.

287.   Ann Reed, interview with author, June 17, 2015.

288.   Mosa, interview with author, January 28, 2016.

289.   Judy Reagan, interview with author, June 10, 2016.

290.   Barbara Swahlen, interview with author, April 19, 2016.

291.   Ronnie Gilbert, interview conducted for *Radical Harmonies*, date unknown, Sophia Smith Collection, Smith College, Northampton, Mass., Dee Mosbacher and Woman Vision Papers.

292.   Toni Armstrong Jr., "Isn't This a Time—The Legend Continues: Ronnie Gilbert," *HOT WIRE*, May 1992.

293.   Ronnie Gilbert, interview conducted for *Radical Harmonies*, date unknown, Sophia Smith Collection, Smith College, Northampton, Mass. Dee Mosbacher and Woman Vision Papers

294.   Toni Armstrong Jr., "Isn't This a Time—The Legend Continues: Ronnie Gilbert," *HOT WIRE*, May 1992.

295.   Ibid.

296.   Ibid.

297.   Chris Soluna, interview with author, April 19, 2016.

298.   Ron Romanovsky, interview with J. D. Doyle, *Queer Music Heritage*, May 2003, http://www.queermusicheritage.com/may2003s.html. Ron Romanovsky co-formed Romanovsky and Phillips. This gay couple

released eight albums and toured extensively in the eighties and nineties. Many of their songs had an LGBTQ theme.

299. Toni L. Armstrong, "Teresa Trull and Barbara Higbie," *HOT WIRE*, July 1985.

300. Teresa Trull, interview with author, April 10, 2016.

301. Toni L. Armstrong, "Teresa Trull and Barbara Higbie," *HOT WIRE*, July 1985.

302. Ibid.

303. April 23, 1989.

304. Ron Romanovsky, interview with J. D. Doyle, *Queer Music Heritage*, May 2003, http://www.queermusicheritage.com/may2003s.html.

305. Olivia promotional material, eighties.

306. Tret Fure, interview with author, January 9, 2015.

307. Ibid.

308. Tret Fure, interview with J. D. Doyle, *Queer Music Heritage*, January 2007, http://www.queermusicheritage.com/jan2007s.html.

309. Ibid.

310. Katrina Rosa, interview with author, April 23, 2016.

311. *Meg/Cris at Carnegie Hall* liner notes, Second Wave, subsidiary of Olivia Records, 1983.

312. Tret Fure, interview with author, January 9, 2015.

313. Meg Christian, interview with Pokey Anderson and Cherry Wolf, KPFT's *Breakthrough*, April 23, 1983, posted at http://www.queermusicheritage.com/feb2012s.html.

314. Tret Fure, interview with author, January 9, 2015.

315. Ginny Berson, interview with author, November 14, 2014.

316. Ibid.

317. Mary Byrne, interview with author, November 17, 2014.

318. Ibid.

319. Theresa Thompson, interview with author, April 19, 2016.

320. Mary Byrne, interview with author, November 17, 2014.

321. Sandra Washington, interview with author, October 6, 2014.

322. Jo-Ed Videotape collection, National Festival 1996, Schlesinger Library, Radcliffe Institute, Harvard University.

323. Boo Price, interview with author, November 10, 2014.

324. Lisa Vogel, interview with author, February 23, 2012.

325. Robin Tyler, interview with author, January 23, 2015.

326. Ibid.

327. Ibid.

328. Ibid.

329. Ellen Elias, "West Coast Women's Music and Comedy Festival 1985," *HOT WIRE*, March 1986.
330. Bonnie J. Morris, *Eden Built By Eves: The Culture of Women's Music Festivals*, (Alyson Books, 1999).
331. Jo-Ed Videotape collection, National festival 1985, Schlesinger Library, Radcliffe Institute, Harvard University.
332. Jorjet Harper, "Southern: The 'Live and Let Live' Festival," *HOT WIRE*, Sept 1990.
333. Debbie Fier, interview with author, February 16, 2016.

Chapter Five
334. Boo Price, interview with author, November 10, 2014.
335. Lisa Vogel, interview with author, February 23, 2012.
336. Ibid.
337. Ibid.
338. For some, DART stood for "Disabled Access Resource Team or Tent" and for others, "Differently Abled Resource Tent."
339. Mary Byrne, interview with author, November 17, 2014.
340. Ibid.
341. Robin Tyler, interview with author, January 23, 2015.
342. Ibid.
343. Bonnie J. Morris, *Eden Built by Eves: The Culture of Women's Music Festivals*, (Alyson Books, 1999).
344. Ibid.
345. Jocelyn Macdonald, "Setting the Record Straight About Michfest," AfterEllen.com, October 24, 2018.
346. Toni L. Armstrong, "The Great White Folk Music Myth, *HOT WIRE*, July 1988.
347. Judith Casselberry, interview conducted for *Radical Harmonies*, date unknown, Sophia Smith Collection, Smith College, Northampton, Mass. Dee Mosbacher and Woman Vision Papers.
348. Ibid.
349. Bonnie J. Morris, *Eden Built by Eves: The Culture of Women's Music Festivals*, (Alyson Books, 1999).
350. Robin Tyler, interview with author, January 27, 2015.
351. University of Illinois Press, 2010.
352. Alix Dobkin, interview with author, September 26, 2014.
353. Ibid.
354. Dianne Davidson, interview with author, July 7, 2014.
355. Robin Tyler, interview with author, January 23, 2015.

356. Ibid.

357. Margie Adam, interview with author, January 27, 2015.

358. Alix Dobkin, interview with author, September 26, 2014.

359. Ibid.

360. Ibid.

361. Boo Price, interview with author, November 10, 2014.

362. Sue Fink, interview with author, August 23, 2014.

363. Judith Casselberry, interview conducted for *Radical Harmonies*, date unknown, Sophia Smith Collection, Smith College, Northampton, Mass. Dee Mosbacher and Woman Vision Papers.

364. November 1983.

365. Michele Gautreaux, "Sweet Linda Devine: An Interview with Linda Tillery," *HOT WIRE*, March 1985.

366. Ibid.

367. Ibid.

368. Toni L. Armstrong, "Casselberry & DuPreé: The Making of Their First Studio Album," *HOT WIRE*, July 1986.

369. Michele Gautreaux, "Sweet Linda Devine: An Interview with Linda Tillery," *HOT WIRE*, March 1985.

370. Ibid.

371. Jo-Ed Videotape collection, National festival 1989. Schlesinger Library, Radcliffe Institute, Harvard University.

372. Mary Watkins, interview with author, January 22, 2016.

373. Toni L. Armstrong, "Moving into the Mainstream: Deidre McCalla's *Don't Doubt It*, *HOT WIRE*, March 1986.

374. Ibid.

375. Judith Casselberry, interview conducted for *Radical Harmonies*, date unknown, Sophia Smith Collection, Smith College, Northampton, Mass. Dee Mosbacher and Woman Vision Papers.

376. Gwen Avery, interview with J.D. Doyle, Queen Music Heritage, November 2011, http://www.queermusicheritage.com/nov2011s.html.

377. Deidre McCalla, interview with author, May 31, 2014.

378. Sandra Washington, interview with author, October 6, 2014.

379. Ibid.

380. Naomi Littlebear Morena (Martinez), interview with author, September 16, 2011.

381. Ibid.

382. Kristie Vogel, "Michigan," January 21, 2016, http://www.michfestmatters.com/michigan-by-kristie-vogel/.

383. Margie Adam, interview with author, October 6, 2011.

384. Toni L. Armstrong, "The P. T. Barnum of Women's Music and Culture: Robin Tyler," *HOT WIRE*, March 1988.

385. *Gay Community News*, November 1981.

386. Toni Armstrong Jr., "What is Women's Music?" *HOT WIRE*, September, 1989.

387. Toni Armstrong Jr., "The Best of Both Worlds: Teresa Trull," *HOT WIRE*, March 1988.

388. William K. Knoedelseder Jr., "Recording Studios," *LA Times*, July 4, 1988.

389. Toni Armstrong Jr., "The Best of Both Worlds: Teresa Trull," *HOT WIRE*, March 1988.

390. Alix Dobkin, interview with author, April 2, 2016.

391. Ginny Berson, interview with author, November 14, 2014.

392. Ibid.

393. Ibid.

394. Ibid.

395. Ibid.

396. January 1989.

397. Ginny Berson, interview with author, November 14, 2014.

398. Robin Tyler, interview with author, January 23, 2015.

399. Margie Adam, interview with author, October 6, 2011.

400. Boo Price, interview with author, November 10, 2014.

401. Margie Adam, interview with author, October 6, 2011.

402. Betsy Rose, "Mulling It Over: In Search of the Cutting Edge, Part One," *HOT WIRE*, November 1987.

403. Nancy Vogl, interview with author, July 24, 2012.

404. Teresa Trull, interview with author, April 10, 2016.

405. Toni L. Armstrong, "The Washington Sisters," *HOT WIRE*, November 1987.

406. Margie Adam, interview with author, October 6, 2011.

407. Ibid.

408. Kay Gardner, "How Did We Get into This Mess?" *HOT WIRE*, July 1986.

409. Ann Reed, interview with author, June 9, 2014.

410. Toni Armstrong Jr., "True Life Adventures in Women's Music: Sue Fink," *HOT WIRE*, May 1991.

411. Ibid.

412. Erica Wheeler, interview with author, January 23, 2015.

413. Sandra Washington, interview with author, October 5, 2014.

414. Ibid.

415. Robin Flower, interview with author, December 5, 2011.

416.   Janis Ian, Jo-Ed Videotape collection, National Festival 1995, Schlesinger Library, Radcliffe Institute, Harvard University.

417.   Ibid.

418.   Ronnie Gilbert, interview conducted for *Radical Harmonies*, date unknown, Sophia Smith Collection, Smith College, Northampton, Mass. Dee Mosbacher and Woman Vision Papers.

419.   Ibid.

420.   Robin Tyler, interview with author, January 23, 2015.

421.   Boo Price, interview with author, November 10, 2014.

422.   Margie Adam, interview with author, October 6, 2011.

423.   March/April 1976.

424.   Toni Armstrong Jr., "Cris," *HOT WIRE*, September 1989.

425.   Kay Gardner, "Charisma and Star Tripping," *HOT WIRE*, March 1987.

426.   Ibid.

427.   Tess Wiseheart, interview with author, February 25, 2015.

428.   Ibid.

429.   Teresa Trull, interview with author, April 10, 2016.

430.   March/April 1976.

431.   Ibid.

432.   Toni L. Armstrong, "Deidre McCalla," *HOT WIRE*, July 1988.

433.   Toni Armstrong Jr., "The Best of Both Worlds: Teresa Trull," *HOT WIRE*, May 1989.

434.   Margie Adam, interview with author, October 6, 2011.

435.   Sue Fink, interview with author, August 23, 2014.

436.   Tess Wiseheart, interview with author, February 25, 2015.

437.   Robin Tyler, interview with author, January 23, 2015.

438.   Ibid.

439.   Sue Fink, interview with author, August 23, 2014.

440.   Ibid.

441.   Ibid.

442.   More stories from the road are offered in the author's memoir, *Drive All Night*, (Bella Books; 2014).

443.   Ginny Berson, interview with author, November 14, 2014.

444.   Robin Flower, interview with author, December 1, 2011.

445.   Sherry Cmiel, interview with author, January 7, 2015.

446.   Meg Christian, Jo-Ed Videotape collection, Southeastern Gay and Lesbian Conference in Birmingham, AL, 1984, Schlesinger Library, Radcliffe Institute, Harvard University.

447.   Margie Adam, interview with author, October 6, 2011.

448.   Mike Nichols and Dave Daley, "Aldermanic Race: "Gotzler Testified in Drug Probe, Her Brother's Plea Deal Alleges Her Business Was

Laundering Money," *Milwaukee Journal Sentinel*, February 2, 1996.

449. February/March 1984.

450. Margie Adam, interview with author, October 6, 2011.

451. Toni L. Armstrong, "Kay Gardner," *HOT WIRE*, March 1986.

452. Ibid.

453. Margie Adam, interview with author, May 7, 2016.

454. Meg Christian, interview with Silvana Moscato, Vito Russo's *Our Time*, episode 3, (1983), https://www.youtube.com/watch?v=GYr9F2Fsuis.

455. Toni Armstrong Jr., "What is Women's Music?" *HOT WIRE*, Sept 1989.

456. Ibid.

457. Ellen Seeling, "The Politics of Instrumental Music," *HOT WIRE*, July 1988.

458. Jean Fineberg, interview conducted for *Radical Harmonies*, date unknown, Sophia Smith Collection, Smith College, Northampton, Mass. Dee Mosbacher and Woman Vision Papers.

459. Toni L. Armstrong, "Kay Gardner," *HOT WIRE*, March 1986.

460. Ruth Barrett, interview with author, August 18, 2011.

461. Mary Watkins, interview with author, January 22, 2016.

462. Ibid.

463. *Sojourner*, September 1983.

464. Michaelle Goerlitz, interview with author, February 14, 2016.

465. Amy Ray, interview conducted for *Radical Harmonies*, date unknown, Sophia Smith Collection, Smith College, Northampton, Mass. Dee Mosbacher and Woman Vision Papers.

466. Amy Horowitz, interview with author, January 30, 2015.

467. Laura Post, "Olivia Artists," *HOT WIRE*, July 1988.

468. Alix Dobkin, interview with author, July 21, 2011.

469. Kay Gardner, "How Did We Get into This Mess?" *HOT WIRE*, July 1986.

470. Laura Post, "Rhiannon and Phranc: Performing in Women's Music and in the Mainstream Scene," *HOT WIRE*, September 1991.

471. Toni Armstrong Jr., "What is Women's Music?" *HOT WIRE*, September 1989.

472. Sandra Washington, interview with author, October 5, 2014.

473. Toni L. Armstrong, "Teresa Trull and Barbara Higbie," *HOT WIRE*, July 1985.

474. Alix Dobkin, interview with author, July 21, 2011.

475. Cris Williamson, "Soapbox" (Letters to the Editor), *HOT WIRE*, January 1990.

476. Toni Armstrong Jr., "What is Women's Music?" *HOT WIRE*, September 1989.

477. Toni L. Armstrong, "The Washington Sisters," *HOT WIRE*, November 1987.

478. Ginni Clemmens with Linda Wagner, "Mulling It Over," *HOT WIRE*, March 1985.

479. Toni Armstrong Jr., "Isn't This a Time—The Legend Continues: Ronnie Gilbert," *HOT WIRE*, May 1992.

480. Tracy Baim and Paula Walowitz, "Rock and Women's Music," *HOT WIRE*, July 1985.

481. Casse Culver, interview conducted for *Radical Harmonies*, date unknown, Sophia Smith Collection, Smith College, Northampton, Mass. Dee Mosbacher and Woman Vision Papers.

482. Ibid.

483. Toni L. Armstrong, "The Washington Sisters," *HOT WIRE*, November 1987.

484. September 1983.

485. Laura Post, "Olivia Artists," *HOT WIRE*, July 1988.

486. Ibid.

487. Holly Near, interview with J. D. Doyle, *Queer Music Heritage*, January 2010, http://www.queermusicheritage.com/jan2010s.html.

488. Phyllis Free, interview with author, April 23, 2012. After her work with Jan Riley and Friends, Phyllis was the drummer for folk-rock band Yer Girlfriend.

489. Ibid.

490. Ibid.

491. LauRose Dancingfire Felicity and Calla Felicity, "Yer Girlfriend: Louisville's Community Band, 1989-96, *Sinister Wisdom*, Spring 2017.

492. Laurie Fuchs, interview with author, June 13, 2012.

493. Sue Fink, interview with author, August 23, 2014.

494. Ibid.

495. Ibid.

496. Toni Armstrong Jr., "True Life Adventures in Women's Music: Sue Fink," *HOT WIRE*, May 1991.

497. Unidentified festival attendee, conversation with author, August 1979.

498. Flash Silvermoon, interview with author, February 16, 2013.

499. Ibid.

500. Robin Flower, interview with author, December 1, 2011.

501. Ibid.

502. Ibid.

503. Ibid.

504. Nancy Vogl, interview with author, July 25, 2012.

505. Robin Flower, interview with author, December 1, 2011.

506.   Ibid.

Chapter Six

507.   Many women wore more than one hat in women's music. They are placed in the section where they are best known. Please note that there were hundreds of women and men working behind the scenes. This is an abbreviated overview of a few of them.

508.   Karen Corti and Toni Armstrong, "A Sometimes Serious Person: An Interview with Maxine Feldman," *Paid My Dues*, Fall, 1977.

509.   Maxine Feldman, interview with Boden Sandstrom for her dissertation, September 24, 1999.

510.   Retts Scauzillo, interview with author, September 2, 2011.

511.   Margie Adam, interview with author, May 8, 2016.

512.   Toni Armstrong Jr., "Women in Live Sound: Myrna Johnston and Shelley Jennings," *HOT WIRE*, January 1992.

513.   Staff writer, "The First Boston Women's Music Festival," *Paid My Dues*, March 1976.

514.   Toni Armstrong Jr., "Women in Live Sound: Myrna Johnston and Shelley Jennings," *HOT WIRE*, January 1992.

515.   Kaia Skaggs, interview with author, February 11, 2016.

516.   Cindi Zuby, interview with author, February 25, 2013.

517.   Margie Adam, interview with author, May 10, 2016.

518.   K. C. Cohen, interview with author, March 15, 2016.

519.   Kris Koth, interview with author, May 26, 2013.

520.   Robin Flower, interview with author, December 1, 2011.

521.   Tret Fure, interview with J. D. Doyle, *Queer Music Heritage*, January 2007, http://www.queermusicheritage.com/jan2007s.html.

522.   See Appendix A for a more complete list of concert producers and venues.

523.   Staff writer, "The First Boston Women's Music Festival," *Paid My Dues*, March 1976.

524.   Catherine Roma, "Women's Culture in Ohio," *HOT WIRE*, Sept 1989.

525.   Lin Daniels, interview conducted for *Radical Harmonies*, date unknown, Sophia Smith Collection, Smith College, Northampton, Mass. Dee Mosbacher and Woman Vision Papers.

526.   Lucy Diamond, "Pokey Anderson, Merle Bicknell, and Tam Martin," *HOT WIRE*, July 1987.

527.   Michelle Crone papers (APAP101), M. E. Grenander Department of Special Collections and Archives, State University of New York, Albany, http://library.albany.edu/speccoll/findaids/eresources/findingaids/

apap101.html.

528. Flash Silvermoon, interview with author, March 31, 2012.
529. Lori Lambert, interview with author, February 22, 2013.
530. Ibid.
531. Linda Wilson, interview with author, March 15, 2016.
532. Ibid.
533. Amy Horowitz, interview with author, January 30, 2015.
534. Ibid.
535. Toni Armstrong Jr., interview with author, April 10, 2016.
536. Julia Cameron Damon, "3 Generations and All My Children," June 12, 2015, http://www.michfestmatters.com/3-generations-and-all-my-children-by-julia-cameron-damon/.
537. Maxine Feldman, interview with Boden Sandstrom for her dissertation, September 24, 1999.
538. Boo Price, interview with author, November 10, 2014.
539. Ibid.
540. Ibid.
541. Retts Scauzillo, interview with author, September 2, 2011.

Chapter Seven
542. Sue Fink, interview with author, August 23, 2014.
543. Toni Armstrong Jr., "A Taste of the Canadian Prairies: Heather Bishop," *HOT WIRE*, May 1990.
544. Ibid.
545. Ibid.
546. March 25, 2002.

Chapter Eight
547. Toni L. Armstrong, "The Great White Folk Music Myth," *HOT WIRE*, July 1988.
548. Ibid.
549. www.NedraJohnson.com, accessed June 14, 2014.
550. Toni L. Armstrong, "The Great White Folk Music Myth," *HOT WIRE*, July 1988.
551. Nancy Vogl, interview with author, July 24, 2012.
552. Robin Flower, interview with author, December 5, 2011.
553. Tracy Baim and Paula Walowitz, "Rock and Women's Music," *HOT WIRE*, July 1985.
554. Mary Watkins, interview with author, January 22, 2016.
555. Tracy Baim and Paula Walowitz, "Rock and Women's Music," *HOT*

WIRE, July 1985.

556. Tret Fure, interview with author, January 9, 2015.

557. Nov 22, 1984.

558. Jean Fineberg, interview conducted for *Radical Harmonies*, edited by Jean in January 2016, original interview date unknown, Sophia Smith Collection, Smith College, Northampton, Mass. Dee Mosbacher and Woman Vision Papers.

559. Ibid.

560. Ibid.

561. Mary Watkins, interview with author, January 22, 2016.

562. Kristan Aspen, interview with author, November 17, 2011.

563. Ibid.

564. Joshua Kosman, "VIEW / R. I. P. Women's Philharmonic, You Were the Perfect Blend of Achievement and Idealism," *San Francisco Gate*, March 4, 2004.

565. Ibid.

566. Leslie Judd, interview with author, February 14, 2016.

567. It is the author's hope that someone will write a book about the feminist and lesbian spoken word artists who appeared at women's festivals and other venues.

568. Feminist dance and theater is beyond the scope of this book. However, the author recognizes its importance and hopes that someone will write a book about each. Over the years, the Michigan and National festivals presented a variety of both, from The Dance Brigade to Carolyn Gage's lesbian plays.

Chapter Nine

569. Ellen Seeling, interview conducted for *Radical Harmonies*, date unknown, Sophia Smith Collection, Smith College, Northampton, Mass. Dee Mosbacher and Woman Vision Papers.

570. Jean Fineberg, interview conducted for *Radical Harmonies*, date unknown, Sophia Smith Collection, Smith College, Northampton, Mass. Dee Mosbacher and Woman Vision Papers.

571. Laura Post, "The Roads to Solo Keyboard Work: Julie Homi and Adrienne Torf," *HOT WIRE*, May 1990.

572. Ellen Seeling, interview conducted for *Radical Harmonies*, date unknown, Sophia Smith Collection, Smith College, Northampton, Mass. Dee Mosbacher and Woman Vision Papers.

573. Jean Fineberg, interview conducted for *Radical Harmonies*, date unknown, Sophia Smith Collection, Smith College, Northampton,

Mass. Dee Mosbacher and Woman Vision Papers.

574.   Jan Martinelli, interview with author, March 2, 2016.

575.   Ellen Seeling, interview conducted for *Radical Harmonies*, date unknown, Sophia Smith Collection, Smith College, Northampton, Mass. Dee Mosbacher and Woman Vision Papers.

576.   Jean Fineberg, interview conducted for *Radical Harmonies*, date unknown, Sophia Smith Collection, Smith College, Northampton, Mass. Dee Mosbacher and Woman Vision Papers.

Chapter Ten

577.   Ruth Barrett, interview with author, August 18, 2011.

578.   Eclipse Neilson, *Motherghost: A Journey to the Mother*, (Star Meadow Press, 2012).

579.   Ruth Barrett, interview with author, August 18, 2011.

580.   Antoinette Johnson-Gross, "Melanie DeMore: Share My Song," *HOT WIRE*, Jan 1993.

581.   Bonnie J. Morris, "Celebrating Jewish Identity at Festivals," *HOT WIRE*, January 1993.

582.   November 1987.

583.   Toni Armstrong Jr., "The Political is Personal in the Deep South," *HOT WIRE*, Jan 1993.

Chapter Eleven

584.   September 30, 1994.

585.   Dianne Davidson, Jo-Ed Videotape collection, National festival 1996, Schlesinger Library, Radcliffe Institute, Harvard University.

586.   Since the focus of this book is on music, this section is only a brief overview. The feminist and lesbian comics deserve a book of their own.

Chapter Twelve

587.   Holly Near, "Soapbox" (Letters to the Editor), *HOT WIRE*, September 1994.

588.   See Appendix B for a list of more performers.

589.   Tara Ayres, interview with author, March 19, 2016.

590.   Motter used both names on www.angelamotter.com, accessed on June 16, 2014.

591.   *Live at IMA*, 1993.

592.   Tret Fure, interview with author, January 24, 2015.

593.   Tret Fure, interview with J. D. Doyle, *Queer Music Heritage*, January 2007, http://www.queermusicheritage.com/jan2007s.html.

594. Ibid.
595. Ibid.
596. Tret Fure, interview with author, January 9, 2015.
597. Cris Williamson, interview with Kathy Belge, *About.com Lesbian Life*, (October 4, 2005).
598. Sue Fitzgerald, interview with author, June 19, 2015.
599. Debbie Fier, interview with author, June 19, 2015.
600. Ibid.
601. Tess Wiseheart, interview with author, February 26, 2015.
602. Julie King, interview with author, April 19, 2016.
603. Country/pop/rock performer k.d. lang released her first album in 1984 and has long been a favorite of lesbians. She came out in 1992.
604. Connie Daily, interview with author, April 19, 2016.
605. Sue Fink, interview with author, August 23, 2014.
606. "Tyler Childers, Rosanne Cash Sound Off at 2018 Americana Honors & Awards," www.rollingstone.com, accessed September 14, 2018.
607. September 1994.
608. Lin Daniels, interview conducted for *Radical Harmonies*, date unknown, Sophia Smith Collection, Smith College, Northampton, Mass. Dee Mosbacher and Woman Vision Papers.
609. Robin Tyler, interview with author, January 23, 2015.
610. Ibid.
611. Sue Fink, interview with author, August 23, 2014.
612. Jocelyn Macdonald, "Setting the Record Straight About Michfest," AfterEllen.com, October 24, 2018.
613. Anne Griffiths, interview with author, March 6, 2016.
614. Letter from Lisa Vogel, posted on Facebook on April 21, 2015.
615. Jocelyn Macdonald, "Setting the Record Straight About Michfest," AfterEllen.com, October 24, 2018.
616. We Want the Land Coalition signed a contract with Lisa Vogel in 2017 to begin purchase of the land. Full purchase should be completed in 2025 or earlier.
617. Teresa Trull, interview with author, April 10, 2016.
618. Toni Armstrong Jr., "Cris," *HOT WIRE*, 1989.
619. Cris Williamson, interview with Kathy Belge, *About.com Lesbian Life*, (October 4, 2005).
620. Robin Slicer, interview with author, April 19, 2016.
621. Elisabeth Brook, interview with author, April 19, 2016.
622. Marianne Barlow, interview with author, April 19, 2016.
623. Nancy Vogl, interview with author, July 24, 2012.

624.   Lori Lambert, interview with author, February 22, 2013.

625.   Sandra Washington, interview with author, October 6, 2014.

626.   Robin Tyler, interview with author, January 23, 2015.

627.   Amy Ray, interview conducted for *Radical Harmonies*, date unknown, Sophia Smith Collection, Smith College, Northampton, Mass. Dee Mosbacher and Woman Vision Papers.

628.   Robin Flower, interview with author, December 1, 2011.

629.   Deidre McCalla, interview with author, May 31, 2014.

630.   Robin Flower, interview with author, December 1, 2011.

631.   Lin Daniels, interview conducted for *Radical Harmonies*, date unknown, Sophia Smith Collection, Smith College, Northampton, Mass. Dee Mosbacher and Woman Vision Papers.

632.   Deidre McCalla, interview with author, May 31, 2014. Reference is to a forthcoming 2014 show with Dianne Davidson and Jamie Anderson in Carrboro, N.C., "We Aren't Dead Yet."

633.   Nancy Vogl, interview with author, July 24, 2012.

634.   Ginny Berson, interview with author, November 24, 2014.

635.   Kristan Aspen, interview with author, November 17, 2011.

Index

Women's music festivals; Women's music/late 1970s; Women's music/1980s; Women's music/post-1980s

Lesbian Tide newspaper, 15, 16, 19, 23, 57, 63, 65, 131, 132, 133, 139, 140, 141, 143, 144, 147, 151, 172

Leslie and the Ly's pop band, 138

Lewis, Laurie, 77, 103, 200, 202

Lewis, Zoe, 202, 218

Lez Zeppelin band, 190

LGBTQ choral movement, 84

LGBTQ rights movement, 2, 21, 61

See also Lesbian culture; Lesbian music

Lifeline band, 104, 159

Lighting. *See* Sound/light technicians

Lightwomoon, River, 232

Lilith Fair, 219, 226

Lima Bean Records, 26

Lindsay, Diane, 52, 81, 82, 112, 179, 180, 201, 202

Lippitt, Betsy, 66, 83, 86, 116

Lockhart, Bonnie, 27, 77, 193

Loggins, Kenny, 151

Lone Star Women's Festival, 120, 216

Long, Aleah, 207

Long Island Women's Music Festival, 50

Love, Laura, 99–100

Lowe, Joan, 7, 10, 32, 64

Lucina's Music venue, 52

Luckett, Erika, 193, 231

Lucy Records, 86

Lynn, Loretta, 36, 44

MacAuslan, Janna, 104, 172, 194, 195

MacColl, Ewan, 22

MacDonald, Betty, 26

MacDonald, Carol, 34, 117, 127, 188, 189, 231

MacKay, Karen, 103

MacRae, Jean, 163

Mah, Leslie, 190

Mahoney, Kathleen, 215

Maiden Voyage band, 117, 125, 146, 192

Mainstream music:

The Arsenio Show and, 225

310 Index

Newport Folk Festival, 123
Newport Jazz Festival, 193
Nicolay, Julie, 11
Nivert, Susan, 196
Nolan, Faith, 182
Northampton Lesbian Festival, 217, 220
Northampton Women's Center, 35
Northeast (New England) Women's Music Retreat (NEWMR), 36, 94, 97, 114, 120, 121, 123, 124, 159, 163, 192, 231
Notzen, Denise, 171, 175
Nugent, Trish, 71, 199
Nyro, Laura, 14, 32, 34, 36, 67, 116, 119, 203–204

Oakenstar, Jess Hawk, 183, 219–220
Obiedo, Ray, 108, 109
O'Brien, Linda, 160
Ochs, Phil, 20
"Ode to a Gym Teacher", 8, 9, 13, 112, 211
Odetta, 87, 106, 137, 216
off our backs, 7, 8, 22, 85, 172, 173
O'Hara, Kiera, 78, 192
Ohio Lesbian Festival, 97, 116, 196, 218, 221, 225, 229
Old Lesbians Organizing for Change, 222
Old Towne School of Folk Music, 71, 108
O'Leary, Jean, 62
Olivia Collective, 7, 8–9, 10, 58–59, 65, 112, 113, 133, 173, 176
Olivia Records, 6, 57, 155
    Americana Music Association honors for, 227
    BeBe K'Roche band and, 28, 69–70
    Berkeley Women's Music Collective album and, 27
    Black performers and, 29
    Carnegie Hall concerts and, 29, 64, 89–90, 91, 110, 112, 156, 174, 233
    The Changer and the Changed album and, 10–11, 59
    contract negotiations and, 175–176
    cruises by, 156, 197, 212, 213, 226
    Davidson, Dianne and, 90–91
    demise of, 215, 226
    distribution systems for, 57–58, 167–168
    expansion/late 1970s and, 57–59
    expansion/1980s and, 85–86
    feminist values, modeling of, 58, 59

Amazon Music Party, 40
attendance at, ii–iii, 57, 85
Boston Women's Music Festival, 23, 29, 42
Campfest, 84, 85, 119
challenging issues with, 121–124
comedy at, 117
community drumming and, 224–225
corporate sponsorships and, 123
cross-community clashes and, 123–124
decline in, 228–229
East Coast Lesbian Festival, 85, 86, 101, 119–120
financial difficulties and, 123
growing number of, 85
Gulf Coast Women's Music Festival, 110, 118–119
health issues and, 123
International Women's Music Festival, 179
Iowa Women's Music Festival, 120, 164
land issues and, 121–122
Lone Star Festival, 120
Long Island Women's Music Festival, 50
Midwest Wimmin's Festival, 40–41
newly established festivals and, 116–120
1980s, festival growing pains and, 113–116
Northeast (New England) Women's Music Retreat and, 36, 94, 97, 120
Ohio Lesbian Festival, 97, 116
Pacific Northwest Women's Music Festival, 49, 190
post-1980s festivals and, 215–217
racism, perceptions of, 124–127
Rhythmfest, 97
S&M community and, 123–124
Sacramento State festival, 15–16, 27, 39–40
San Diego Women's Music Festival, 13–14, 41–42
Sisterfire Festival, 31, 64, 94, 98, 119
Sisterspace and, 49
Southern Women's Music and Comedy Festival and, 118
Southern Women's Music Festival, 120
transgender community and, 124
Virginia Women's Music Festival, 159
weather conditions and, 123
West Coast Women's Music and Comedy Festival, 85, 116
West Coast Women's Music and Cultural Festival and, 94, 116–118

Bella Books, Inc.

Women. Books. Even Better Together.

P.O. Box 10543
Tallahassee, FL 32302

Phone: 800-729-4992
www.bellabooks.com

CPSIA information can be obtained
at www.ICGtesting.com
Printed in the USA
LVHW091022141119
637167LV00001BA/1/P